Matthew Henry

Matthew Henry

Pastoral Liturgy in Challenging Times

JONG HUN JOO

Foreword by Todd E. Johnson

☙PICKWICK *Publications* • Eugene, Oregon

MATTHEW HENRY
Pastoral Liturgy in Challenging Times

Copyright © 2014 JONG HUN JOO. All rights reserved. Except for brief quotations in critical publications or reviews, no part of this book may be reproduced in any manner without prior written permission from the publisher. Write: Permissions. Wipf and Stock Publishers, 199 W. 8th Ave., Suite 3, Eugene, OR 97401.

Pickwick Publications
An Imprint of Wipf and Stock Publishers
199 W. 8th Ave., Suite 3
Eugene, OR 97401

www.wipfandstock.com

ISBN 13: 978-1-62564-761-0

Cataloguing-in-Publication Data

Joo, Jong Hun

    Matthew Henry : pastoral liturgy in challenging times / Jong Hun Joo.

    xxii + 208 p. ; 23 cm. Includes bibliographical references.

    ISBN 13: 978-1-62564-761-0

    1. Henry, Matthew, 1662–1714. 2. Liturgics. 3. Public Worship. 4. Pastoral care. 5. Theology, Practical. I. Title.

BV4831 H4 J66 2014

Manufactured in the U.S.A.   10/16/2014

Dedicated
to my wife Sangye
and children Gloria (Hayoung) and Robert (Hajin),
companions in worshipping God

Contents

Foreword: On the Unseen Wisdom of Palm Trees and Matthew Henry
by Todd Johnson | ix
Acknowledgments | xiii
Introduction | xv

1 English Presbyterian Worship in the Restoration and Aftermath: The Liturgical Context of Matthew Henry | 1

2 The Life and Thought of Matthew Henry: Word-Centered Piety | 41

3 Matthew Henry on Christian Worship: Communion with God in Liturgical Forms and Patterns | 78

4 Matthew Henry's Theology of the Sacraments: English Presbyterian Piety of Baptism and the Lord's Supper | 115

5 Reformed Tradition in Henry's Presbyterian Public Worship Service | 156

6 Conclusion: Liturgical Resources for Renewal of Public Worship in Henry's Theology and Practice of Worship | 188

Bibliography | 201

Foreword
On the Unseen Wisdom of Palm Trees and Matthew Henry

I GREW UP IN a forest. The Allegheny Forest to be precise. The Allegheny mountains of western Pennsylvania are literally carpeted with trees. Before Drake discovered oil in those mountains, logging was the primary industry in northwestern Pennsylvania. And logging cleared the mountains, leaving them bald. After the oil boom hit, the hills were populated instead with oil derricks, a sort of sparse, small-scale forest—or so the pictures record.

By the time I was born, the forest has recaptured the hills, hiding the derricks and muffling their sound as they pumped thick, black crude oil out of the ground. I spent many years of my boyhood biking on the oil-lease roads that crisscrossed the hills around my home with my friends. I learned about trees there. I learned that in a light rain the trees would keep those dirt roads underneath me dry and rideable. I learned that on hot summer days it would still be cool under the trees. I learned how to climb trees—all kinds of trees—there, and came to know differences in branches and leaves and bark and many things there. I also learned that as tall and majestic as the trees above me were, they were equally intricate and extensive beneath me. As much as trees provided shelter, roots provided a hazard, as a root in the road could spell a spill on one's bike. Knowing roots were a crucial part of knowing a tree.

But today I write this on my patio in southern California with tall palm trees swaying in the Santa Ana breezes. Palm trees do not look like other trees, particularly the ones of my youth. But they are trees after all, so I assumed they were still trees underground. As tall and durable as these trees are, they must have an extensive system of roots to afford them such stability.

But they do not. They defy my expectations of a tree. The roots of a palm tree are like a fibrous web of tendrils extending from a ball-like bulb in the ground. As roots continue to die and be replaced by new ones, they do not grow to the extent of the trees I had come to know so well as a boy.

But I assumed they did. But thanks to the unique root system they do have, they are able to thrive in arid, windy climates, even while they grow to dizzying heights. There is wisdom unseen in their design. Sometimes things look a lot different when you dig a little bit.

And so I am thankful for the digging Dr. Jong Hun Joo has done to unearth the very unique roots that are the foundation for Matthew Henry. Matthew Henry is best known for his exhaustive, verse-by-verse Bible commentary. It is one of, if not the, most cited biblical commentaries in the English language and it has few peers in terms of expanse and influence. A less well-known fact is that Henry was primarily a pastor and secondarily a biblical scholar. However, what you will learn in this book is how scripture, prayer and worship operated as the trinity of Henry's piety and pastoral care. The Bible was certainly central for Henry, but it was read within the context of prayer, personal and gathered, and he gave instructions for how to pray, and how to worship and how to appropriate the scriptures as an individual, a congregation, and as a family.

These are Henry's roots. His faith was not founded upon exegesis and scripture study. But his exegesis and scripture study was rooted in his passion for the devout life and a living relationship with a living God. Henry was spiritual, even liturgical. This was the ground of his biblical work and the aim of it as well.

Now in this work by Dr. Joo, we have for the first time a careful analysis of the spiritual and liturgical pulse of Matthew Henry's pastoral ministry and piety. Through the careful description and analysis of Henry's life and times, one comes to understand the crucible that formed his beliefs and faith. Further you will learn about the influences on Henry's thought and his convergence and divergence from those influences. But foremost, you will see for the first time a clear exposition of the centrality of worship and prayer in Henry's life. The careful and thoughtful work in unearthing this unknown side of Henry is not only a welcome gift historically; it is a precious gift to the soul. For Dr. Joo's work is not one that ends in theological and historical detail, but honoring the ministry of Henry, promotes the quality and themes of Henry's insights into private and corporate prayer as resources for today's church. If there is a guide for a church in challenging times, it just might be Matthew Henry.

So delight in this book and its unique foundation in the spiritual and liturgical perspectives of Matthew Henry. Henry, like the palm tree, has such unique roots that it allowed him to negotiate the challenging winds of his days even as his biblical scholarship soared to new heights. Might you find rootedness in the wisdom of Jong Hun Joo's careful recovery of Matthew Henry's pastoral voice. It just might be the understanding you need in your life today.

Sometimes things look a lot different when you dig a little bit.

Todd E. Johnson
Fuller Theological Seminary
Good Friday 2014

Acknowledgments

It is a privilege for me to express my grateful heart to many people and institutions that helped me with publishing this book. Most of all, I would like to appreciate Todd Johnson. Dr. Johnson has taught me Christian worship not only in the doctoral seminar room but also through his way of life. He has modeled for me what it means to be a pastoral scholar. I learned pastoral heart, humility, and excellence in scholarship from him. He even encouraged me by writing the foreword for this book. I cannot fully express my grateful heart for his sacrifice for encouraging and guiding me in my academic improvements and life formation. I am also grateful to William Dyrness. Dr. Dyrness taught me how to understand and engage culture, a crucial issue of contemporary worship with a theological perspective. He also advised me on this book to make my argument clearer from a keen scholarly perspective.

I also owe much appreciation to three institutions that assisted me for this work in significant ways. These are Okhanheum Scholarship Committee of Sarang Community Church, Scholarship Committee of Boondang Central Church, and Choong Hyun Mission Church. These three institutions allowed me to spend much time and energy on researching and writing this work by prayers and financial supports. There are other special people I would like to recognize. Dr. Kukwon Shin, professor at Chongshin University, strongly recommended that I study Christian worship and encouraged me to be a contributing scholar for worship renewal. Dr. John Witvliet, Director of Calvin Institute of Christian Worship, advised me to delve into liturgical resources in the theology and practice of Matthew Henry's worship as a crucial foundation of contemporary worship renewal at the beginning stage of this book. I also appreciate the editorial team of Pickwick for their kind and professional help.

Acknowledgments

Last, and most important of all, I want to thank my wife, Sangye, and two children, Ha-young (Gloria) and Ha-jin (Robert). My wife, Sangye, has been with me every step of my life journey for about twenty years by being a faithful partner. I deeply thank Sangye for all the support and love that she has given me on this journey. My two children, Gloria and Robert, were patient with my absence at home while I was in the library and working place. They always make me smile and motivate my life with vibrant energy. Soli Deo Gloria!

Jong Hun Joo
In the Season of Lent, 2014

Introduction

TODAY'S CHURCH IS VEXED with questions about worship: what it is, how you do it, what it accomplishes, to name a few. And there is no shortage of books offering answers to these questions. So where should one turn for insight on how to apply biblical principles to the local church's worship? This book attempts to offer a model of how both solid biblical understanding and effective practice of worship can be realized in churches today. And this model is anything but contemporary.

Matthew Henry (1662–1714) was a Presbyterian minister who interpreted the nature of Christian worship from within his Reformed tradition and applied it in his pastoral ministry. This book seeks to define Christian worship from this Reformed perspective and to explore how it can be a resource in our contemporary context of freedom of worship by exploring Henry's theology and practice of worship.

QUESTION AND TOPIC

For contemporary Christian people, the question of how to worship God is one of the most significant issues we face. It relates both to our ecclesiastical activity and to our daily lives. During the nearly fifty years since the Second Vatican Council in 1962, Protestant churches have also attempted to renew their worship services according to their own beliefs, convictions, and theologies, resulting in a variety of responses.[1] In particular, Reformed

---

1. As John Witvliet clearly summarized in the syllabus for the seminar "The Transformation of Christian Worship": "the last four decades have witnessed remarkable changes in the practice of Christian worship across Catholic and Protestant communities. One notable feature of all the change is how diverse it is. Rarely has the church been reforming in so many different directions at the same time. The Charismatic Movement, Liturgical Movement, Church Growth Movement, Hymn Renaissance, the Ecumenical Movement,

churches have engaged in this quest by updating their worship books and providing congregations with liturgical sources for various ecclesiastical, ethnic, and cultural contexts.² It might seem that the Reformed tradition could transform their worship services solely by supplying churches with copious liturgical resources. However, as churches in this tradition have found, an abundance of liturgical resources does not guarantee success in the transformation of the public worship service. In fact, there are many expectations of what success might look like. Worship renewal is not a process of simply adopting new styles and forms of worship. Rather, it is a complex pastoral work, requiring wisdom from the tradition, understanding of the congregation and the context, and careful engagement with the people at every step. For example, new but fixed forms or styles of worship could never serve as absolute models for Reformed churches, since Reformed churches (like most Protestant churches today) does not seek a single pattern for their worship services for all churches.

Therefore, the Reformed churches can serve as a model to negotiating the landmines of worship renewal: How can Reformed churches offer worship services that express the Reformed tradition while adapting to a rapidly changing world where often congregants are ignorant of that tradition, its values and practices? This is especially true in the midst of a marketplace that is overflowing with worship resources and liturgical expressions, to an extent that it might be called a time of a liturgical smorgasbord if not liturgical indulgence. For example, the Reformed tradition strongly holds the authority and authenticity of the Bible as the key principle and guide in every area of Christian faith, though this is not unique to that tradition. So the question can be asked in a more specific way: How in our present context of liturgical plenty do we discern an authentic biblical foundation for worship? Answering this question is significant for contemporary churches as they negotiate tradition of worship practice, while considering a pluriformity of options for liturgical innovation.

This book attempts to give a thorough and detailed answer to this question by articulating Matthew Henry's theology and practice of worship

---

and Postmodern cultural patterns have each transformed worship in many denominations and traditions."

2. Refer to Presbyterian worship sources such as the *Book of Common Worship* and *Prayers for Sunday Services: Companion Volume to the Book of Common Order*. *The Worship Sourcebook* as an ecumenical Reformed worship book was published in 2004. The Calvin Institute of Christian Worship has been leading in providing contemporary churches with abundant liturgical resources in various ways.

Introduction

in his specific context, as a case study of Reformed Presbyterian worship and a liturgical resource for contemporary Christian churches.

Keeping the question above in mind, this work mainly deals with the context, theology, practice, and Reformed characteristics of Matthew Henry's worship. Through exploring Henry's worship as a whole, this book, on the one hand, seeks to give a fuller vision of Reformed Presbyterian worship as an example of applied Reformed theology. It is not enough to understand what English Presbyterian worship is by simply stating the "Puritan Regulative Principle"[3] or interpreting the *Westminster Directory*. By focusing on Henry's practice as a case study, this work will also demonstrate that Reformed Presbyterian worship in Henry's ministry is not a limited or exaggerated expression of Reformed worship,[4] but rather a good example of *sola scriptura*-based worship as a creative interpretation of a Reformed understanding of worship. On the other hand, this particular study articulates general principles for Protestant worship, then and now, that can serve pastors, liturgical ministers, and worship leaders in their service to Christ and church. By offering Henry's liturgical resources in relation to the theological and liturgical context of his day, contemporary churches may learn how to develop public worship according to the Scriptures in their own contexts.[5]

---

3. Simply put, the Regulative Principle states that true worship is only what is commanded by God; false worship is anything not commanded. This was the Puritans' view of worship. Hughes Old commented (personal e-mail, December 17, 2009) that "the regulative principle is more appropriately called the Anabaptist principle of worship. The Anabaptists, however, got it from Tertullian, whom most of the Reformers regarded as a rigorist. Bucer, Zwingli and Oecolampadius were fully aware that Tertullian ended his days in a Montanist sect. The Reformers were well aware of the dangers of Montanism."

4. See Gore Jr., *Covenantal Worship*, and Farley, "What Is Biblical Worship? Biblical Hermeneutics and Evangelical Theologies of Worship," presented at the Evangelical Theological Society, San Diego, California, November 14, 2007. These two scholars contend that Puritan Regulative Principle is a limited and exaggerated form of the Reformed principle. They suggest a new approach to Reformed worship: the Covenantal approach to worship with reference to "adiaphora" (R. J. Gore Jr.); a more whole perspective of biblical theology without ignoring the Old Testament (Michael Farley).

5. For example, Korean Presbyterian churches can find liturgical resources in Henry because of their solid biblical foundation for church ministry. They began with the Bible in their worship even before shaping their theology. The liturgical foundation of Reformed Korean worship was founded on the principle of biblical worship in a simple style following the Nevius Method. Cf. Joo and Kim, "The Reformed Tradition in Korea," 484–91. For more detailed information on the Nevius Method of mission, see Nevius, *Methods of Mission Work*, and Allen, *The Nevius Plan for Mission Work*.

Introduction

Worship for Matthew Henry and his English Presbyterian community was not merely an adoption of theological doctrine in a ritual form from either Calvin or the Westminster Assembly. Culture and context also influenced the form and content of Henry's approach to worship. As such, this provides an example of liturgical inculturation, a crucial concept in a world of increasingly shifting cultural patterns. By studying Henry's work in his context, we have a helpful paradigm for contemporary churches to apply principles for integrating worship in their specific contexts.

MAIN THEMES

In articulating Henry's theology and practice of worship, this book will address several themes, including the use and place of the Bible in worship, a Reformed and broadly evangelical vision and practice of worship, and the implications of Henry's practices for the creative contextualization of this Reformed worship. These three themes are relevant to all churches' contemporary ministry, as they seek to develop and implement fresh worship practices.

A consistent vision of the Reformation was that of the primacy of the Scriptures in confession, ecclesiastical ministry, and Christian life; the Bible as Word of God is believed to be at the center of the Christian faith. Christian worship as a liturgical rite, then, should also be under the guidance of the Bible. The issue in theology centers not on accepting the authority of the Bible but on how to interpret and apply it to every area of human life, including the rites of liturgy.

The English Presbyterian tradition sought to protect the primacy of the Bible in their worship services, as well as in life. They were convicted of the sufficiency of the Word of God, following Calvin and the decision of the Westminster Assembly, indicated in the *Confession*, *Catechism*, and *Directory*. Although specific situations differ, contemporary Protestant churches share this conviction as well: the Bible is sufficient and authoritative in all areas of human life, including the worship service. For example, Calvin emphasized the primacy of Scripture regardless of ministerial context, as well:

> But if, without any regard to circumstances, you would simply know the character belonging at all times to those human traditions which ought to be repudiated by the church and condemned by all the godly, the definition which we formerly gave is clear and certain—viz. that they include all the laws enacted by men,

Introduction

without authority from the word of God, for the purpose of either of prescribing the mode of divine worship, or laying a religious obligation on the conscience, as enjoining things necessary to salvation.[6]

This Reformation principle is still common currency in contemporary churches.

METHODOLOGY

Liturgical studies uses three main approaches to the issues of worship: theology, history, and ritual study (practice). In order to understand the theology and practice of Henry's worship, this book uses the methods of these three disciplines. First, by delving into mainly his primary sources such as the *Bible Commentary* and treatises on the sacraments, the way in which Henry understood worship and the sacraments will be explored in detail. Second, regarding this work's approach to history, Henry's worship, as an English Presbyterian worship, will be interpreted as a case study of worship in the late seventeenth and the early eighteenth centuries by comparing and evaluating his worship with previous examples of Reformed worship. Third, in order to investigate how and to what extent Henry followed Reformed tradition in his worship ministry, this book will primarily look into his practice or ritual, considering related liturgical texts as necessary. This third method is especially necessary for understanding Henry's worship because he did not use a formulary for worship as a main text. Using these three methods, this book will discern how Henry understood and practiced English Presbyterian worship as an example of worship in his context and, further, will suggest how contemporary churches can appropriately develop and articulate their worship in their contexts based on the principles found in Henry's worship.

OUTLINE OF CHAPTERS

In order to accomplish its objectives, this book will proceed according to the following outline. First, Henry's worship ministry came out of his own specific context. In order to understand Henry's emerging Reformed Presbyterian worship, it is first necessary to examine his liturgical context.

---

6. Calvin, *Institutes of Christian Religion*, 4.10.16.

Introduction

Chapter one will examine Henry's liturgical context, giving particular attention to the political situation out of which it emerged. The Act of Uniformity (1662) and the Act of Toleration (1689) were two important political enactments of the English monarchy; together they had profound implications for Henry's ministry. Henry was born in 1662, the year in which the Act of Uniformity was passed, and he began his ministry as a Presbyterian divine right after the Act of Toleration was passed. Henry began his ministry in a time of freedom of worship. Contemporary churches also function in an era of freedom of worship. In this regard, a period of freedom of worship as Henry's liturgical context was not much different from that of contemporary worship, though many other cultural shifts have changed the landscape of worship today.

Before delving into Henry's understanding and practice of worship, chapter two will investigate Henry's life and thought. It will do so by examining biographies, funeral sermons delivered on the occasion of his death, and critical analyses of his thought. Although he was influenced by Puritan theologians and ministered as a Nonconformist, this chapter will argue that it is more appropriate to identify Henry as an English Presbyterian divine. Moreover, Henry published many books concerning Christian piety in addition to the *Bible Commentary*. Most scholars have been interested in him only as a Bible commentator. However, in order to understand Henry's thought, it is also necessary to examine all other works by Henry. By looking at his other works besides his *Commentary*, this chapter will show that communion with God as a pattern of relationship between humanity and God lies at the core of Henry's thought.

Chapters three and four, the main body of this work, will examine Henry's theology of worship and sacraments. The premise of these two chapters is that Henry developed his understanding of English Presbyterian worship as an expression or realization of communion with God. This was at the heart of his understanding of worship. Chapter three will examine how Henry constructed his understanding of Christian worship as a liturgical pattern of communion with God based on his reading and interpreting the Bible. Chapter four will investigate his understanding of the sacraments as concrete guides for a Christian's communion with God in daily life as well as essential rites of the church. These two chapters will show readers to what extent Henry followed the Reformed tradition he received, which emphasizes the Bible and discipleship in everyday life in its understanding of Christian worship and the sacraments. To assess the

Introduction

relevance of Henry's work to today's context, these two chapters will appraise Henry's strengths and weaknesses as a prelude to the application of his thought for contemporary churches.

Chapter five will examine the practice of Henry's public worship. The main focus of this chapter is not on the theological understanding of Henry's worship but on the practice of Henry's public worship. To state that Henry had a clear understanding of Reformed worship does not guarantee that he practiced public worship in accord with how he thought about it. Most Protestant theologians follow Geoffrey Wainwright's argument in his book *Doxology* for primacy of belief in worship: *lex credendi, lex orandi* (the rule/law of faith leads the rule/law of prayer).[7] However, regardless of specific issues on the debate of the relationship between *lex credendi* and *lex orandi*,[8] the real practice of a given worship service must be examined and interpreted in order to find the underlying assumptions and beliefs that shape those practices. By comparing Henry's public worship service with previous Reformed worship services such as John Calvin's Liturgy, John Knox's Genevan Liturgy, the *Westminster Directory*, Richard Baxter's Reformed Liturgy, and Philip Henry's public worship, this chapter will show that Henry developed liturgical practices not by simply adopting previous patterns but by creatively applying them to his own context with permeating Reformed aspects.

Through this work, this book anticipates that contemporary churches can glean helpful insights from Henry's liturgical insights and practices. Henry inherited a tradition associated with Calvin, Knox and *The Westminster Directory*. Yet his work of receiving, honoring that tradition through the lens of Biblical primacy in his day, becomes a model for all churches today.

---

7. See Wainwright, *Doxology: The Praise of God in Worship, Doctrine, and Life: A Systematic Theology*.

8. Geoffrey Wainwright emphasizes theological reflection over the worship service in the relationship between each sphere; Edward Kilmartin looks into the dynamic interrelationship between the worship service and faith. Cf. Wainwright, *Doxology*, 218–86; Kilmartin, *Christian Liturgy*. In contrast, Aidan Kavanagh and David Fagerberg established another paradigm in terms of liturgical theology: worship is the primary theology and theological reflection is the secondary theology; primary theology (*lex orandi*) establishes secondary theology (*lex credendi*), and so they emphasize primary theology over the secondary theology. Cf. Kavanagh, *On Liturgical Theology*; Fagerberg, *Theologia Prima*.

xxi

1

English Presbyterian Worship in the Restoration and Aftermath

The Liturgical Context of Matthew Henry

WHEN MATTHEW HENRY (1662–1714) began his ministry at Chester in 1687 as a nonconformist Presbyterian divine, the liturgical context of England had been in a state of flux in many ways for twenty-five years. The liturgical changes of this English Restoration era shaped the historical context of Matthew Henry's developing Presbyterian worship ministry. Henry learned and experienced Presbyterian worship mainly from English nonconforming dissenters within the Restoration era (1660–1689), and he ministered at Chester and Hackney for twenty-seven years during the period of liturgical indulgence that began in 1687, until his death in 1714. During this thirty-year period, Matthew Henry made little change in the structure and method of private and public worship. He practiced and led worship without changes from inward or outward causes in this period of toleration towards the liturgy. His decisions on worship for the congregations both in Chester and Hackney were shaped from learning and experiencing English Presbyterian worship during the persecution of the nonconforming dissenters. Thus, liturgical changes in the Restoration era could be regarded as the main context for Henry's understanding and implementation of Presbyterian worship.

This chapter does not attempt to analyze the general issues about the English Restoration[1] or the historical case of any specific territories in England;[2] instead it attempts to examine the transition of English Presbyterian worship in the Restoration era as Henry's liturgical context. At that time, the policy of the king and decision of parliament directly determined the manner of worship since every religious policy was sanctioned by the state. Thus, in order to understand changes in worship of that period, it is necessary to comprehend liturgy within the political and religious context. Recent research has given historians new perspectives on various aspects of the Restoration era.[3] With help from historical research, this chapter will focus on how English Presbyterian worship was changed by the restoration of the monarchy. What was the vision of English Reformed Presbyterian ministers at the beginning of this period? What were the main changes—and the causes of these changes—in English Presbyterian worship under the condition of persecution? How did English Presbyterians respond to political freedom and what were Matthew Henry's choices regarding the liturgy in a context of toleration? By answering these questions, this chapter will illustrate the way English Presbyterians upheld the Reformed principle of worship during the Restoration era and will explore the liturgical context in which Matthew Henry began his ministry.

THE VISION OF ENGLISH REFORMED PRESBYTERIAN WORSHIP

In 1660, two years before Henry's birth, the nation experienced the restoration of the English monarchy. For the Puritan nonconformists the Restoration meant a period of continuous religious persecution and strife. The persecution for the nonconformists, the Presbyterians, Independents, Baptists, and Quakers, did not begin outside of any context; they were "all dissenters from the church as established by law."[4] The persecution of them

---

1. For example, this chapter does not engage in the debates that look at the English Restoration from a peculiar viewpoint, such as the "revisionist" perspective, which regards Protestants as having played a largely negative role in sixteenth-century England in terms of anti-Catholicism. For this debate and issue, see Finlayson, *Historians, Puritanism, and the English Revolution*, chap. 5, and McClendon et al., *Protestant Identities*.

2. For example, Ramsbottom, "Puritan Dissenters and English Churches."

3. For understanding recent scholarship on the Restoration era, see Harris et al., *The Politics of Religion in Restoration England*, especially chap. 1.

4. Spurr, "From Puritanism to Dissent, 1660–1700," 238.

was the result of repeated decisions of Charles II and the Parliament and the nonconformists' rejections of the religious politics of the state. In order to understand how and why the English Presbyterians refused to follow the religious politics of the king and parliament and were thus persecuted, it is first necessary to examine their exact situation when the Restoration began. We need to explain the English Presbyterians' vision of worship and how they attempted to realize this vision within Restoration in England. The English Presbyterians' vision of worship at the beginning of the Restoration era can be seen best in the work of Richard Baxter (1615–1691). Richard Baxter's "Savoy Liturgy" or "Reformed Liturgy" (1661) shows the elements of the English Presbyterian vision when the Restoration began, although it was not implemented in the Presbyterian congregations in history. This section will investigate three points in Baxter's liturgy: why Baxter tried to write and use a new book of worship; what it included in the form and content of worship; and to what extent it can be seen as Reformed worship.

Political and Religious Attempts to Unify the Anglican and Presbyterian Form of Worship

When the restoration of the monarchy began in 1660, Charles II "issued a declaration [Declaration of Breda] promising 'a liberty to tender consciences . . . that no man shall be disquieted, or call in question, for differences of opinion in matters of religion which do not disturb the peace of the kingdom.'"[5] Regardless of the motives,[6] this declaration of Charles II shows his desire for religious toleration. John Spurr assessed Charles's policy on toleration by saying that "[he] intended to bind the bleeding wounds of his English kingdom, to abolish all notes of discord, separation, and difference of parties, by pardoning past crimes, extending liberty in religion to those of a tender conscience, and referring all disputed property titles to parliament."[7] Bard Thompson, liturgical historian, also pointed out the liturgical significance of Charles's choice of religious toleration by

---

5. Watts, *The Dissenters*, 221.

6. According to Watts, two explanations are possible: "that the years of religious strife, involuntary exile, and the pursuit of pleasure had taught the king a worldly skepticism which looked on all religions with tolerant indifference; or alternatively, that the king was a sincere, though secret, Roman Catholic who wanted toleration only because it would mean security for his hated co-religionists and would constitute a first step towards the restoration of papal influence in England" (ibid.).

7. Spurr, *The Restoration Church of England*, 30.

mentioning that "the Church of England would become sufficiently comprehensive to include some of the Puritans."[8] While some toleration in liturgical practice was given, both the Anglicans and the nonconformists attempted to take their religious places with the restoration of the monarchy by reintroducing their own liturgy. Among these attempts, the English Presbyterians also endeavored not to lose this opportunity to unify the Anglican and Presbyterian liturgy with their own Reformed convictions. Richard Baxter's Reformed Liturgy in 1661 can be regarded as an English Presbyterian political and religious effort to unify liturgy based on his Reformed convictions about worship.[9]

Unifying Liturgy

However, the English Presbyterian vision for the national church during this short period of liturgical toleration was not accomplished. One of the religious issues that Charles II faced was the tension between the Church of England and the nonconformist Puritans. Anglican bishops, on the one hand, and other nonconformists, on the other hand, had their own visions at that time. The Cavaliers in the Parliament who defended their king and church "were determined to restore the Prayer Book."[10] Anglican bishops "chided the ministers for their adulation of the Reformed churches and surmised that a more profitable norm would be the liturgy of the ancient Greek and Latin Churches."[11] There "was [also] the spontaneous recovery of the Church of England in the counties, cathedral cities and parishes of England."[12] In practice, "the local gentry occasionally encouraged a return to the Prayer Book by prosecuting those clergy who failed to use it under Elizabethan statutes."[13] Moreover, the Independents would not follow Baxter's reformation of worship but insisted, "Scripture gave no warrant to prescribed forms of prayer."[14] They even "feared that this settlement [based on the tolerant principle of Charles' declaration from Breda] would lessen

---

8. Thompson, *Liturgies of the Western Church*, 375.

9. To Baxter, "unify the liturgy" meant an attempt to establish a more Reformed liturgy as a national form of worship for all Protestants in England.

10. Davies, *Worship and Theology in England*, 2:363.

11. Thompson, *Liturgies of the Western Church*, 276.

12. Spurr, *Restoration Church of England*, 36.

13. Ibid., 37.

14. Davies, *Worship and Theology in England*, 2:375.

their own chances of a toleration."[15] Thus, "in 1661–2 the movement towards this form of church [a broad-based national church] was stopped in its tracks."[16]

Under these conditions, English Presbyterians needed to overcome serious attacks from Anglican bishops and radical nonconforming Independents in order to accomplish their vision of unifying liturgy. Thus, while facing this conflict, English Presbyterians attempted to unify the liturgy with the help of the monarchy. One of the attempts was producing the "Exceptions against the Book of Common Prayer;" the other was the "submission of Baxter's 'Reformation of the Liturgy.'"

Thompson categorized the list of "Exceptions" that the Presbyterian commissioners prepared against the *Book of Common Prayer* into two divisions: (1) general objections to principles and characteristics of the Book, and (2) specific criticisms of details in the Book:

> Of the general objections, some touched the nature of worship. The Puritans asked for a comprehensive, Scriptural liturgy. . . . They opposed any type of uniformity that would stifle extempore prayer or deprive the minister of all discretion in the conduct of worship. . . . They deemed the Book defective. . . .
>
> Of the specific criticisms, some were designed to achieve a greater correspondence between Scripture and liturgy, others to serve the clarity of the biblical message. Thus, the doxology should be restored to the Lord's Prayer, the apocryphal *Benedicite* replaced by a psalm or hymn. . . . The lessons should be read, not sung, and preaching more strictly enjoined. . . . Holy Communion should no longer be given to any persons except those who were prepared to receive it. . . . They thought it well to restore the Black Rubric of the 1552 Prayer Book, with its discourse against adoring the elements.[17]

However, Anglican bishops defeated this effort by declaring "that the liturgy could not be circumscribed by Scripture, but rightfully included those matters which were generally received in the Catholic Church."[18]

While the Presbyterian commissioners articulated the "Exceptions," In an attempt to help resolve the tension between the Anglicans and the nonconformists, Baxter submitted his "*Reformation of the Liturgy*, which

15. Spurr, *Restoration Church of England*, 37–38.
16. Spurr, "From Puritanism to Dissent," 236.
17. Thompson, *Liturgies of the Western Church*, 376–77.
18. Ibid., 387.

was in fact a complete service-book and thereafter acquired the name, 'the Savoy Liturgy.'"[19] Baxter by himself produced the alternative Reformed order of service with the anticipation of the approval of the Presbyterian liturgy by the king and parliament. Baxter's Reformed Liturgy can be understood as an alternative liturgical book written at the restoration of the monarchy in order to unify services of the State with a Reformed liturgy. As Davies commented, "[W]hile the *Westminster Directory* was a compromise between Presbyterians and Independents, the 'Reformed Liturgy' represents the liturgical convictions of one party, the English Presbyterians."[20]

Although this liturgical book was formulated by him alone, Baxter's attempt to unify two liturgical traditions was not initiated by himself; this unified ideal liturgy was an earlier vision of English Presbyterians. When English Presbyterians saw the possibility of the restoration of the monarchy, "it was hoped that in return for Presbyterian support of his efforts to regain the throne, Charles would accept limitations upon his powers as King and agree to the establishment of Presbyterianism instead of Anglicanism."[21] That is why English Presbyterians tried to take a central place at the beginning of the Restoration. As Douglas Lacey pointed out, the English Presbyterian ministers "were thinking primarily of their hope to gain Charles II's acceptance of Presbyterianism as the established religion."[22] However, Baxter's Reformed Liturgy failed to take a place as an alternative to the *Book of Common Prayer*. In reality, "it has received little attention at its own time."[23]

On July 24, 1661, the Savoy Conference closed without achieving any reconciliation. Regardless of the result, it is clear that English Presbyterians attempted to unify liturgy by producing the list of the "Exceptions" and "Reformed Liturgy." The English Presbyterian commissioners and Baxter "objected to set liturgy as it totally excluded the gift of prayer and because of the 'Romish Forms' still in it."[24]

---

19. Ibid., 377. He quickly produced this Reformed Liturgy within two weeks.
20. Davies, *Worship and Theology in England*, 2:434.
21. Lacey, *Dissent and Parliamentary Politics in England*, 4.
22. Ibid., 6.
23. Davies, *Worship and Theology in England*, 2:433.
24. Williams, "The Puritan Concept and Practice of Prayer," 360.

English Presbyterian Worship in the Restoration and Aftermath

With a Reformed Vision

While Baxter wanted, through the Savoy Conference, to unify the liturgy, he did not attempt to achieve just one uniform liturgy in order to overcome the tension among the Protestants in England. Furthermore, by unifying the liturgy he endeavored to achieve a Reformed vision of worship for the restoration of the monarchy.

First of all, Baxter did not seek to unify the liturgy simply for the purpose of a unified liturgy; he did his best to make Presbyterian worship an official liturgy of the State when the restoration of the monarchy provided the opportunity. To put it another way, he attempted to develop Reformed liturgy in his specific context. Before the Restoration began, *The Westminster Directory* of 1644 had been in use among Presbyterians and Independents for about sixteen years. As Davies pointed out, "The *Directory* of 1644 produced jointly by Presbyterians and Independents was a compromise, exacting too little for the Presbyterians and too much for the Independents."[25] As a Presbyterian minister Baxter anticipated the establishment of Presbyterianism by articulating a more Reformed liturgy when the opportunity was given.

Second, it is clear that Baxter's effort to unify the liturgy was initiated by a "Reformed vision." Williams summarized the Puritans' liturgical reformation: "According to *The Westminster Directory*, the Puritans' criticisms of *the Book of Common Prayer* were not from any love of novelty. They were motivated by desire for a liturgy reformed in accordance with the Scriptures."[26] Baxter's Reformed vision in his Savoy Liturgy can be summarized as follows:

> The Savoy Liturgy was constructed of *biblical speech*. It was a realization of the Puritan desire to have an exact correspondence between worship and the *Word of God*. Baxter was persuaded that such a liturgy would comprehend all manner of Christians: all would be satisfied by the infallible truths and apt phrases drawn out of *God's own Word*; and all would be free to interpret this liturgy "according to the sense they have in *Scripture*."[27]

---

25. Davies, *Worship and Theology in England*, 2:406.
26. Williams, "The Puritan Concept and Practice of Prayer," 357.
27. Thompson, *Liturgies of the Western Church*, 381, italics added.

Thus, it was important that Baxter's development of a Reformed worship sought to do so according to the Scriptures when he sought to unify the liturgy.

The Form and Content of Baxter's Reformed Liturgy

Although it was not used in English Presbyterian congregations, Baxter's Reformed Liturgy needs to be examined in more detail in order to understand what English Presbyterians wanted to achieve in liturgy at the restoration of the monarchy. When Baxter submitted a petition to the Savoy Conference, he categorized it in two parts, which show the Reformed vision of worship at the beginning of the Restoration: "A Petition for Peace" and "the Reformation of the Liturgy."[28]

"A Petition for Peace" literally means a petition "to the most reverend archbishop and bishops, and the reverend their assistants commissioned by his majesty to treat about the alteration of the Book of Common Prayer"[29] with twenty sections in the style of an apologetic letter. In addition, "the Reformation of the Liturgy" includes specific requests for alteration of worship. The contents of the Reformation of the Liturgy are as follows:

> The Ordinary Public Worship on the Lord's Day
> The Order of Celebrating the Sacrament of the Body and Blood of Christ
> The Celebration of the Sacrament of Baptism
> Of Catechizing, and the Approbation of Those That Are to be Admitted to the Lord's Supper
> Of the Celebration of Matrimony
> The Visitation of the Sick, and Their Communion
> The Order for Solemnizing the Burial of the Dead
> Of Extraordinary Days of Humiliation, and Thanksgiving, and Anniversary Festivals
> Of Prayer and Thanksgiving for Particular Members of the Church
> Of Pastoral Discipline, Public Confession, Absolution, and Exclusion from the Holy Communion of the Church

---

28. The whole title of this petition is "A Petition for Peace: with the Reformation of the Liturgy. As It was Presented to the Right Reverend Bishops, by the Divines Appointed by His Majesties Commission to Treat with Them about the Alteration of It" (1661).

29. Subtitle of this petition.

In addition to these ten sections, it includes an appendix composed of "a Larger Litany, or General Prayer: to be used at Discretion" and "the Church's Praise for our Redemption; to be used at Discretion."

To understand the changes the English Presbyterians attempted to make to the contemporary Anglican worship, it is useful to focus on the form and content of the Lord's Day worship. The elements of the Lord's Day worship (without Communion service) developed by Baxter are listed below:

> A Short Prayer (with shorter alternative)
> The Creed (sometimes Athanasius Creed)
> The Ten Commandments
> Scripture Sentences: for the right informing and affecting the people, and moving them to a penitent believing confession
> The Confession of Sin and Prayer for Pardon and Sanctification (with shorter alternative)
> Lord's Prayer
> Scripture (Gospel) Sentences: for the strengthening of faith and raising the penitent
> Sentences what must be and done for the time to come for the salvation
> Reading Psalm 95 or 100 or 84 followed by the Psalms in order for the Day
> Reading a Chapter of the Old Testament
> Singing a Psalm or Te Deum
> Reading a Chapter of the New Testament
> Prayer for the King and Magistrates
> Sing or Reading Psalm 67 or 98 or Some Other Psalm or Benedictus or Magnificat
> Prayer for the State, Necessities of the Church, and the Subject of the Sermon
> Sermon upon Some Text of Holy Scripture
> Prayer for a Blessing on the Word of Instruction and Exhortation
> Benediction

This "Ordinary Public Worship on the Lord's Day" of Baxter's is not an innovation unrelated to previous Puritan worship. At the same time, his suggested Lord's Day worship is distinctive from *The Westminster Directory* in its structure and form. Baxter's suggested Lord's Day worship is a more Presbyterian liturgical pattern than that of *The Westminster Directory for the Publique Worship of God* (1644). *The Westminster Directory* was "an authentic creation of the Puritan spirit and the truest exemplar of Puritan worship."[30] This *Directory* was prepared by the Westminster Assembly, which convened on July 1, 1643, in order to "reform the standards of the church in a manner 'most agreeable to God's holy word.'"[31] After serious debate on the form and freedom of worship, the Assembly produced a *Directory*, "as opposed to a liturgy, which outlined the main headings of worship, and described the substance of each element in such a way that by altering here and there a word, a man may mould it into a prayer."[32]

The Westminster Directory includes these main elements of Lord's Day worship:[33]

> Prayer
> Public Reading of the Holy Scriptures
> Singing the Psalm
> Public Prayer before the Sermon (long prayer)
> Preaching of the Word
> Prayer after the Sermon
> Singing the Psalm
> (Celebration of the Communion)

These elements are much simpler than that of Baxter's Savoy Liturgy.

A characteristic of *The Westminster Directory* is the Puritan seeking for liturgical freedom from the Anglican Church. The Puritans opposed any rubric that did not allow them to lead free prayers. The order of *The Westminster Directory* was prepared by the Puritans including Presbyterians, Scot commissioners, and Independents. Also, that order was not called a "liturgy" but a "directory." As Thompson commented, "it [the directory] was a monumental effort to comprehend the virtues of form and freedom."[34] To Baxter, this *Directory* was not enough to realize the vision of Presbyterian worship. That is why he attempted to suggest a more Presbyterian liturgical pattern of worship by articulating the Reformed Liturgy

---

30. Thompson, *Liturgies of the Western Church*, 353.

31. Ibid., 349.

32. Ibid.

33. The complete contents of *The Westminster Directory* are the Assembling of the Congregation, Public Reading of the Holy Scripture, Public Prayer before Sermon, Preaching the Word, Prayer after the Sermon, the Sacrament of Baptism, the Sacrament of the Lord's Supper, the Sanctification of the Lord's Day, the Solemnization of Marriage, the Visitation of the Sick, Burial of the Dead, Public Solemn Fasting, the Observation of days of Public Thanksgiving, Sing the Psalms, and An Appendix touching Days and Places of Public Worship.

34. Thompson, *Liturgies of the Western Church*, 353.

when the opportunity was given. To understand Baxter, we must examine the nature of a Presbyterian pattern of worship in the Reformed Liturgy.

Reformed Characteristics of Worship in the Savoy Liturgy

Baxter's "Ordinary Public Worship on Lord's Day" reveals several Reformed characteristics. Most of all, Baxter's liturgy places worship on a biblical foundation. The original copy of the "Ordinary" includes biblical texts for each element. The scriptural texts quoted for each element consist of not just a simple verse but various proofs from the Old Testament to the New Testament. All the eighteen elements above have a biblical foundation and relation. Baxter even provided scriptural texts for the content of prayer.

When considering these numerous biblical texts, it is hard to believe that he composed this worship order in two weeks. It is certain that he had prepared this type of worship order beforehand. Baxter's massive book *Five Disputations of Church Government and Worship* (1659; 492 pages) already expressed his conviction about biblical worship. In the section of "Whether a Stinted Liturgy, or Form of Worship, be a Desirable Means for the Peace of these Churches?" he clearly wrote in Prop. 7: "The safest way of composing a stinted liturgy, is to take it all, or as much as may be, for words as well as matter out of the Holy Scriptures."[35] With this thesis, he gave sufficient reason for his conviction by concluding, "there are no other words that may be preferred before the word of God, or stand in competition with them."[36]

Second, Baxter's liturgy has a biblical direction, which means that it is composed of biblical form and content. Among the eighteen elements of worship in the Savoy Liturgy given above, the content of most of the elements come from the Bible: "The Ten Commandments," "Scripture Sentences," "The Lord's Prayer," "Scripture (Gospel) Sentences," "Reading a Psalm," "Reading a Chapter of the Old Testament," "Singing a Psalm," "Reading a Chapter of the New Testament," "Sing or Reading a Psalm," and "Sermon." In addition, the words and forms of prayers in his liturgy are based on Scripture. He did not directly quote any prayers from the Scriptures. Instead he intentionally composed prayers using the content and language of the Scriptures. He attempted to produce a flexible biblical pattern of prayer in contrast to Anglican fixed prayers. Moreover, Baxter directed worship music to follow a biblical form by continuing to sing the

---

35. Baxter, *Five Disputations of Church Government and Worship*, 378.
36. Ibid., 379.

psalms. Reformers, as Thompson mentioned, "urged the singing of psalms in church as an instrument of praise and a means of attaining common worship."[37] Thus, Baxter attempted to use biblical principles to direct the form and content of Lord's Day worship.

Third, Baxter's liturgy is related to piety, which emphasizes holiness of life. In place of *The Westminster Directory*'s "Prayer after Sermon" Baxter has a "Prayer for a Blessing on the Word of Instruction and Exhortation." Thompson pointed out that Baxter's emphasis on holiness of life followed Calvin's tradition: "while he [Baxter] did not use the law as Calvin preferred—to incite the penitent to true piety—he achieved *the same* great emphasis upon holiness of life by certain other devices, namely, by the Scriptural sentences that evoked sanctity, by the Exhortation at the close of communion, by the exercise of Discipline."[38] In this way, Baxter tried to integrate life and liturgy in the new form of worship.

Fourth, Baxter's liturgy has a Reformed characteristic in that it emphasized "ongoing reformation" of worship. One of the reasons that he submitted "a Petition for Peace" was to alter the *Book of Common Prayer*: "the Common Prayer Book as differing from the Masse-Book, being not so old, and that which might then be the matter of a change, is not so unchangeable itself, but that those alterations may be accepted for ends so desirable as are now before us."[39] With this Reformed conviction, Baxter humbly asked the Savoy Conference to give the Presbyterians freedom: "the cause of the Non-conformists has been long ago stated . . . you have no reason to suspect them of any considerable change. Grant us but the freedom that Christ and His Apostles left unto the Churches."[40] That is why he included some flexibility in his Reformed Liturgy by adding alternative prayers.

Although Baxter's Savoy Liturgy arose from a clear Reformed vision, this vision was not realized in practice. Contrary to their expectations, English Presbyterian worship was changed under a new political and social context. Thus, it is necessary to examine how English Presbyterian worship changed during the Restoration in order to more clearly understand Matthew Henry's liturgical context.

---

37. Thompson, *Liturgies of the Western Church*, 188.
38. Ibid., 383, italics added.
39. Baxter, *Petition*, 9.
40. Ibid., 20.

CHANGES IN ENGLISH PRESBYTERIAN WORSHIP UNDER PERSECUTION IN THE RESTORATION ERA

The year of 1661, one year before Matthew Henry was born, was a crucial moment for English Presbyterian worship. Richard Baxter's "Petition to for Peace: with the Reformation of the Liturgy" was rejected by the Savoy Conference in 1661. Moreover, the Conference not only denied Baxter's "Petition" but also more actively required all clergy to follow the decision of Parliament by "requiring them to declare their unfeigned assent and consent to all and everything contained and prescribed in and by the book entitled the Book of Common Prayer."[41] Changes of English Presbyterian worship in the Restoration era were explicitly connected to this political imposition on religion. To put it another way, changes of English Presbyterian worship were mainly motivated not so much by the inward needs or theological convictions of the ministers as by political and social causes.

English Presbyterian worship changed in significant ways between 1661, the year of Baxter's Reformed Liturgy's failure, and 1687. After 1687, the year of the Act of Indulgence, and 1689, the year of the Act of Toleration, English Presbyterian worship began to embrace the new experience of freedom. This section will focus on the period of persecution—1661 to 1687—by examining the main causes and changes of the English Presbyterian worship in that period. English nonconformists were severely persecuted by the "Clarendon Code," the series of enactments passed by the Cavalier Parliament:[42] Corporation Act (1661), Act of Uniformity (1662), Conventicle Act (1664, 1670), and Five Mile Act (1665). Although their main purpose was not to directly persecute English Presbyterians alone,[43] these enactments had a huge impact on English Presbyterian worship. The three most important arenas of change related to English Presbyterian worship during the period of persecution involved Anglican attacks on English Presbyterians in relation to their worship resource, Presbyterians dissenters' experience of hardship and its effect on their worship, and a new emphasis on family piety and life.

---

41. Ramsbottom, "Puritan Dissenters and English Churches," 7.

42. "The period of persecution is usually associated with the name of Charles's Lord Chancellor, the Earl of Clarendon" (Watts, *Dissenters*, 223).

43. All nonconformists such as Presbyterians, Baptists, Independents, and Quakers were persecuted by the Clarendon Code.

Anglican Attacks on English Presbyterians in Relation to Worship Resource

One of the great changes in English Presbyterian worship during the period of persecution was not to use any prescribed liturgies or liturgical texts as rubrics. They just took the Bible as the primary worship resource for both the foundation and the direction of worship. As Davies pointed out, "the Presbyterians had no objection to set prayers as such, but could not agree that the Book of Common Prayer was in all things conformable to the Word of God."[44] When the political authorities required them to follow a fixed liturgy from the *Book of Common Prayer*, English Presbyterians chose a new way of worship. Their response to the political enactments of the Act of Corporation (1661) and Act of Uniformity (1662) relates to the liturgical resource. In response to these political requirements, English Presbyterians moved away from a written liturgical book or manual as their worship resource since they did not want to follow the idea of fixed prayers.

Presbyterian Response to the Corporation Act

The Corporation Act in 1661 was the first policy of the Restoration to cause change in English Presbyterian worship. This enactment required "all mayors, aldermen, councilors, and borough officials to swear loyalty to the king and to take 'the sacrament of the Lord's Supper, according to the rites of the Church of England.'"[45] One of the purposes of this political requirement was "to destroy the political influence of the Presbyterians and other sects."[46] "The Corporation Act had shown that parliament knew how to strike a shrewd blow at the centres of Puritan power."[47] The response to this political enactment was this:

> Although there were efforts to defeat this resolution, and although about one-third of the Presbyterian-Congregationalist group of members in the Commons either refused to attend or to follow the prescribed Sacramental procedure, in the end all but one of them did comply with the requirement even though obviously with reluctance and undoubtedly with reservations. Thus did

---

44. Davies, *The English Free Churches*, 92.
45. Watts, *Dissenters*, 223.
46. Plum, *Restoration Puritanism*, 24.
47. Ibid., 7.

English Presbyterian Worship in the Restoration and Aftermath

these members bend to the exigencies of the day, and occasional conformity as practiced by Puritans for political purposes has its beginnings.[48]

This was the beginning of persecution, as Davies described:

> This [Act of Corporation] prohibited any Nonconformist henceforth from holding office in any city or municipal corporation, a ban that fell heavily on the Presbyterians in particular, because many of them held office in the City of London, and in other corporations. This, however, was only the beginning of the persecution.[49]

In addition to the political persecution of nonconformists, this Act also had religious significance in relation to English Presbyterian worship. Although its political aspect can be regarded as the main purpose of the Corporation Act, it specifically required those who sought public office to follow "the rite of the Church of England" based on the *Book of Common Prayer*. For approximately the past sixteen years, *The Westminster Directory of Public Worship* (1644) was decreed as the national formulary of worship and had taken the place of the *Book of Common Prayer* as "the product of the Westminster Assembly of Divines appointed by Parliament."[50] However, English Presbyterians, as nonconformists, criticized the *Book of Common Prayer* and even attempted to establish a more Reformed liturgy as a national form of worship with Baxter's Savoy Liturgy. To them, Parliament's political enactment requiring them to follow the rite of the Church of England meant religious persecution in terms of worship. In this way, through the Corporation Act, English Presbyterians not only lost the opportunity to recover Baxter's Reformed Liturgy but also were required to follow the *Book of Common Prayer*. So the failure of a more Reformed liturgical form led to the English Presbyterians' even greater hesitation to take any liturgical book as their direction for worship.

---

48. Lacey, *Dissent and Parliamentary Politics*, 19.
49. Davies, *English Free Churches*, 92–93.
50. Davies, *Worship and Theology in England*, 2:344.

Matthew Henry

The Influence of the Act of Uniformity on Change of Liturgical Text

The Act of Uniformity was more actively "intended to eliminate the Presbyterians."[51] Nonconformist Presbyterian ministers were ejected from the national church—a result they had not expected: "instead of healing the nation's divisions and easing the path to conformity for moderate Presbyterians, this 'sharp act' [Act of Uniformity] virtually ensured that they would be forced out of the national church."[52] Spurr clearly summarized the core demand of the Act of Uniformity:

> The Act presented four specific difficulties to the scrupulous: to qualify for a clerical living it was necessary to give "unfeigned assent and consent to all and everything contained and prescribed in and by" the Book of Common Prayer, including the sacraments and ceremonies, psalter and ordinal; to subscribe to the Thirty-Nine Articles, of which three concerned church government; to renounce the obligation of the Solemn League and Covenant for yourself and all others, and forswear "to endeavour any change or alteration of government either in church or state"; and finally, to have received ordination from the hands of a bishop.[53]

In brief, one liturgical purpose of this enactment, as Ramsbottom indicated, was to "make the Book of Common Prayer once again the only legal form of public worship."[54]

All nonconformists including English Presbyterians needed to choose whether or not to consent to this political enactment regarding liturgy. As Charles Whiting pointed out, "the Act of Uniformity required the clergy to take the oath of canonical obedience, a phrase which many of them misinterpreted or misunderstood, and to swear obedience to the ordinary according to the cannons of the Church."[55] The Act of Uniformity pointed to several reasons for penalizing the nonconformists': "'viciousness of life,' 'errors in doctrine,' 'superstitious innovations in worship,' and 'malignancy against the Parliament.'"[56] Regarding worship, it also "stipulated that the morning and evening prayers therein contained shall upon every Lord's

---

51. Plum, *Restoration Puritanism*, 24.
52. Spurr, *Restoration Church of England*, 42.
53. Ibid., 43.
54. Ramsbottom, "Puritan Dissenters and English Churches," 6.
55. Whiting, *Studies in English Puritanism*, 17.
56. Ibid., 6.

Day and upon all other days and occasions and at the times therein appointed be openly and solemnly read by all and every minister or curate in every church, chapel or other place of public worship."[57]

Although some Presbyterians remained in the official ministry as Puritan clergymen,[58] a great number of the nonconforming Presbyterians were ejected; "it is traditional that the number of the ejected on St. Bartholomew's Day, 1662, was 2000,"[59] even though it is impossible to get the exact numbers. The ejection of Presbyterian ministers influenced changes in worship in significant ways. They could not securely worship using the Reformed forms such as *The Westminster Directory* or Reformed Liturgy. The Act of Uniformity was not optional but mandatory for all Puritan clergymen, and their Reformed Book of Worship (Reformed Liturgy) was denied by Anglican power. But the English Presbyterian divines who attempted to establish a Reformed liturgy as a national form of worship at the beginning of the Restoration era did not want to comply with the political enactment requiring "unfeigned assent and consent to everything in the Book of Common Prayer." Their strong rejection of the *Book of Common Prayer* was the most serious change in this period. The English Puritans' criticisms of the *Book of Common Prayer*, as Roy Williams pointed out, "were not from any love of novelty. They were motivated by desire for a liturgy reformed in accordance with the Scriptures."[60] As a result, their only choice—if they would not conform to the rubric of the Church of England—was to make the Bible, the traditional Reformed resource of worship, their liturgical foundation and direction.

---

57. Ramsbottom, "Puritan Dissenters and English Churches," 7.

58. Owing to their willingness to continue in their places, some Puritan clergymen remained in the official ministry well after 1662. In fact, according to Spurr, "the overwhelming majority of the English parish clergy simply endured the changes brought about in 1660–62 as they had those of the previous decades" (*Restoration Church of England*, 42–43). According to Ramsbottom, "no doubt a few among them were motivated more by fear of losing their livelihood than by deep commitment to godly religion" ("Puritan Dissenters and English Churches," 105).

59. Whiting, *Studies in English Puritanism*, 10. Horton Davies also agreed that "almost two thousand of the most conscientious ministers in England refused to comply with the new and stringent terms of conformity and lost their livelihoods" (*Worship and Theology in England*, 2:439). In another way, Harry Plum indicated that "considerable number decided to remain within the Anglican church, but it is impossible to say how many" (*Restoration Puritanism*, 25).

60. Williams, "The Puritan Concept and Practice of Prayer," 360.

Persecution and English Presbyterian Dissenters' Worship

The Act of Uniformity indeed forced Puritanism into dissent. English Presbyterians who did not conform to the Act of the Uniformity were ejected from the national church and all ejected nonconformists were soon called "dissenters." However, all dissenters did not become complete nonconformists. Some dissenters instead "adopted the practice of occasional or partial conformity."[61] Either way, the concept of "dissenter" is related to the service of worship: "on legal grounds Dissent was not determined by the relative frequency with which Conventicles and Anglican services were attended. If a person attended any Nonconformist service at all, he became a Dissenter according to the law."[62] Moreover, the dissenters "asked chiefly to be left alone to worship God in their own way."[63] In the period of persecution from 1662 to 1687 English Presbyterian dissenters underwent religious persecution but continued to keep public worship according to their convictions even though they had to change in some ways. The changes in English Presbyterian worship during this period relate to their hardship and dissenting life under persecution.

Persecution and Experience of Hardship

In the Restoration era, Parliament reestablished the Anglican Church and protected it by the political enactments called articulated above. Tim Harris indicated that all of these parliamentary laws "aimed at destroying the dissenting influence in towns."[64] In response, dissenters everywhere at first "tried to seize the municipal government."[65] Moreover, "there was great opposition to the enforcement of the Conventicle Act."[66] Presbyterians also "did their best to keep their flocks together, and by the pains they took in praying and preaching, to show how much superior their way was to the Episcopal way."[67] Although there was serious opposition to the parliamentary laws, nonconformists Presbyterian pastors had already left the

---

61. Lacey, *Dissent and Parliamentary Politics*, 15.
62. Ibid., 25.
63. Watts, *Dissenters*, 2.
64. Harris, "Introduction: Revising the Restoration," 16.
65. Whiting, *Studies In English Puritanism*, 397.
66. Ibid., 399.
67. Ibid., 394.

Anglican Church with their denial of the *Book of Common Prayer*. Thus, English Presbyterian dissenters, with other dissenters, began to suffer persecution. In practice, Watts pointed out, "the Dissenters were powerless by themselves to influence political events."[68]

The persecution made a huge impact on the dissenters' life and their worship. Most of all, as James Bradley indicates, "from the ejection of some 2000 Nonconforming ministers, lecturers, and fellows of colleges in 1662, through the penal period of Dissent to 1689, and on into the early years of Queen Anne's reign, heterodox and orthodox dissenters alike experienced imposition and exclusion, and they were constantly under the threat of repression."[69] The hardship that the dissenters experienced was not light:

> The ministers were not only excluded from preferments, but cut off from all hope of a livelihood, as far as the industry and craft of their adversaries could reach. . . . Though they were as frugal as possible, they could hardly live. Some lived on little more than brown bread and water, many had but eight or ten pounds a year to maintain a family, so that a piece of flesh had not come to their tables in six weeks time; their allowance would scarce afford them bread and cheese.[70]

Although some deprived dissenters had benefactors for their ministries and lives, it is certain that their hardship caused great sufferings. The Act of Uniformity caused the greatest harm to the dissenters: "the persecution to which the ejected and their followers were liable, persecution which meant fines, imprisonment, and sometimes death in prison, increased the bitterness, and hardened the schism."[71]

With the Act of Uniformity, the first Conventicle Act in 1664 "completed the transformation of Puritanism into Dissent."[72] The Conventicle Act directly persecuted dissenters' worship by "forbidding five or more people from meeting together for worship except in accordance with the liturgy of the Church of England."[73] This Act made any non-Anglican gathering of five or more people over the age of sixteen illegal. Following the Conventicle Act, in 1665 the Five Mile Act forbade nonconformist

---

68. Watts, *Dissenters*, 252.
69. Bradley, "The Religious Origins of Radical Politics," 194.
70. Whiting, *Studies in English Puritanism*, 20.
71. Ibid., 32.
72. Lacey, *Dissent and Parliamentary Politics*, 15.
73. Watts, *Dissenters*, 225.

ministers to reside within five miles of any town where they had ministered prior to that year. Lacey indicated the significance of the Five Mile Act:

> The significance of the Five Mile Act was political and constitutional in character as well as religious, for Nonconformist ministers were to swear that they would not at any time endeavor any alteration of government in Church or State if they wished to stay within five miles of any borough sending burgesses to Parliament, or any place where they had held a Church preferment after the Act of Oblivion or preached to an unlawful assembly.[74]

This Five Mile Act made it seriously difficult for the dissenters to be near and minister to their congregations legally. Yet in the local church setting, as Plum pointed out, "this act was not as effective as one would suppose since the removal of all ministers from one congregation only established them in closer contact with others."[75] Nevertheless, the persecution of the dissenters did not stop until the Act of Indulgence in 1678. Especially, another Conventicle Act in 1670 made dissenters' ministry much more difficult by prohibiting them from any ministerial work by law.

However, persecution by the parliamentary laws did not succeed in eliminating all of the dissenters' ministry.[76] There are several reasons for the failure. Most of all, the persecution was "sporadic, varying in intensity from place to place and from year to year."[77] England did not have a strong centralized administration, which could make "the full implementation of the penal code well nigh impossible."[78] For that reason, "the persecution of Dissenters was largely at the discretion of local magistrates."[79] Moreover, in the middle of this period, there were two huge natural disasters: the plague (1665) and the fire of London (1666). These two unforeseen situations gave the dissenters an opportunity for their ministry:

> The Great Plague persuaded many of the conformist clergy to flee from London. The churches stood empty amid a population

---

74. Lacey, *Dissent and Parliamentary Politics*, 54.

75. Plum, *Restoration Puritanism*, 33.

76. "[I]n spite of its severity it had failed to accomplish its purpose, and many liberal Anglicans had come to doubt its effectiveness.... the local officials were less interested in the success of the Anglican church; some were disgusted with the severity of its methods and many were sympathetic with the persecuted" (ibid., 30).

77. Davies, *Worship and Theology in England*, 2:448.

78. Watts, *Dissenters*, 244.

79. Greaves, *Enemies under His Feet*, 130.

> haunted by the fear of disease and death. This was a challenge which the ejected ministers felt they could not ignore. They took possession of the vacant pulpits, and the people listened meekly to their message of judgment and mercy. . . . To the nonconformists it [the Fire of London] was apparent that they were living in exceptional times. When God had a controversy with this people those who had heard his call could not be silent.[80]

Thus, the Clarendon Code did not completely prohibit dissenters from attending to their ministry.

However, it is true that the political enactments aimed at all dissenters persecuted both ministers and people. This religious persecution caused dissenters not only hardship but also stimulated changes in worship.

Presbyterian Dissenters' Beliefs about and Practice of Public Worship during Persecution

The hardship that Presbyterian dissenters suffered along with other denominational dissenters under the persecution affected changes in their life and the service of worship. In his book *Studies in English Puritanism from the Restoration to the Revolution, 1660–1688*, Whiting delineated the Dissenting life in detail.[81] English Presbyterian dissenters' life and religion were not different from those of other dissenters in general. According to Whiting, the Puritan Dissenting religious life could be summarized with one sentence: "the Puritans founded the whole of their religion on the Bible."[82] Although there was severe persecution, the Puritan dissenters, including Presbyterians, held to their religious conviction that the Bible was the guide of their actions. They kept Sunday as "a day of prayer and worship, and sometimes of fasting, too."[83] Even under the persecution, they observed the Lord's Day. Yet while they continued public worship, English Presbyterian worship was changed in several ways.

First of all, for the first several years, English Presbyterians did not give up their vision of Presbyterian worship for the whole English church.

---

80. Cragg, *Puritanism in His Great Persecution*, 14. For more detailed explanation also refer to Spurr, *Restoration Church of England*, 52–55.

81. Refer to chap. 10, 443–73.

82. Whiting, *Studies in English Puritanism*, 443.

83. Ibid. Puritans including English Presbyterians found the basis of Lord's Day not from the tradition but from the Bible, especially in the story of creation.

Presbyterians attempted to unify liturgy with their vision as we have seen in the case of Richard Baxter. Watts summarized the Presbyterian intention for worship: "From the point of view of the Presbyterians at least the practice [of remaining in the Church of England] was theologically defensible, and some Presbyterians had continued to communicate with the Church of England after 1662 with a design to show their charity towards that church."[84] With this intention, they continued their hope for unifying liturgical tradition, especially before the Conventicle Act in 1670: "the Presbyterians long hoped for reunion, and abstained for some years from perpetuating the schism by ordaining successors, though when they did so, they did not intend a direct act of separation; Presbyterians kept on hoping to get back on their own terms of a very modified episcopacy."[85] That is why "Baxter and his friends considered it a duty not to cut themselves off from the services of the established church, and they were scrupulous to arrange their private meetings at times which did not conflict with public worship."[86] This Presbyterian expectation of unified worship continued until the great persecution in 1681.[87] As a Presbyterian dissenter, even after the Act of Indulgence in 1687, Philip Henry did not give up the Reformed vision of a unifying liturgy, fearing "that the sanctioning of separate places of worship would help to overthrow what he still called 'our parish-order.'"[88] Moreover, with charity toward the national church, Henry "attended Anglican services in Whitewell chapel for nearly 30 years."[89] However, "the idea of reuniting all the sects into one national Church becomes increasingly recognized as hopeless."[90]

Second, English Presbyterians as dissenters did continue their public worship,[91] attempting to "maintain at all costs the worship of its forefathers

---

84. Watts, *Dissenters*, 265.

85. Whiting, *Studies in English Puritanism*, 451.

86. Cragg, *Puritanism in the Great Persecution*, 15.

87. Cf. Whiting, *Studies in English Puritanism*, 373; Philip Henry, father of Matthew Henry, began to be regarded as nonconformist, not as Presbyterian in the year of 1681. This implies that Philip Henry did try to realize the Presbyterian vision of worship even in the first years of persecution. Cf. Henry, *An Account of the Life and Death of Mr. Philip Henry*, chap. 7.

88. Watts, *Dissenters*, 248.

89. Spurr, "From Puritanism to Dissent," 241.

90. Whiting, *Studies in English Puritanism*, 23.

91. According to Spurr, "in the Restoration church, worship was no subsidiary duty to be relegated to a Sunday, but a constant obligation in the daily life of the Christian" (*Restoration Church of England*, 331).

as a sacred obligation."[92] As Ramsbottom pointed out, to the Puritan public worship was essential: "just as before the Civil War, corporate worship remained as an essential part of godly religion. Puritanism had always comprehended more than an individual's relationship with God."[93] However, most Presbyterian dissenters did not initiate "their own worship service" departing from the parish church at the beginning of the Restoration era. According to Spurr's analysis, Presbyterian dissenters joined public worship and also held private meetings that included both sermons and prayers.[94] Their own distinctive meetings were progressively developed in the middle of persecution in "a form for godly fellowship and teaching, which was presumably felt to be lacking in the parish."[95] Whiting described well how dissenters performed the service of worship:

> There was, of course, a certain amount of variation at the discretion of the minister, but they usually said or sang psalms (though the Baptists were much divided on the lawfulness of singing), the minister prayed extemporaneously once or twice, read a portion or portions of Scripture, of which he gave an exposition, and preached a sermon, which would seldom or never be less than an hour long.[96]

Thus, English Presbyterian Dissenting worship was simple: "Singing a psalm," "prayer," "reading, expounding, and preaching the Scriptures." Cragg explained the time frame in detail: according to him, the normal length of worship was about three or four hours.[97] Times varied place to place: "they might worship from 4 a.m. to 8 a.m.; perhaps from 6 a.m. to 10 a.m. or even from 2 a.m. to sunrise."[98]

Third, persecution led English Presbyterians to change their worship space. The Anglican Church did not allow any dissenters to use church buildings for their worship space because of the prohibition of nonconformist liturgy. Dissenters needed to find their own secret places for worship.

---

92. Davies, *Worship and Theology in England*, 3:112.
93. Ramsbottom, "Puritan Dissenters and English Churches," 139.
94. Spurr, "From Puritanism to Dissent," 243–44.
95. Ibid., 234. Spur added to his comment by saying that "this might be a matter of providing more inspiring worship than the dry stuff of the Prayer Book. There were many complaints of the ineffectualness of the liturgy."
96. Whiting, *Studies in English Puritanism*, 447–48.
97. Cragg, *Puritanism in the Great Persecution*, 161.
98. Ibid.

When the Conventicle Act was passed, the nonconformists worshipped "in barns, forests, fields, simple houses in the back alleys of towns, and anywhere except in churches."[99] Among these places, they mainly gathered at private houses for their worship: "very commonly groups of members met together in the evening in a private house."[100] When the persecution became lenient, the dissenters "began to erect new meeting houses in which to worship."[101] In contrast, when persecution became intense, the dissenters invented a new space in their own creative way, as Davies explained:

> The Nonconformists invented some ingenious ways of defeating the constables and their informers. Some made use of architectural conveniences. Simpler devices were also successful in aiding concealment. The door of a room used for worship was often hidden by moving a great cupboard against the entrance. Sometimes a table was spread with food, so that, in an emergency, a religious gathering might be made to look like a festive occasion. When persecution was at its fiercest, worship was held at the dead of night, in the open air, in the woods or orchards, caves or dens of the earth, in shops or barns. It was a return to the church of the catacombs.[102]

In this way, the dissenters' domestic experience of worship became their public service. This history caused the English Presbyterian dissenters' meeting house to become "a place of heart-felt worship, devoted prayer, and warm fellowship."[103] To the dissenters, the private house became a crucial religious place for their worship. This expansion of religious space for spiritual experience was an important change for English Presbyterian worship.

Emphasis on Family Piety and Life

Persecution of the Restoration period not only caused English Presbyterian dissenters to change their worship space but also reinforced some aspects of Reformed worship. One is family piety; the other, emphasis on life or

---

99. Davies, *Worship and Theology in England*, 2:444; Whiting, *Studies in English Puritanism*, 448.
100. Whiting, *Studies in English Puritanism*, 448.
101. Cragg, *Puritanism in the Great Persecution*, 41.
102. Davies, *Worship and Theology in England*, 2:448.
103. Watts, *Dissenters*, 5.

English Presbyterian Worship in the Restoration and Aftermath

integration between worship and life. English Presbyterian dissenters' articulation of family worship and their emphasis on life are clearly shown in the period of persecution.

Family Worship

Keeping family worship as a part of Reformed liturgical piety was a crucial contribution of the English Presbyterian dissenters. Since the Conventicle Act officially prohibited the dissenters from gathering for public worship, there was no safe liturgical place for them during the period of persecution. Despite strict restrictions, many dissenters kept their family devotion even during the persecution. Family worship was distinctive from the Lord's Day public worship. The dissenters did not initiate family worship at that time; it was already articulated and practiced in the time of the Reformation.[104] English Presbyterian dissenters attempted to keep family worship as a crucial method of piety in their historical context.

The manner of family worship was very simple: in the morning and evening, they prayed, sang a psalm, and read the Scriptures.[105] Whiting illustrates the dissenters' family worship:

> At night, especially on Sunday nights, the members of the family were collected together, the children, servants and apprentices were catechized on the sermons they had heard, psalms were sung, and the head of the family offered prayer, and sometimes, chiefly on Sunday nights, a sermon by some well-known Puritan divine was read.[106]

Among the Presbyterian dissenters, Philip Henry is well known for practicing family worship in his home. While he grew up in the period of persecution, Matthew Henry experienced the way that his father, Philip Henry, led family worship. In this practice, "he [Philip Henry] was uniform, steady, and constant, from the time that he was first called to the charge of a family, to his dying day."[107] He regarded family worship as "a family duty," yet at the same time, he "managed his family worship, so as to make it a pleasure, and not a task to his children and servants."[108] Thus, Philip Henry made his

---

104. Old, "Daily Prayer in the Reformed Church of Strasbourg," 121–38.
105. Henry, *Account of the Life and Death of Mr. Philip Henry*, 73.
106. Whiting, *Studies in English Puritanism*, 449.
107. Henry, *Account of the Life and Death of Mr. Philip Henry*, 72.
108. Ibid., 79.

house "a little church."[109] Family worship was not only for Sunday evening but also for every day: "in most pious homes not only Sunday but every day began and ended with family devotions."[110]

English Presbyterians kept family worship as their central form of piety because it has a strong biblical foundation. In his lecture on family worship, Philip Henry declared the biblical foundation of family worship: "many look upon family worship as an upstart. But it was in Adam's family, in Noah's, in Abraham's, Isaac's, and Jacob's. In the New Testament we read of the Church in the house. The Old Puritans saw many corruptions in worship, yet they waited upon God in it."[111] Moreover, emphasis on family worship was a Reformed asset developed in the time of the Reformation. As Williams pointed out, "the Reformation's emphasis on the family began to take on new dimensions with the development of family worship in the late sixteenth century."[112] Based on both biblical foundation and Reformed tradition, English Presbyterian dissenters continued family worship even during the persecution.

In brief, family worship was significant to dissenters in the persecution. According to Cragg, "the corporate devotions of the family were only one phase of a life carefully regulated and severely disciplined throughout."[113] Family worship made families a crucial place for spiritual renewal. That is why "Baxter and Henry refer to their pious homes with a fondness that speaks of close and loving relationship."[114] In the period of persecution, dissenters experienced family worship as crucial to their spiritual formation. They realized that the privilege and duty of shaping Christian faith belonged not only to the clergy but also to each family.

Emphasis on Everyday Life

In the period of persecution, English Presbyterian dissenters also emphasized the everyday life as having significance for the life of worship. Persecution caused people to concentrate on the direct relationship between God and the human being without any outward mediator such as liturgy.

---

109. Ibid., 73.
110. Watts, *Dissenters*, 313.
111. Henry, *Account of the Life and Death of Mr. Philip Henry*, appendix 15.
112. Williams, "The Puritan Concept and Practice of Prayer," 389.
113. Cragg, *Puritanism in the Great Persecution*, 143.
114. Williams, "The Puritan Concept and Practice of Prayer," 391.

English Presbyterian Worship in the Restoration and Aftermath

Although they did not ignore public gathering for worship, English Presbyterian dissenters paid more attention to their relationship with God under the persecution. The terms "rite" or "liturgy" hardly appear in the dissenters' writings about worship after Richard Baxter's Savoy Liturgy in 1661. Dissenters reacted to the Anglican Church's legal requirement to follow the fixed forms of worship in the *Prayer Book* by emphasizing one's personal relationship with God: "personal dealings with the LORD were at the heart of puritan piety."[115] Instead of a liturgical book, dissenters wrote and read various pietistic books. That is why "the dissenter was rarely without a godly book."[116]

Moreover, the persecution broke up a worshipping community into Dissenting groups. However, this means "scattering the seed" because Puritanism in the persecution "became more a matter of life than it had ever been before."[117] Philip Henry also integrated religion, worship, and life: "to be religious is also to serve God. The gift of God is eternal life; this service of God is to wait upon him daily and duly in the duties of his immediate service and worship. If you do not pray, and read, and hear, you are not God's servants."[118] For him, worship means a daily practice of praying and reading God's Word in addition to public worship. Daily life must involve walking with God.

English Presbyterian dissenters' private prayer or meditation could be regarded as an individual way of worshipping God with an emphasis on everyday life. As Spurr commented, prayer, and meditation alone as an individual manner of piety "was a constant feature of dissenting life with the family, or in private gatherings."[119] According to Cragg, in the period of persecution, "the life of the individual, though related in so many ways to other people, was continually renewed and sustained in secret."[120] In order to relate everyday life to God, Philip Henry also offered a caution not to neglect private prayer: "be sure you look to your secret duty; keep that up whatever you do. The soul cannot prosper in the neglect of it."[121] He "made

---

115. Spurr, "From Puritanism to Dissent," 259.
116. Ibid., 258.
117. Cragg, *Puritanism in the Great Persecution*, 86.
118. Henry, *Account of the Life and Death of Mr. Philip Henry*, appendix 12.
119. Spurr, "From Puritanism to Dissent," 259.
120. Cragg, *Puritanism in the Great Persecution*, 48.
121. Henry, *Account of the Life and Death of Mr. Philip Henry*, 69.

conscience of closet-worship, and did abound in it, not making his family worship to excuse for that."[122]

English Presbyterian dissenters' emphasis on everyday life could be seen in the communion of the church. They connected life with church communion: "Holiness of life was essential to church communion."[123] Cragg indicated the direct relationship between life and the table by pointing out that "the relevance of discipline became apparent as soon as a congregation began to celebrate the sacrament of the Lord's Supper."[124] Presbyterian dissenters had a strong conviction for "fencing the Table": "unless the table were fenced against unworthy communicants, the sacrament would be brought into disrepute, righteousness would be jeopardized, the distinction between right and wrong obliterated, and all order in the church destroyed."[125] In one way, their emphasis on life was to keep the table holy; in another way, their purpose in stressing life was to shape every aspect of their lives as Christians. Dissenters, according to Cragg, "noted with the deepest concern any conduct that might reflect unfavorably upon the Gospel, and bring the cause of Christ into ill repute."[126] Thus, the final purpose of their emphasis on holiness of life was "to help men and women to 'walk in uprightness of life.'"[127]

English Presbyterian dissenters' emphasis on everyday life could also be seen in ministerial life. Ministers did not regard themselves only as leaders of worship; they committed themselves as life-care pastors. When the plague began in 1665 during the persecution, nonconformist pastors showed their concerns for the lives of people. Plum explained well the Dissenting nonconformists' concern for people's lives in hardship:

> When the plague began in 1665 and grew worse day by day, many of the conformist ministers fled their posts, partly because they were timeservers only and partly because services were largely discontinued and the Anglicans had not yet developed the habit of visiting the homes and carrying on the pastoral work. Many, of course, fled through fear. The Nonconformist clergy very readily stepped into the breach, took up the pastoral work, ministered to

---

122. Ibid.

123. Cragg, *Puritanism in the Great Persecution*, 168. This topic will be dealt with in detail in chap. 4.

124. Ibid.

125. Ibid.

126. Ibid., 169.

127. Ibid.

the sick, buried the dead, and preached in the vacant pulpits unless the authorities forbade.[128]

Visiting homes could be understood as a Puritan pastoral care. Even during the persecution, nonconformist dissenters committed themselves as pastors by caring for their congregations in their hardships. In this way, the dissenters' concern for the life of people led the minister to not only be "liturgical leader" but also "pastor" for all aspects of life.

ENGLISH PRESBYTERIAN WORSHIP DURING LITURGICAL LIBERTY

Although to most historians "the year of 1689 when the Toleration Act was passed by Parliament would seem the end of the period of religious persecution,"[129] liturgical liberty began with the Act of Indulgence in 1687.[130] Historically, the persecution of dissenters continued until the year 1687. In fact, "the government began to adopt a tougher policy towards Nonconformity"[131] up until 1687. By 1685, when the persecution was at its peak, "the jails were filled to overflowing: many people went to prison and suffered in fines or fled abroad."[132] However, right after this fierce persecution and the death of Charles II in February 1685, "in 1686 came a dramatic reversal in royal policy."[133] In April 1687, "this policy was completed by a Declaration of Indulgence."[134] Moreover, the Toleration Act was passed by Parliament in 1689. With these two political enactments, English Presbyterian dissenters' worship encountered a new situation.

---

128. Plum, *Restoration Puritanism*, 28.

129. Ibid., 82.

130. Although there was a rumor that some kind of liberty would be extended to the nonconformists in the year of 1667–68, the year after the plague and great fire, nothing officially happened: "Negotiations were undertaken, hints were dropped in public, the King's speech to Parliament spoke of religious union and composure, bills were prepared, but nothing was ever brought before the Parliament" (Spurr, *Restoration Church of England*, 56–67). Matthew Henry was ordained as a Presbyterian Dissenting divine and began his liturgical ministry at Chester in 1687.

131. Spurr, *Restoration Church of England*, 57.

132. Plum, *Restoration Puritanism*, 52.

133. Watts, *Dissenters*, 257.

134. Ibid.

Most of all, the nonconformist ministers "were exempt from the penalties of the Act of Uniformity and of the Five Mile Act."[135] Moreover, as Matthew Henry clarified in the biography of his father, these two acts "not only tolerated but allowed the Dissenters meeting."[136] However, English Presbyterians were dissatisfied with the context of liturgical liberty given by the Act of Indulgence and the Toleration Act. Despite this dissatisfaction, no one attempted to restore Baxter's Reformed vision of worship by advocating any worship book or manual. They just continued their corporate worship as they did in the time of persecution, but now under the condition of freedom.

English Presbyterians' Dissatisfaction with Toleration

Both the Act of Indulgence and the Act of Toleration gave dissenters new opportunity for their worship. The Act of Toleration politically sanctioned the gathering of dissenters by suspending "the penal laws against orthodox Dissent in England."[137] As John Marshall pointed out, "the Toleration Act of 1689 in England marked a major advance in English legislative practices of tolerationism by providing Parliamentary indulgence of nonconforming worship, but such toleration of worship and belief was provided in 1689 only to Trinitarians."[138] Although persecution of dissenters stopped in the period of liturgical indulgence, English Presbyterian dissenters were not satisfied with the decision of Parliament. There are two main reasons for their discontent.

First, the liberty to worship was not given only to English Presbyterians but to all dissenters who confessed a Trinitarian faith. It also allowed even Roman Catholics to worship in private houses.[139] During the persecution, English Presbyterian dissenters did not completely forsake the Reformed vision of worship that Baxter had in mind: liturgical comprehension.[140] Presbyterian ministers "may well have been more reluctant than their lay

---

135. Ibid., 259.
136. Cf. chap. 8.
137. Bradley, "Religious Origins," 187.
138. Marshall, *John Locke, Toleration and Early Enlightenment Culture*, 127.
139. Watts, *Dissenters*, 247.

140. Baxter attempted to take the Reformed Liturgy as a rubric for all Protestants in England in order to comprehend various worship services.

adherents to accept a separate existence."[141] Thus, conservative English Presbyterian dissenters "had their own reasons for disliking the Indulgence for, as always, toleration's victory meant comprehension's defeat."[142] That is why "the Declaration of Indulgence was received by Dissenters with mixed feelings."[143] The liturgical indulgence of the Act of Toleration "marked the victory of the Independent concept of toleration over Presbyterian hopes of comprehension."[144]

Likewise, although the Declaration of Indulgence suspended the penal laws against both Protestant and Catholic dissenters, it did not mean that Presbyterian dissenters could take a leading place in society. They were "powerless by themselves to influence political events"[145] even after the Declaration of Indulgence. Watts regarded this failure of the Presbyterian vision as "the metamorphosis of Presbyterianism from the religion of a national church to that of a Dissenting sect."[146] Although "religious settlement reduced the Church of England from the *national* to merely *established* church,"[147] Anglicans were not silent about the liturgical indulgence. Even in the context of liturgical liberty, "Anglican apologists advanced various arguments to justify the government's persecution of dissenters and they stressed the necessity of a national church and the harmfulness of religious disunity and schism."[148]

As a result, English Presbyterian dissenters could not even attempt to restore Baxter's Reformed vision of worship in the context of the new liturgical freedom. Spurr clearly summarized the Presbyterian dissenters' situation in the period of toleration:

> While many Presbyterians did not want to leave the national church at the Restoration—indeed they repeatedly sought a reunion or "comprehension" with the church—yet they gradually accepted that their future lay with the sects and eventually all of

---

141. Spurr, "From Puritanism to Dissent," 247.
142. Watts, *Dissenters*, 248.
143. Ibid., 247.
144. Ibid., 260.
145. Ibid., 252.
146. Ibid., 260.
147. Spurr, *Restoration Church of England*, 104.
148. Zagorin, *How the Idea of Religious Toleration Came to the West*, 242.

the nonconformists came to think of themselves as willing separatists, as dissenters.[149]

Their political position also applies to worship: instead of liturgical comprehension which meant unifying liturgy by formulary or manual of worship, they developed dissenters' worship.

Continuing Dissenters' Worship

In the new context of freedom of worship, instead of liturgical comprehension, English Presbyterian dissenters continued to worship God in the way articulated in the period of persecution. Davies analyzed the "effects of persecution on religion and worship."[150] According to him, there are nine influences of persecution on religion and worship: inflexibility in the defense of free prayer, great flexibility in worship, more concern for interiority of worship, closeness of the bond between minister and people, heightened importance of serious biblically based preaching, emphasis on personal religion, emphasis on the love of liberty, creation of a religious and cultural divide between the church and the chapel outlooks, and growing comradeship of Presbyterian and Independent ministers. All these effects upon English Presbyterian dissenters continued in the period of liturgical liberty. They even elaborated the manner of dissenters' worship in their new context of indulgence. English Presbyterian dissenters took this liturgical plurality as "the advantage of giving a wider set of options to the people of God" and "greater creativity in the attempt to produce a worthier worship."[151] First, they did not articulate any prescriptive liturgical resources. Second, they developed their own use of music in worship. Third, they established the meeting house as their main worship space.

Continuing Dissenters' Worship without Articulating a Liturgical Manual

First and foremost, English Presbyterian dissenters did not articulate any prescriptive liturgical manual or resource under the new condition of liberty.

---

149. Spurr, "From Puritanism to Dissent," 244.

150. Davies, *Worship and Theology in England*, vol. 2, chap. 12, "Nonconformist Worship," 449–55.

151. Ibid., 535.

At the beginning of the Restoration, as indicated above, they attempted to replace the *Book of Common Prayer* with new Reformed liturgical book. However, when freedom of worship was granted, they did not attempt to unify their liturgy with any prescribed written manual or directory.

Neither *The Westminster Directory* nor Baxter's Reformed Liturgy eliminated the worship manual or book; they just criticized any fixed prescribed worship that did not allow for flexibility.[152] However, from the dissenters' perspective, any prescribed worship could be against the second commandment. They thought that there was no absolute foundation and direction for worship except the Bible.[153] This implies that "in Scripture is revealed how he is to be worshipped. It is a sin to introduce anything into 'religious worship not instituted by God himself.'"[154] English Presbyterian dissenters "were motivated by desire for a liturgy reformed in accordance with the Scriptures"[155] as their sole guide. Plum summarized the Presbyterian attitude toward the Bible regarding worship:

> They [the Presbyterians] accepted the Scripture first as a general guide of religious affairs and had never opposed the government of King and Parliament. They believed that in religion the Scriptures should be the rule of faith and worship, that man should be given latitude in his reading and interpretation, that man's conscience was the final arbiter of this faith when he had honestly studied the Scriptures, and that the whole history of English Presbyterianism had shown the Presbyterian to be consistent in this effort.[156]

Thus, in the context of liturgical indulgence after 1687 English Presbyterian dissenters followed the Reformed tradition of Calvin in preferring a Bible-based liturgy; however, they differed from the previous Presbyterians in that they did not articulate any liturgical manual or directory. As Spurr concluded, they "made a literal application of the scriptures to their lives

---

152. *The Westminster Directory* did not blame the established liturgy; Baxter's Savory Liturgy just "objected to set liturgy as it totally excluded the gift of prayer and because of the 'Romish Forms' still in it." Williams, "The Puritan Concept and Practice of Prayer," 358.

153. Ibid., 342.

154. Ibid., 371.

155. Ibid., 358.

156. Plum, *Restoration Puritanism*, 57.

and worship."[157] They took only the Bible as their liturgical foundation and guide.

Second, English Presbyterian dissenters in the period of indulgence continued the manner of worship followed in the period of persecution. Matthew Henry delineated his father's worship practice after the Act of Toleration of 1689:

> He began his morning family worship on Lord's Day: reading, expounding, singing Psalm, praying.... He began, in public, just at nine o'clock, winter and summer. His meeting place was an outbuilding of his own, near adjoining to his house, fitted up very decently and conveniently for the purpose. He began with prayer; then he sung Psalm cx, without reading the line; next, he read and expounded a chapter in the Old Testament in the morning, and in the New Testament in the afternoon. He looked upon the public reading of the scriptures in religious assemblies to be an ordinance of God, and that it tended very much to the edification of people by that ordinance, to have what is read expounded to them.... After the exposition of the chapter, he sung a psalm, and commonly chose a psalm suitable to the chapter he had expounded; and would briefly tell his hearers how they might sing that psalm towards God, in the singing of it; his hints of that kind were of great use, and contributed much to the right performance of that service.... After the sermon in the morning, he sung Psalm 117, without reading the line.[158]

Philip Henry, a conservative Presbyterian dissenter, continued the Word-centered worship of the dissenters even in the context of liturgical indulgence. In family worship, all of the forms and contents were guided by the Word: Reading and expounding the Word, singing the Word (psalm), and praying based on the Word. Public worship likewise placed the Word at the center: praying based on the Word; sing the Word (psalm); reading, expounding, and preaching the Word.

His pattern of Lord's Day worship was almost the same as that of *The Westminster Directory*. However, there are two differences between Philip Henry's worship and *The Westminster Directory*. First, although their forms seem to be similar, Henry did not use any liturgical manual or directory for the Lord's Day worship. He just followed the pattern of dissenters' worship. Second, *The Westminster Directory* did not emphasize the importance

---

157. Spurr, "From Puritanism to Dissent," 262.
158. Henry, *Account of the Life and Death of Mr. Philip Henry*, 190–91.

of discipline. However, Henry included discipline as an important part of worship, especially in relation to the Lord's Supper. Mathew Henry pointed out his father's restoring the discipline as a "peculiar excellence."[159]

Music in Dissenters' Worship

It is important to notice the place of music in English Presbyterian dissenters' worship in the period of liturgical freedom. Restoring the role of music in worship was one of their contributions to public worship service. With the freedom and openness of worship, "enthusiasm was reintroduced in the praise."[160] Although there was praise in dissenters' worship in the period of persecution, they could not loudly sing praises in the service of worship within unsanctioned meeting houses. They could sing psalms without any serious difficulties only in their family worship.[161]

Under liturgical liberty, however, English Presbyterian dissenters developed their emphasis on music in worship by composing hymn books. As Watts commented, "the Dissenters made a major contribution of their own to English worship."[162] Their contribution was the singing of hymns: "at the time of the passing of the Toleration Act the singing of hymns was largely unknown to English congregations, whether they met in parish churches or in Dissenting meeting-houses."[163] As Bryan Spinks pointed out, "it was from Dissent that hymnody first made its regular appearance in public worship."[164]

However, they did not ignore the role of the sermon; they added music as another important aspect of worship. Davies commented on their new stress on music: "there was a stress on the sociable aspect in worship; whereas the chief stress in Puritan worship was on the downward, revelational movement of God in sermon and Sacrament, now *a new stress was given to the hymns* and to the importance of the congregation."[165] In practice, the Act of Toleration "had made it safe for churches to advertise their

---

159. Ibid., 196.

160. Davies, *Worship and Theology in England*, 3:99.

161. Philip Henry led his family worship without ceasing even in the period of persecution, and unlike in public worship, he continued to sing psalms in his family worship.

162. Watts, *Dissenters*, 308.

163. Ibid.

164. Spinks, *Liturgy in the Age of Reason*, 251.

165. Davies, *Worship and Theology in England*, 3:99, italics added.

presence by song."¹⁶⁶ In this way, the role of music in worship became more crucial in this period.

The Meeting House and Dissenters' Worship

Changing the place of worship is also an important phenomenon in the era of greater freedom. Before the Act of Toleration, the dissenters' place of worship typically "was not a specifically constructed meeting-house but a private dwelling, barn, or rented room."¹⁶⁷ Dissenters' meeting houses were secured by Parliament during the period of Toleration. Watts explained how the meeting houses became the main place of dissenters' worship after the Toleration Act:

> Consequently once the Toleration Act had legalized Nonconformist worship most Dissenting churches sought to provide themselves with permanent places of worship, and in Nottingham the foundation stone of the Congregationalists' Castle Gate meeting-house was laid only five days after the Act received the royal assent. Over the next twenty years meeting-houses sprang up in most of the towns and many of the villages of England and Wales, visible and permanent reminders of the failure of the established church to extinguish or comprehend Dissent.¹⁶⁸

With the liturgical freedom, meeting houses became the main space of dissenters' worship. Davies reports the number of meeting houses in the Toleration:

> From that year of great relief for Nonconformity, 1689, to the end of the century, a total of 2418 buildings were registered for public worship by Presbyterians, Independents, and Baptists, besides many Quakers' meeting-houses. From that era there survive a considerable number of Dissenting meeting-houses.¹⁶⁹

---

166. Watts, *Dissenters*, 308.
167. Ibid., 303.
168. Ibid., 304.
169. Davies, *Worship and Theology in England*, 2:64. This was an important effect of the Act of Indulgence in 1687 and Act of Toleration in 1689. Davies also pointed out that a significant number of meeting houses were built right after the liturgical indulgence: "they immediately made plans for either temporary or permanent meeting-houses. Between 1688 and 1690, 796 temporary and 143 permanent nonconformist chapels were erected, while between 1691 and 1700 another 1,247 temporary meeting-houses were erected and 32 permanent ones" (ibid., 2:455).

They did not construct buildings that looked like churches at that time. Meeting-houses built in this period "have all the charm and simplicity of the domestic architecture of the period."[170] Davies also analyzed shapes and characteristics of dissenters' meeting houses: "the typical-impression made by a late seventeenth-century meeting house is that of a square with a double row of windows looking like a rather squat and wholly staid domestic building, utterly lacking any sense of the numinous."[171] This meeting house, according to Davies, had two distinguishing characteristics: "an emphasis on form, which is often lost in flashy splendor or intricacies of detail, and this expressed clarity, simplicity, and dignity; a preference for sobriety in color, which meant white or grey, with the brown of the woodwork as a contrast."[172]

The internal arrangements were also as simple as the outside appearance. Although there might be minor differences, the interiors are quite similar. Christopher Stell illustrated Saint Nicolas Street Meetinghouse, in Ipswich, built in 1693 as an example of an old dissenters' worship place.[173] The internal arrangements, according to him, "are now predictable, with galleries on three sides and the pulpit on the fourth; the four substantial columns are still in place, two freestanding and two aligned with the gallery fronts."[174]

The meeting house was a house suitable for English Presbyterian dissenters' public worship at the time of liturgical toleration. To them, "a domestic atmosphere, with the people gathered around the preacher, was all that the faithful desired, a building of good proportions and seemly construction, which is itself the basis of all good architecture."[175] Thus, when it comes to function of space, the meeting houses were intentionally structured for the purpose of preaching with consideration for the communion table: "In Puritan meeting-houses the primacy was given to the pulpit with its central position and high stairs, often one on each side, and a subordinate position was given to the Communion table, though not as

---

170. Watts, *Dissenters*, 305.

171. Davies, *Worship and Theology in England*, 2:60.

172. Ibid., 61.

173. Stell, "Puritan and Nonconformist Meetinghouses in England," 62–65. Also there is a brief history on Matthew Henry's worship place (his Chapel): see Roberts, *Matthew Henry and His Chapel*.

174. Davies, *Worship and Theology in England*, 2:65.

175. Ibid., 81.

secondary as is often supposed."[176] The place of the pulpit in the meeting house demonstrates that the Word is at the center of Dissenting worship.

CONCLUSION: LITURGICAL PLURALITY AS THE CONTEXT OF MATTHEW HENRY'S WORSHIP MINISTRY

The Act of Toleration of 1689 established the dissenters as a permanent part of English religious life. As Spinks concluded, "Dissent became a permanent legal reality in England."[177] English Presbyterian dissenters were also regarded as part of the Dissenting body of Christians in England. They did not attempt to unify liturgy by articulating any liturgical book as Baxter did, though some Presbyterians unofficially visited bishops to ask for "comprehension in the face of the Catholic monarch's greater scheme of toleration which would include Catholics."[178] Through the period of persecution, nonconformists, which were composed of the Separatists and the Puritans, were more clearly divided into four main Dissenting groups: Presbyterians, Baptists, Independents, and Quakers. With the Act of Toleration, all of these groups began to worship with freedom. English Presbyterian dissenters did not take this Toleration as an opportunity for unifying liturgy by providing an alternative to the *Book of Common Prayer*. Unifying liturgy at that time was an unrealistic anticipation for them because there was no one strong Reformer like Calvin or Knox in England. Moreover, in England, as Bradley pointed out, "there was never a centralized judicatory among the Presbyterians."[179]

The dissenters' liturgical context after 1687 can be described as "liturgical plurality."[180] Matthew Henry, as a Presbyterian divine, also ministered

---

176. Ibid., 11.

177. Spinks, *Liturgy in the Age of Reason*, 251.

178. Ibid., 48. When the Restoration began, Presbyterians attempted to comprehend liturgy for the churches in England. However, at this time, clergies of the Church of England tried to reconcile between them and the dissenters by renewing the *Book of Common Prayer* as a new liturgical comprehension. This attempt failed because "the Dissenters already had a legal basis to their existence, and were virtually on an equal footing with the established Church. Thus they refused to be content with small alterations in the Liturgy and cannons" (Fawcett, *The Liturgy of Comprehension*, 25).

179. Bradley, "Religious Origins," 234.

180. Spinks distinguished the liturgical context of the Glorious Revolution as "Liturgical Plurality." Cf. Spinks, *Liturgy in the Age of Reason*, chap. 3: "The Glorious Revolution and Liturgical Plurality."

in the context of liturgical plurality. Plum positively described this context for the dissenters:

> The period from 1689 to 1715 marked an era of growth in the numbers of dissenters, in their organization, and in their confidence. The Act of Toleration gave opportunity for open and public worship, and throughout the reign meeting houses grew in number. Funds were found from the faithful. Wealthy members donated houses or furnished money to build them.[181]

It is true that Toleration gave the dissenters opportunity for open and public worship. All dissenters except Roman Catholics and Unitarians could worship God without any legal restrictions with the exception of the necessity of registering their places of worship. Matthew Henry should choose his own position toward that liturgical plurality which resulted in liturgy with liberty.

In the time of liturgical plurality, Matthew Henry did not attempt to unify liturgy as the early English Presbyterians did at the beginning of the Restoration. Instead, he defended the place of dissenters and their ways of worship as his first ministerial task. One of the reasons for the persecution was because the dissenters separated themselves from the Church of England by rejecting the requirements of the established Church. They were regarded as schismatics: "the vast majority of the thousands of Protestant dissenters who suffered for their religious commitments in Restoration England were punished for a separation from the Church of England that was understood as 'schism' and not 'heresy.'"[182] Thus, it was Henry's first and foremost task to defend English Presbyterian dissenters' life and worship as an appropriate choice in the liturgical indulgence. For this purpose, Henry wrote *A Brief Inquiry Into the True Nature of Schism* (or *A Persuasive to Christian Love and Charity*: 1689) as his first publication.

Henry followed the Reformed tradition by rejecting the *Book of Common Prayer* as English Presbyterian dissenters' rubric for worship; at the same time, he did not follow Baxter's approach of rejecting one liturgy and seeking to replace it with another. He took over the Reformed "principle" of worship, not a "fixed form" of worship. Following the principle, not the form, the manner of English Presbyterian dissenters' worship did not matter to him so long as it was biblical, which is at the core of the Reformed principle. In his *A Brief Inquiry Into the True Nature of Schism*, Henry

---

181. Plum, *Restoration Puritanism*, 89.
182. Marshall, *John Locke, Toleration, and Early Enlightenment Culture*, 124.

admitted to the dissenters' worship being a kind of "schism" by mentioning that "the meetings of the dissenters are commonly charged with being schismatical."[183] However, he argued that dissenters' worship was not against the Bible:

> The common outcry is, that it is the setting up of altar against altar; which is not so; for at the most it is but altar by altar; and though I have often read of one body, and one Spirit, and one hope, and one LORD, and one faith, and one baptism, and one God and Father yet I could never find a word in all the New Testament of one altar, except Jesus Christ.[184]

Henry did not agree that each different way of worship in each different group is wrong or against the Bible.

For Henry, the issue was not difference but the attitude behind the difference: "it is not so much our differences themselves, as the mismanagement of our differences, that is the bane of the church, burning up Christian love with the fire of our contentions."[185] What needs to bond each different group is "not an act of uniformity in point of communion, in the same modes and ceremonies; but true love and charity in point of affection."[186] In the liturgical plurality or indulgence, Henry did not seek uniformity of liturgy but "unity of affection" for each different way of worshipping:

> By all this it is evident that unity of affection is the thing to be labored after, more than uniformity in modes and ceremonies. . . . what if we should now strive which should love one another best, and be most ready to do all offices of true charity and kindness, and bury all our little feuds and animosities in that blessed grave of Christian love and charity?[187]

Thus, Henry approved of the English Presbyterian dissenters' worship with liberty in the Toleration. In addition, Henry suggested and implemented a specifically Reformed manner of worship suited to the time of liturgical indulgence, which will be explored in a later chapter.

---

183. Henry, "A Brief Inquiry into the True Nature of Schism," 359.
184. Ibid., 361.
185. Ibid., 359.
186. Ibid., 356.
187. Ibid., 361.

2

The Life and Thought of Matthew Henry
Word-Centered Piety

MATTHEW HENRY WAS AN English Presbyterian minister whose life and thought clearly presented a practical application of the Scriptures to ordinary life. He was the second son of Philip Henry (1631–1696), a nonconformist Presbyterian pastor who was ejected from the national church with the Act of Uniformity in 1662.[1] Henry was born in the same year. His life began with the persecution of the nonconformist dissenters. Under this persecution, he did not have the privilege to learn in a public educational institution. He studied under a private tutor, William Turner,[2] and his father, Philip Henry, and through a nonconformist private academy that was organized by Thomas Doolittle (1630–1707).[3] In addition, Henry was influenced by other Puritan or Presbyterian theologians such as John Owen (1616–1683) and Richard Baxter (1615–1695).[4] When the persecu-

---

1. For details on the Act of Uniformity and the nonconformists' ejection from the National Church, see chap. 1, 18–21.

2. Williams, *Memoirs of the Life*, 1–3.

3. Ibid., 9–13; thus, when Henry was young, he learned Reformed and Presbyterian theology and ministry mainly under Philip Henry, William Turner, and Thomas Doolittle.

4. It is clear that Henry was influenced by John Owen (1616–1683) through his father's teaching because Philip Henry was a friend of Owen. Henry was also influenced by Richard Baxter through a personal meeting when Baxter was in prison. Although Henry did not follow Baxter in terms of practice of worship, he took Baxter's advice on Christian life as written in a letter to his father: "[Baxter] gave [me] some good counsel to

tion ended with the Act of Indulgence in 1687, Henry began his ministerial work for a Presbyterian congregation at Chester, a small countryside town of England. He spent most of his time with them, and later he spent only about two years with the congregations at Hackney until his sudden death in 1714 at the age of fifty-two.[5]

While he was ministering in both rural and urban areas, he was diligently publishing his writings on various pious and pastoral issues mainly based on his sermons[6] as well as the *Bible Commentary*. Henry is most well known for his six-volume *Bible Commentary*,[7] especially in contemporary evangelical circles. His *Bible Commentary* is still read by many pastors for sermon preparation. However, this *Bible Commentary* does not present a full picture of Henry's life and thought. Henry's *Bible Commentary* is one among his many contributions, even though it has been the primary representative of his life's work. It is necessary to examine and analyze his life and thought beyond his *Bible Commentary* in order to understand how he lived out and thought about Christian faith and life.

Thus, this chapter will explore Henry's life and thought by analyzing his own works and others writings about him. It will first make a historical survey of the research on Henry's life and thought while analyzing each approach to understanding him. This analysis will clearly show us to what extent Henry's life and thought has been examined. Next, analyzing his sermons and published works, Henry's thought will be organized into major themes. Finally, this chapter will examine his methodology in how he developed his thought.

---

prepare for trials, and said the best preparation for them was a life of faith, and a constant course of self denial. He thought it harder constantly to deny temptations to sensual lusts and pleasures, than to resist one single temptation to deny Christ for fear of suffering" (ibid., 22).

5. After visiting his old congregation at Chester, while he was coming back to Hackney, Henry "was suddenly taken ill at Nantwich and was seized with apoplexy on June 22, 1714: and, after laying three hours speechless, with his eyes fixed," died. He was buried in Trinity Church, Chester. See ibid., 163–64.

6. There are forty-four titles in *The Complete Work of Matthew Henry* besides his *Bible Commentary*. However, many of his original manuscripts, including his diary, are not easily accessible for contemporary readers.

7. Henry finished his commentaries for Genesis up to Acts before his death. The remaining parts of the New Testament were completed by several ministers based on Henry's Exposition notes. On the specific assistance of these ministers, see Williams, *Memoirs of the Life*, 308.

HISTORICAL SURVEY ON UNDERSTANDING MATTHEW HENRY'S LIFE AND THOUGHT

Several attempts have been made to describe Henry's life and thought. These efforts can be categorized in two main forms: biographies and shorter writings dealing with specific concerns. Writings on Henry began with the publication of funeral sermons by several of his comrades. John Reynolds preached a funeral sermon "on Thursday, June 24, prior to removing the body [of Henry] from Nantwich."[8] According to Williams, "the news of Mr. Henry's death on reaching the metropolis awakened inexpressible sorrow."[9] There were many voices of lamentation from the dissenting pulpits. Two more funeral sermons for Henry were delivered at Hackney, and both of them—by Daniel Williams[10] and William Tong[11]—were published. Each of them briefly interpreted and evaluated Henry's life at the end of their sermons. Besides these funeral sermons, there are some major works: William Tong's biography of Henry (1716);[12] John William's comprehensive biographical sketch on Henry (1828); Charles Chapman's short description and evaluation on Henry's life (1859);[13] and lastly, Alexander Grosart's analysis of Henry's life and work (1879).[14] After Grosart, there has been only one book related to Henry—not about Henry's life but a historical sketch on Henry's Chapel.[15] These four resources on Henry were published in the eighteenth and nineteenth centuries. In the twentieth century, there has been no major study on Henry's life except for brief descriptions in dictionaries or in the introductions of republished works by Henry.[16] The primary

8. Williams, *Memoirs of the Life*, 164. Reynolds, *Sermon Upon the Mournful Occasion*.

9. Williams, *Memoirs of the Life*, 164.

10. Williams, *Funeral Sermon Upon Occasion*. He preached on June 27, 1714.

11. Tong, *Funeral Sermon Preached*. He preached on July 11, 1714.

12. Tong, *An Account of the Life and Death*.

13. Chapman, *Matthew Henry, His Life and Times*. Prior to Chapman's work, there is one short biography on Henry: no name, "Memoirs of the Rev. Matthew Henry," 5–33.

14. Grosart, "Matthew Henry."

15. Roberts, *Matthew Henry and His Chapel*.

16. London, "Biographical Sketch of the Rev. Matthew Henry," 4–50; Harman "Introduction," 13–26; Duncan, "Editor's Introduction," v–viii; Packer, "Introduction," 7–18; Old, "Matthew Henry," 521–24; Wykes, "Henry, Matthew," 582–84; Wainwright, "Henry, Matthew," 495. For his preaching ministry, see Old, *The Reading and Preaching of the Scriptures*, 5:24–33. See also Gummer, *Bible Themes from Matthew Henry*; Routley, "Charles Wesley and Matthew Henry," 345–51; Crump, "The Preaching of George Whitefield and His Use of Matthew Henry's Commentary," 19–28; most recently, Pederson,

sources on Henry, including his *Complete Works*, have been published with revisions in more readable format.[17] This section attempts to analyze how Henry's life and thought have been understood and interpreted by several biographers and commentators. Analysis of their writings will enable us to clarify the aspects that have been explored in Henry's life and thought.

First Descriptions of Henry from Funeral Sermons (1714)

Although the biographies on Henry could be the main sources for exploring his life and thought, it is helpful to begin by looking over the earliest descriptions on Henry. Funeral sermons were delivered by preachers who knew him well. The published funeral sermons on Henry give us some perspectives for understanding him even though the main points of each were about the meaning of death. As indicated above, there are three available funeral sermons on Henry: John Reynolds' "Sermon Upon the Mournful Occasion of the Funeral of the Reverend and Excellent Mr. Matthew Henry, Minister of the Gospel" (1714), Daniel Williams' "Funeral Sermon Upon Occasion of the Death of the Reverend Mr. Matthew Henry" (1714), and William Tong's "Funeral Sermon Preached at Hackney on Occasion of the Much Lamented Death of the Reverend Mr. Matthew Henry" (1714).

First, John Reynolds, a minister of Salop, preached a funeral sermon in Nantwich, where Henry died, on June 25, 1714. He delivered his sermon on the "good and faithful servant" based on Matthew 25:21. Reynolds did not evaluate Henry's life and thought in detail, but commented generally on Henry's life as a faithful servant by mentioning that "you [Henry] have, in your world, diligently serv'd your LORD and ours."[18] He also indicated that all aspects of Henry's life were as faithful as his ministry, indicating that "the Henry's shall be illustrious in all that they have done faithfully, both to the Brethren and to Strangers."[19] Apart from this, his funeral sermon did not touch upon any specific characteristics of Henry's life.

Matthew Henry Daily Reading.

17 Baker Books published *The Complete Works of Matthew Henry* in 1979 (2nd ed., 1997). Before this publication, the only comprehensive collection of Matthew Henry's, except the *Bible Commentary*, was published with the title *The Miscellaneous Works of Mr. Matthew Henry* in 1827 (1833). Beside the *Complete Works*, several of Henry's writings were published as monographs.

18. Reynolds, *Sermon upon the Funeral Occasion*, 6.

19. Ibid., 15.

The Life and Thought of Matthew Henry

Second, Daniel Williams preached his funeral sermon based on Romans 14:8. After expounding it and exhorting the audience, he described Henry's life. Williams clearly referred to Henry as a Presbyterian minister, not a minister of the Established Church (Church of England) or of the dissenters: "upon the maturest thoughts, he [Henry] chose to be a Presbyterian minister."[20] According to Williams, Henry intentionally dedicated himself to be a Presbyterian minister. At the same time, he also pointed out that Henry was hospitable to all "pious" Conformists, saying that "with his Non-conformity, he highly esteemed all pious Conformists, and kept up a Christian Charity towards such as differed from him."[21] Moreover, Williams clearly interpreted Henry's life as a perfect model of a minister of the gospel/Bible:

> He always accounted the Work of the ministry the most honorable employment; and was to his death a singular honor to it, by his unweary'd diligence, and exemplary conversation. . . . the business of his life was, both to improve in meetness for it, and to fulfill the ministry he had received of the LORD . . . and thereby he commended the close study of the Scriptures; for the whole Bible being fix'd in his head as well as heart.[22]

In this way, as Williams described, Henry was a Presbyterian minister who sought for the Bible in his heart as well as in his mind for his ministerial success.

Third, William Tong also delivered his funeral sermon at Hackney, Henry's second ministerial congregation, in 1714. Tong preached his funeral sermon based on John 13:36. He regarded Henry's life as illustrating a "tasting the powers of the world to come, not in a superficial manner, but by deep and satisfying experience."[23] He regarded Henry's *Bible Commentary* as his main contribution, exclaiming that "in them you have his clear head, his warm heart; his life, his soul appears to be in them; prize them more, read them more than ever you have done."[24] Lastly, Tong suggested

---

20. Williams, *Funeral Sermon*, 30. This is important in that some preferred to refer to Henry as a Puritan Dissenting clergy. However, as Williams pointed out, Henry was a Presbyterian divine who knew well the teaching of Puritans.

21. Ibid., 30–31.

22. Ibid., 31.

23. Tong, *Funeral Sermon*, 28.

24. Ibid., 31. Tong also said that "while you are seriously perusing those excellent books, besides many other books published by him, you will seem to your selves to have Mr. Henry still with you" (ibid.).

two remaining tasks to honor Henry. The first was to write on Henry's life and character. Tong hoped to write a biography on Henry, noting that "I hope this will be more fully done in an account of his exemplary life."[25] Two years after Henry's death, Tong wrote his biography. The second task was to edit and publish the remaining parts of Henry's *Bible Commentary*, which Henry had not finished publishing.[26] Thus, Tong concluded his preaching by saying:

> I hope those that have attended long upon the ministry of good Mr. Henry, and taken down his expositions upon that part of the Bible that yet remains, whether in the publick assembly or in his family, will carefully gather up those precious fragments, that none may be lost, and will communicate them to the world in the best way they can, that his great work may be finished, and be as much as possible his own performance.[27]

He also participated in publishing the remaining parts of Henry's *Bible Commentary* by editing his notes on Expositions. In this way, Tong briefly indicated Henry's contributions to the current and future generations, along with pointing out the tasks to be accomplished in order to honor Henry.

William Tong's Account of the Life and Death of Henry (1716)

Tong was a friend of Matthew Henry. He wrote the first biography of Henry in 1716, entitled *An Account of the Life and Death of Mr. Matthew Henry, Minister of the Gospel of Chester, Who Died June 22, 1714, in the Fifty-Second Year of His Age*. As evident in the title, Tong dealt with Henry's life with special reference to his being a "minister of the gospel." Tong organized the account of Henry's life as ministerial preparation and conduct.

First, Henry's early life, according to Tong, was a preparation for the ministry of the gospel. Tong indicated Henry's familiarity with the Bible and preaching. "[Henry] was able to read a chapter in the Bible very distinctly at about three years old, and with some observation of what he read.... he

---

25. Ibid., 32.

26. He published the expositions until the Act in 1714. Before his death he had made some preparations for the next volume, and this work was completed by many friends and ministers who had manuscripts and knew his style and method. For the specific information on this work, see Williams, *Memoirs of the Life*, note N.

27. Tong, *Funeral Sermon*, 36.

very early put away childish things."[28] Also, even when Henry was young, "he loved to imitate preaching, not in a childish manner, but with a propriety, gravity and judgment far beyond his years."[29] Moreover, Tong explored Henry's preparation and excellent qualifications for the ministry by pointing out Henry's own confession in "Mercies Received":[30]

> That I have had a liberal education, having a capacity for, and been bred up to the knowledge of the languages, arts, and sciences; and that, through God's blessing on my studies, I have made some progress therein; that I have been born in a place and time of gospel light; that I have had the Scriptures, and means for understanding them, by daily expositions and many good books; and that I have had a heart to give myself to and delight in the study of them.[31]

In this way, Tong interpreted Henry's early stages of life as preparation of the ministry of the Gospel.

Second, after his preparation, Henry dedicated the last half of his life primarily to the ministry of the gospel by expounding and preaching the Scriptures. In chapter 4 of *An Account of Life and Death of Matthew Henry*, Tong explored the way Henry ministered at Chester. He spelled out two areas of Henry's gospel ministry: family and public. As a minister of the gospel, Henry served his own family and his church. Most of all for Henry, according to Tong, family was not just within the home but was also the house of God or "the gate of heaven." Tong explained his experience of Henry's home: "I have known those that, upon their first acquaintance there, were surprised to see so much beauty of holiness, and were ready to say, 'Surely God is in his place; this is no other than the house of God, and the gate of heaven.'"[32] This is a confession not just about the structure of the family but about domestic worship. Tong pointed out that family worship was crucial for Henry: "he strictly observed his father's example, both in all the parts and circumstances of it; he was constant in family worship; whatever happened, or whoever was present, this duty was never neglected

---

28. Tong, *Account of Life and Death of Matthew Henry*, 2.
29. Ibid., 4.
30. Henry wrote "Mercies Received" on October 18, 1682, when twenty years of age.
31. Tong, *Account of Life and Death of Matthew Henry*, 6.
32. Francis Lee wrote a short essay on Henry's life and work with reference to his home life. See Lee, "The Covenantal Home Life of Rev. Matthew Henry." Tong, *Account of Life and Death of Matthew Henry*, 19.

morning or evening."³³ Moreover, Tong delineated Henry's ministerial conduct for his congregations. He consistently ministered in several areas: expounding, preaching, and praying in the service of the Lord's Day; lecturing and catechizing on weekdays; visiting the sick; visiting and preaching to the prisoners; and so on.³⁴

Tong pointed out Henry's two major strengths in his ministry along with preaching: public prayer and exposition of the Scriptures. In terms of prayer, Henry "had a wonderful faculty of engaging the attention, and raising the affections of his assembly."³⁵ Likewise, "the exposition of the Scriptures was a very pleasant part of his work, both in his house and in the house of God."³⁶ Moreover, Tong emphasized Henry's role as a minister of the gospel by analyzing his sermon topics in detail. He organized the sermon topics and Scripture verses from Henry's twenty-five years of preaching ministry at Chester.

Tong's *An Account of the Life and Death of Matthew Henry* has been the basis for understanding Henry's life and ministry from birth to death. All subsequent biographies have been explicitly or implicitly based on Tong's description of Henry. John Williams, another biographer of Henry, highly regarded Tong's credentials in writing on Henry, pointing out that Tong's friendship with Henry was a crucial asset in his *Account*: "As the result of long and close intimacy, and of strict fidelity in the application, so far as they went, of facts, its worth cannot be questioned. It is, the Dissenting historians very justly observe, 'highly valuable for laying open to us the soul of Mr. Henry himself.'"³⁷ Lastly, Tong excellently described Henry's life with references to the Scriptures. His *Account of Henry* clearly presents the Bible as at the center of Henry's preparation and practice of ministry.

Nevertheless, Tong's account of Henry's life is limited in two ways. First, although it may seem to be enough to understand Henry as a minister, a biography should also include personal details and descriptions of his public life as well as of his ministerial conduct in order to more appropriately interpret and evaluate his life and thought. Second, there are some inaccuracies in Tong's account. Williams pointed out that "they may be found, notwithstanding many excellencies, in the glaring imperfections

---

33. Tong, *Account of Life and Death of Matthew Henry*, 19.
34. Ibid., 24.
35. Ibid., 27.
36. Ibid.
37. Williams, *Life of the Rev. Matthew Henry*, v.

which disfigure Mr. Tong's account: in it awkward, and somewhat repulsive arrangement in its entire omission of some features of Mr. Henry's character; and its meager illustration of others."[38] Thus, although it is a good basis for understanding Henry's life, Tong's account needs to be revised with more complete picture.

John Williams's Memoirs of Henry (1828)

A nonconformist memorialist, John Bickerton Williams (1792–1855), published the second and more comprehensive biography of Henry. He was "a collateral relative of the family of the seventeenth-century nonconformist divines Philip and Matthew Henry."[39] He was an attorney and "was elected an alderman of Shrewsbury, and in 1836 became mayor, the first dissenter so appointed."[40] He published several works on the Henry family.[41] He corrected and enlarged *The Life of the Rev. Philip Henry* by Matthew Henry in 1825 and devoted his time to writing *Memoirs of the Life, Character, and Writings of the Rev. Matthew Henry* (*The Life of the Rev. Matthew Henry*) in 1828.

When he began collecting manuscripts by Henry, Williams used Tong's *Account of the Life and Death of Henry* as a basis. While making that collection, he found several mistakes in Tong's biography of Henry. Thus, he attempted to write a more comprehensive and correct biography. He clearly indicated his method, "I have attempted the union of chronology with that method of biography which is sectional."[42] With this method and based on Tong's account, Williams organized his own biography of Henry into three categories: life, character, and writings. This method is clearly evident in the title of his book: *Memoirs of the Life, Character, and Writings of the Rev. Matthew Henry*.

---

38. Ibid., vi.
39. Fletcher and Reynolds, "William, John Bickerton," 249.
40. Ibid.
41. Ibid. Those works are "Eighteen Sermons of the Rev. Philip Henry, M.A., from Original Manuscripts" (1816); "A Memoir of Henry's Daughter Sarah Savage" (1818); "Memoirs of Philip Henry (1825) and Matthew Henry" (1828); "A Memoir of Sir Matthew Hale" (1835); two series of "Letters on Puritanism and Nonconformity" (1843 and 1846).
42. Williams, *Life of the Rev. Matthew Henry*, vii.

In the first part Williams delineated Henry's life from his birth to death in detail based on various original manuscripts compared with Tong's *Account*. He treated Henry's life by dividing it into time periods of two to five years, and he attempted to include every major event of Henry's life with as much detail following the time line. Each chapter includes a list of heading to explain its content. Readers can imagine the whole life story of Henry from just these statements. The second part of *The Life of the Rev. Matthew Henry* was about his character and piety toward God, based on various manuscripts such as Henry's writings, diaries, and letters. The intention of this part of the biography was to show Henry as an example to believers: "whether considered as a Christian, or a minister, in private life, or in public, he [Henry] was an example to believers—in word, in conversation, in charity, in spirit, in faith, in purity."[43] Third, Williams organized and analyzed Henry's writings and several accounts on him by others. He introduced Henry's writings in chronological order with brief comments on each work. He also collected and added many documents helpful for understanding Henry's thought and practice.[44]

Williams' work has several strengths. First, its most important contribution was his work of collecting and organizing the many original manuscripts by and on Henry. Although he used Tong's *Account* as a basic resource, Williams corrected and rearranged information in the previous source. Further, Williams collected many of Henry's diary entries. These primary sources were crucial in understanding Henry since they presented Henry's thoughts and feelings.[45] In this way, Williams' biography became a standard for Henry's life and thought.

Second, Williams attempted to interpret Henry's life and character from a nonconformist perspective. In the biography, Williams indicated Henry's nonconformist position by pointing out that "Mr. Henry frequently styled the Bartholomew ejection, a fatal day; a day to be remembered with sorrow, on account of the silencing of so many ministers."[46] He also placed Henry as a key figure in the nonconformist tradition, regarding him as "a

---

43. Ibid., xix.

44. Williams added sixteen notes; these notes include accounts about Henry from his friends and relatives, Henry's sermon methods and subjects, Henry's addresses, states of Henry's family, etc. See Williams, *Life of the Rev. Matthew Henry*, 217–311.

45. This implies that that diaries and letters were understood to be important ways that people left their thoughts and feelings at that time.

46. Williams, *Life of the Rev. Matthew Henry*, 184–85.

The Life and Thought of Matthew Henry

connecting link between the early Puritans and modern Nonconformists."[47] In fact, although Henry cannot be regarded as a Puritan, as Williams pointed out, in his life and works Henry knew and reflected "their doctrine, their manner of life, their purpose, their faith, their long-suffering, their charity, their patience, their persecution, and their afflictions."[48] In relation to this, it is clear that Williams intended to promote in his contemporary audience a nonconformist piety from the life and thought of Henry.[49]

Third, Williams' analysis of Henry's sermon subjects and Scripture verses was also a significant contribution. Based on Tong's *Account of the Life and Death of Henry*, Williams analyzed the sermon topics and corresponding Scriptures for the Lord's Day services and sacramental occasions during Henry's twenty-five years at Chester. Williams furthermore pointed out that Henry's characteristic in his preaching ministry was not so much Puritan fervor as the variety of topics: "Mr. Henry was not so much remarkable for his fervor than for the variety which he so admirably kept up in his ministrations."[50] In order to prove that "Henry took a wide range in the choice of his subjects," Williams quoted "the methods of subjects Henry preached upon for twenty five years together at Chester"[51] from Tong's *Account*. This information has been the basis for contemporary research on Henry's preaching. For example, Hughes Old referred to Williams' information on Henry's preaching ministry in order to understand the reading and preaching of the Scriptures in worship in his time period.[52]

Although Williams organized Henry's life and character by collecting and analyzing the data in a comprehensive way, he did not thoroughly treat Henry's thought. He dealt with Henry's character in detail; but he did not fully analyze Henry's thought within his books and manuscripts. He left that task to later generations. In this way, although he gave the most comprehensive information on Henry, Williams' *Life of Rev. Matthew Henry* needs to be supplemented by examining Henry's thought in more detail from other primary works. Williams' biography can be a good resource for further research.

---

47. Ibid., xvii.

48. Ibid., xviii.

49. When it comes to piety, Williams described Henry's character in much detail in a chapter organized into six sections. See ibid., 165–218.

50. Ibid., 118.

51. Ibid., 273.

52. See Old, *The Reading and Preaching of the Scriptures*, 4:24–33.

Charles Chapman's Memorial and Tribute (1859)

Thus, in order to understand Henry's thought as well as his life, it is necessary to analyze Henry's other writings. Charles Chapman filled in where Williams was lacking with an analysis of Henry's thought. Chapman published *Matthew Henry, His Life and Times: A Memorial and a Tribute (1859)* thirty years after Williams' *Life of the Rev. Matthew Henry*. Chapman's book was revised based on lecture he delivered in Music Hall, Chester. Chapman laid out his intention for his book:

> I do not pretend to offer a substitute for the excellent Memoirs that have been published by the late Sir John Bickerton Williams, and others; nor to discuss in tedious detail the many topics of importance suggested by the events of Matthew Henry's Life and Times.[53]

Rather than offer a substitute for Williams' work or discuss Henry's life and times in detail, Chapman's aim was to provide his audiences with a work of "brevity and point, combined with interest"[54] in relation to understanding Henry's life and character. Chapman apologized for the brevity of his work on Henry, mentioning that "in short, my design has been with respect to those, that have not read the story [Williams biography of Henry], that I may prompt them: and of such as have, I humbly pray them to admit the excuse of time, of numbers, and due course of things, which cannot in their huge and proper life, be here presented."[55]

Chapman organized his book into five parts: preliminary, historical, narrative, descriptive, and final. First, the preliminary part clarified Chapman's precise reason for his own work. He attempted to connect his Independent congregations in Chester to Henry's teaching by pointing out that "[his] church is descended from, and is the representative of, an orthodox Church which enjoyed the privilege of listening to the sound evangelical teaching of Matthew Henry."[56] At the same time, he endeavored to warn the Independent churches' congregations that "there was a gradual decline

---

53. Chapman, *Matthew Henry, His Life and Times*, v–vi.
54. Ibid.
55. Ibid., vi.
56. Ibid., 3. Chapman was convinced that "he [Henry] held, taught, and published those great fundamental truths respecting the fallen condition of mankind, the Divine nature of Jesus Christ, the vicarious nature of His death, and the need of a renewal of heart by the Holy Spirit, which we in England consider to be very essence of true scriptural doctrine, and the basis of all permanent Christian activity" (ibid.).

from sound doctrine on the part of the minister, and through him, of some of the congregation."[57]

Second, unlike the previous two biographers, Chapman described in a separate section the historical context in which Henry's life and character were shaped. With the premise that "everyman is best seen in the original sphere of his action, surrounded by the persons and objects that shaped the particular course of his conduct," Chapman outlined Reformation history in England from the sixteenth century to the early eighteenth centuries as historical background. He presupposed that the Reformed tradition in England sought to operate according to the principle of "*the right of private judgment upon the sacred Scriptures.*"[58] He also indicated persecution of the nonconformists as background to Henry's of life and thought. Although he did not count Henry in the Puritan circle, Chapman attempted to show that Henry's life and character was influenced by the persecution that the nonconformist faced beginning in the year of his birth.

Third, Chapman described Henry's life, ministry, and character in the narrative section. Chapman stressed that Henry was a nonconformist minister for Chester. He described the narrative of Henry's life in a simple but clear way. His final description of Henry's life and ministry is that he was a faithful minister for Chester:

> His affection for Chester was strong. Here he began his ministry; here he had experienced the sweetest social joys; and felt the deep sorrows of affliction and bereavement; here his first wife lay interred; here he had been the means of raising a strong Nonconformist church in times of persecution and trouble.[59]

Thus, the life and ministry in Chester lies at the core of understanding Henry: "for twenty-five years, he had preached, prayed, watched, and wept, and here the Divine Redeemer whom he honored, had cased the joys of religion to abound in his heart."[60]

Fourth, the descriptive and final parts are evaluations of Henry in terms of his character and influence. While Williams tried to merely analyze Henry's character, Chapman attempted to extract some applicable lessons from Henry. He summarized two aspects of Henry's character: "his

---

57. Ibid., 6.
58. Ibid., 19, italics original.
59. Ibid., 71.
60. Ibid.

continued firmness and Christian gentleness."[61] According to Chapman, "we may see in [Henry] how strong religious convictions may be held and made practical, and at the same time a kind, generous spirit toward others expressed."[62] Henry's firm and gentle character had a huge impact on his contemporaries and even today. According to Chapman, Henry "exerted great influence for good in a season of considerable difficulty and moral degeneracy."[63] Chapman also did not ignore the distinction of Henry's piety in private and domestic life. In addition, he suggested the relevance of Henry's life for his own day: "this kind of power now exercised by Matthew Henry upon us who are living, is perhaps equal or superior to that of any other person with whose private life we are acquainted."[64] Chapman introduced his readers to Henry's *Bible Commentary* as a great contribution of Christian piety. He summarized the aim of Henry's *Commentary* as "to let the truth be seen and appreciated."[65]

Chapman organized the life, character, and contribution of Henry in his context with "brevity and point" according to his own specific concern. His book cannot be considered a biographical description of Henry but rather an evaluation of Henry's life and character. Chapman stressed Henry's contribution to his contemporaries and succeeding generations as a model of piety in times of difficulty. No doubt Chapman accomplished what he intended through his book: "I wish all to remember that what we admire in him is, that, by the Grace of God, he, in the midst of temptations to ease and indulgence, and amidst persecutions and cares, was enabled to subdue so much of the man, and to exhibit so much of what is Heaven-born."[66] A major strength of Chapman's book was his evaluation of Henry's *Bible Commentary*. Chapman pointed out that Henry's was the first commentary written in plain English: "it is to Matthew Henry's honor, that he was the first to deviate from the practice of learned men of past ages, by publishing in plain, understandable English, not in learned Latin."[67] Chapman summarized the contribution of Henry's *Bible Commentary*: "Did he break down the barriers which the scholastic habits of centuries had raised,

61. Ibid., 101.
62. Ibid.
63. Ibid., 102.
64. Ibid., 125.
65. Ibid., 134.
66. Ibid., 8.
67. Ibid., 131.

and afford assistance to his fellow-countrymen to explain the treasures and enjoy the consolations of the revealed Will of God."[68]

Although Henry's *Commentary* was his most significant work, Chapman appeared not to investigate Henry's other works. He briefly mentioned four other writings by Henry.[69] However, to thoroughly comprehend Henry's thought, it is also necessary to explore his other works. These other works were not just byproducts that were edited posthumously; Henry himself published these writings. Thus, while Henry's life and character have been thoroughly examined, there has been little explanation of his thought.

Alexander Grosart's Treatment of Henry as a Representative Nonconformist (1879)

There have been no attempts to write a new biography of Henry since Williams published *The Life of the Rev. Matthew Henry* (1828). There also has been no monograph on Henry since Chapman wrote *Matthew Henry, His Life and Times* (1859). Twenty years after Chapman's work, however, there was an attempt to interpret Henry from a specific perspective: Alexander Grosart's (1827–1899) *Representative Nonconformists: With the Message of Their Life-Work for Today* (1879). In his book, Grosart treated four representative nonconformists: John Howe, Richard Baxter, Samuel Rutherford, and Matthew Henry. He published this book based on his "Spring Lecture of the Presbyterian Church of England for 1879" that was delivered in "the College," London.[70]

Grosart intended to connect the teachings and lessons of four representative nonconformists to his contemporary situation. He wrote, "my main design is from SELECTED CHARACTERISTICS of the Life and Life-work of these Representative Nonconformists to incite and quicken to higher and nobler service of The Master in our day and generation."[71] In order to draw out lessons for his contemporary audience, Grosart used "didactic," "hortatory," and "moralizing" methods to convince that "facts

---

68. Ibid., 131–32; Chapman said further that "the Commentary itself is one that, on its own merits, deserves to be read and re-read by all classes of society" (ibid., 134).

69. Memoirs of his father, Philip, *Communicant's Companion*, "On Prayer," and "Various Sermons." See Chapman, *Matthew Henry, His Life and Times*, 126.

70. There is no specific information about this college.

71. Grosart, *The Representative Nonconformists*, viii.

and characteristics if simply toddle do not leave the impression which they might and ought."[72] With this intention and these methods, Grosart briefly described Henry's life and estimated his life-work.

According to Grosart, the central characteristic of Matthew Henry was "sanctified common-sense."[73] From the late-nineteenth-century perspective, Grosart criticized the lack of common sense in the church:

> The most uncommon thing I meet with is just this that we vaingloriously call "common-sense." The scarcest article I find in pulpit and pew is this "common-sense." The want of the times is more of it. What with sensationalism and picturesque sentimentalism and quasi-philosophical speculation on the unrevealed and the indeterminable on this hither side, and supra-subtle judgment on what is and what is not authentic and authoritative in the text of Holy Scripture, I am forced to think of many as living in balloons.[74]

He was convinced that in Henry's life and work, readers can find "superlatively good plain common sense clear of the accretions alike of traditionary and sectarian oppositions."[75] According to Grosart, the "sanctified common-sense" was the "supreme characteristic of Matthew Henry's Commentary."[76]

"Sanctified common-sense" means "fine sanity" and common sense that "goes further than all acquired aids, in practically dealing with the Bible and men's souls."[77] So, "it must be sanctified common-sense; common-sense per se is not enough, nor is sanctity per se enough."[78] These two, according to Grosart, were combined in Henry. Grosart argued that Henry articulated sanctified common-sense by connecting Puritan virtue to his contemporaries: "By his 'common-sense' he fell in with the tendency of things in the eighteenth century, while in its being 'sanctified' common-sense, he retained the virtue of Puritanism in the seventeenth for the eighteenth century."[79] Furthermore, in the remainder of the section on Henry in *Representative Nonconformists*, Grosart argued that Henry brought sanctified common-sense to his reading of the Bible and put it into the *Bible*

72. Ibid., ix.
73. Ibid., 286.
74. Ibid.
75. Ibid.
76. Ibid., 286–87.
77. Ibid., 288.
78. Ibid.
79. Ibid., 289.

Commentary. In addition to sanctified common-sense, other characteristics of Henry's *Bible Commentary* included "brevity and wisdom; pungency and ingenuity; savouriness and quaint-felicities of wording."[80]

Grosart clearly and successfully accomplished his goal of revealing the characteristics of Henry's life and work. While focusing on Henry's *Bible Commentary*, he articulated the significance of "sanctified common-sense." He also indicated Henry's contribution to the eighteenth century by pointing out that he developed the piety and virtue of the Puritans for contemporary Christians.[81] Grosart argued that "the sanctified common-sense of Matthew Henry leads us farther into the secrets of the LORD, than the most vaunting and most learned exegesis, whether of native growth or foreign."[82] Moreover, Grosart appropriately places Henry as a nonconformist Presbyterian divine, not a Puritan: "Matthew Henry accepted a call to a 'dissenting congregation' (Presbyterian) in Chester";[83] "by heritage and training and deliberate choice Matthew Henry was a Presbyterian."[84]

Contemporary Approaches and Conclusion on the Best Picture of Henry

In the twentieth century, there have been few attempts to explore Henry's thought. After a long period of silence, though, new approaches on Henry have recently been emerging. There are now some brief descriptions of Henry's life and works as articles in dictionaries such as *The Dictionary of Major Biblical Interpreters*, *Oxford Dictionary of National Biography*, and *The Dictionary of Biblical Interpretation*. There are also some scholars who are interested in Henry's ministry and thought for our contemporary Reformed tradition. For example, Hughes Old researched Henry's thought in

---

80. Ibid., 313–42.

81. As Grosart pointed out in a footnote, Matthew Henry was influenced by his father, Philip Henry. Philip Henry was a Presbyterian nonconformist who kept the Puritan virtues during his life. Matthew Henry followed many legacies of Puritans that he learned from his father. Cf. Grosart, *Representative Nonconformists*, 289.

82. Ibid., 344.

83. Ibid., 269.

84. Ibid., 282. Again this point is important in that many people are confused in identifying Henry as a Puritan clergyman, not as a Presbyterian divine. In order to connect English Presbyterian tradition to contemporary Presbyterian churches, Henry's place in terms of tradition is very important.

his essay, "Matthew Henry and Puritan Disciplines of Family Worship,"[85] and in a chapter on daily prayer in *Worship*. He regards Henry's ministry and thought as important Reformed legacies. In addition, J. Ligon Duncan III, author of "A Method for Prayer by Matthew Henry,"[86] is interested in Henry's thought, especially Henry's practice of prayer. Third, Allan Harman treated Henry's life, family devotions, and background to his writings very well in the Introduction to *Family Religion*. Most recently, Randall Pederson published *Matthew Henry Daily Reading* as a resource for spiritual devotion promoting Word-centered piety based on Henry's *Bible Commentary*.

This research on Henry shares some common characteristics. First, two biographers, William Tong and John Williams, offered us a starting point for further research on Henry by describing and interpreting his life. Using enough sources, they both described Henry's life from birth to death in detail. These two biographical works on Henry have been foundational for understanding Henry's life. Second, Henry's spiritual character in relation to piety was articulated in detail by two authors: John Williams and Charles Chapman. These two authors interpreted Henry's character, exploring his life and practice, with special reference to his piety, which they emphasized as the main aspect of Henry's character. In this regard, these two books are good resources on Henry's character. Third, when it comes to Henry's thought, most authors focused exclusively on his *Bible Commentary*. Although the *Bible Commentary* is a representative work, Henry published many other works that express his thought. In particular, for example, he wrote various pious and liturgical books and treatises such as "The Secret Communion with God," "Meekness and Quietness of Spirit," "Family Religion," "Baptism," "The Communicants' Companion," and so on. Thus, as I have argued, in order to comprehend the characteristics of Henry's thoughts it is necessary to investigate his other writings along with his *Bible Commentary*.

The various approaches to Henry's life and thought give contemporary readers a much clearer picture of Henry. Most of all, Henry was not a Puritan minister but a Presbyterian minister influenced by Puritans, as Grosart delineated.[87] In order to connect him to Reformed thought, this distinction is crucial since all Puritans could not be categorized as Reformed ministers. Henry began his ministerial life with a Presbyterian ordination. Before be-

---

85. Leith, *Calvin Studies*, 69–91.
86. Kapic and Gleason, *The Devoted Life*, 238–50.
87. See n84 above.

The Life and Thought of Matthew Henry

ing ordained as a Presbyterian clergyman, he deeply considered whether to be a clergyman of the Church of England.[88] However, he chose to be a pastor of a Presbyterian congregation at Chester. In addition, Henry was trained mainly under his father, Philip Henry, who was a Presbyterian minister. While the dissenters were prohibited from entering the colleges, Philip Henry equipped his son Matthew with Presbyterian theology and ministry at home. Not all dissenting nonconformists were Presbyterians. Some of them were Independents, Baptists, and Quakers. So, it is more helpful for contemporary readers to understand Henry's life and thought not so much a nonconformist Puritan[89] as a Presbyterian minister who can be interpreted as a figure in the Reformed tradition. Henry's life and thought provide a clear example of an English Presbyterian minister at the beginning of the English Revolution.

In addition, Henry was a pastor who developed a godly life based on the Bible. Henry has been regarded as a Bible commentator, and many researchers and biographers identified him as that. Although it is certain that his main contribution was his *Bible Commentary*, it is not enough to regard him as a Bible commentator. He was a minister who sought out a piety based on the Bible. That was why he published various pious and ministerial works besides the *Commentary*. Following the Reformed tradition, Henry attempted to relate all areas of human life to God. He articulated a patterned relationship of the human with God through his many works and in his life. He tried to relate the human to God through ordinary life as well as rituals of worship, and in this regard Henry's life and thought should be interpreted from a perspective of piety.[90] Thus, in order to more fully understand Henry, contemporary readers should investigate how, in his various works, including the *Bible Commentary*, he attempted to connect the human to God in both ordinary life and through ritual such as the worship service.

In sum, Henry's contribution to Christian piety and Reformed liturgy is significant, though apart from the *Bible Commentary* his sermons and other works are little known to contemporary Christians. There have been few attempts to analyze his contributions for piety and liturgy. Most research on Henry has been focused only on his *Bible Commentary* and brief

---

88. Williams, *Life of Mr. Matthew Henry*, 44.

89. This is Williams's perspective on Henry's life and thought.

90. The main theme of piety is communion with God, which will be defined in detail in the following section.

descriptions of his life. This is a limited approach considering his various works and ministerial contributions. To put it another way, while most research emphasize his way of interpreting and applying the Scriptures, there have been few attempts to interpret and understand the main ideas of all his thought and his theological method of developing it. Thus, although the *Bible Commentary* shows us his theology in some way, it would be better to analyze it together with his other works to more fully understand his thought.

HENRY'S THOUGHT: HIS WORKS, THEMES, AND THEOLOGICAL METHOD

Besides his *Bible Commentary*, for which Evangelical circles know him best, Henry wrote many other books and treatises. He cultivated godly life in himself and others through his writing and preaching ministry. His teachings treated various issues in relation to personal piety and ecclesiastical ministry. This section will develop Henry's thought by answering these questions: What kinds of writings did Henry leave? What subjects did he deal with in his preaching ministry? What was Henry's main thought in his works and sermons? What influenced Henry's thought? What is the theological method that he used to develop his thought?

Henry's Works (besides *the Bible Commentary*) and Sermons

Henry wrote many works in his plain English style. Many of the works have been revised in modern English. Although he began to write his diary from 1689, the year of his marriage,[91] we know little from his diaries except for what biographers have quoted. There were also many letters to and from Henry, but we know little of them except what is illustrated in the biographies. Because of this limitation, this work will treat the thought of Henry only through available works, most of which are included in *The Complete Works of Matthew Henry*.[92] The two volumes of *The Complete Works* in-

---

[91]. "In 1689 being now the head of a family, he began to keep a diary of all the remarkable passages of providence that occurred to him." Tong, *Account of the Life and Death of Mr. Matthew Henry*, 17.

[92]. *The Complete Works* was published in 1979 (1997) and included most of Henry's works; several works are also published as monographs with an added brief introduction to Henry's life and thought. Also, some works are not included in the *Complete Works*,

The Life and Thought of Matthew Henry

clude forty-four of his sermons, treatises, and tracts. In addition, there are not many published manuscripts of his sermons. However, with the help of Tong, Williams analyzed Henry's sermon topics and Scriptures in chronological and topical order, which is a good resource for understanding Henry's thought for his preaching ministry.

Published Works Except the Bible Commentary[93]

Henry began to publish his works in 1689, two years after being ordained and beginning as a Presbyterian minister. The first publication was "The True Nature of Schism: A Persuasive to Christian Love and Charity (1689)," in which he argued that a schism does not necessarily mean being opposed to orthodox Christianity when defending the nonconformist position.[94] For the next five years while he concentrated his time and energy on ministry, Henry did not publish any work until 1694. After that he published works regarding piety and ministry. *The Complete Works* contain many works except for the funeral sermons and biographical writings.[95] Among them are

---

for example, "The Sabbath," "The Promises of God," and "The Worth of the Soul." See Henry, *Daily Communion with God; Christianity No Sect; The Sabbath; The Promises of God; the Worth of the Soul*. Also, Allan Harman recently edited Henry's unpublished sermons: *Matthew Henrys' Unpublished Sermons on The Covenant of Grace*.

93. For "The Exposition on the Old and New Testament," Williams analyzed the composition and process in detail. See Williams, *Memoirs of the Life*, note N.

94. Refer to chap. 1.

95. William Tong's chronological order of Henry's works differs slightly from that of John Williams. Here, I follow Williams's chronological order. Henry's works except funeral sermons can be listed in the following chronological order:

1689	The True Nature of Schism
1694	Family Hymns
1698	Meekness and Quietness of Spirit
1702	A Scripture Catechism
1703	Plain Catechism for Children
1704	The Right Management of Friendly Visits
1704	A Church in the House
1704	The Communicant's Companion
1705	Four Discourses against Vice and Immorality
1707	Great Britain's Present Hopes and Joys Opened
1710	A Method of Prayer
1710	Disputes Received
1710	Concerning the Work and Success of the Ministry
1711	Faith in Christ and Faith in God
1711	The Forgiveness of Sin

two works with uncertain publication dates: *A Treatise on Baptism*[96] and "The Christian Religion Is Not a Sect."

Henry published these works mostly based on his sermons. When he officially began to publish his works in 1698,[97] he already had been preaching for ten years.[98] With special concerns, he revised his selected sermons and lectures that were delivered in Chester and other cities from these years. He also added his own brief introduction to the beginning of each work. While indicating the date of publication in the "to the Reader" section, he explained the reason of publication as well, giving a thesis for each work for readers to know what he intended in his published works. In brief, through his published works, Henry attempted to show his thoughts on various issues such as personal piety, ministry, the young generation, and so forth. Henry selected his works in order to show his thought on pietistic and ministerial issues.

Unpublished Sermons

Although he selected and published some of his sermons, Henry did not publish all his sermons, and few after him have taken on that task. So it is very difficult to access all of Henry's sermons.[99] Besides the published sermons in *The Competed Works*, there are not many manuscripts that

1711	Hope and Fear Balanced
1712	To the Societies for Reformation of Manners
1712	Directions for Daily Communion with God
1712	Popery: A Scriptural Tyranny
1713	Sober Mindedness
1713	Christ's Favor to Little Children
1713	The Catechizing of Youth
1713	Self-Consideration and Self-Preservation
1714	The Pleasantness of a Religious Life

96. According to Harman, *A Treatise on Baptism* was published in an abridged form in 1783 by Thomas Robins. See Henry, *Family Religion: Principles for Raising a Godly Family*, 26.

97. *Family Hymns* was published in 1694 with only a brief essay on psalmody and revised in 1702 with large additions. Cf. Williams, *Memoirs of the Life*, 224. Also, Henry began his publication of "The Exposition of the Old and New Testament" in November 1704. Cf. Williams, *Memoirs of the Life*, 235.

98. John Williams analyzed the subjects and the Scriptures of Henry's sermons from 1687 to 1698. See Williams, *Memoirs of the Life*, 273–79.

99. Most of his funeral sermons are accessible. However, not all his sermons for the Lord's Day are extant beyond the title and Bible verses.

readers can access. In 2002, Allan Harman edited and published Henry's unpublished consecutive sermons that were delivered from December 20, 1691, to June 26, 1692, in his book *The Covenant of Grace*. Except for these works, we have only the titles comprising subjects and Scriptures of his sermons for twenty-five years.[100] Tong, as a friend and biographer of Henry, "received [the subjects of sermons] as it was drawn up by [Henry] a little while before he left that place [Chester]."[101] Williams quoted Tong's analysis of the subjects that Henry preached upon for twenty-five years.

Henry began a series of topical sermons in July 1687.[102] After then, he followed a certain pattern of subject in his preaching. Based on Williams' analysis,[103] Henry's preaching topics at Chester for twenty-five years can be summarized in chronological order as follows:

July 1687—September 1687	A Sinful State
October 1687—July 1689	Conversion
August 1689—January 1691	A Well-Ordered Conversation
February 1691—July 1692	The Covenant of Grace (God, Christ, and the Holy Spirit in the Covenant)
August 1692—April 1694	Sanctification
May 1694—December 1695	Worship (Ordinances, Opportunities, Of the Manners, Of the Mediator)
January 1696—April 1696	Concerning Our Duty to Our Neighbors
May 1696—May 1698	Reasonableness of Being Truly Religious
June 1698—December 1712	A Body of Divinity[104]

---

100. This is a sufficient resource since Henry had ministered for twenty-seven years: twenty-five years at Chester and two years at Hackney.

101. Tong, *Account of Life and Death of Matthew Henry*, 101.

102. However, he already began his sermon at Chester in June the same year. The first sermon that he preached at Chester was "For I determined to know nothing among you, but Jesus Christ and Him crucified" from 1 Corinthians 2:2. Williams, *Memoirs of the Life*, 273–74.

103. Williams, *Memoirs of the Life*, note F; Tong, *Account of the Life and Death of Matthew Henry*, 163–210.

104. Henry began this subject and did not finish it until 1712. Tong confessed Henry's intention about this subject: "he began a body of divinity, which was his constant Sabbath

- Concerning God
- Concerning the Word of God
- Concerning the Works of God
- Concerning the Angels
- Concerning Man
- Concerning Sin
- Concerning our Redemption by Jesus Christ
- Concerning the Application of the Redemption
- Concerning the Divine Law
- Concerning the Gospel Rule of Faith and Repentance
- Concerning Gospel Ordinances[105]
- Concerning the Church
- Concerning the Four Last Things

This is the general pattern of Henry's preaching on the Lord's Day.

There are several characteristics of this scheme. First, Henry approached his preaching ministry thematically. He did not follow the rule of *Lectio Continua* in his preaching. *Lectio Continua* was applied to the expounding of the Scriptures, which was another part of the worship service. He arranged his sermon not as based on the Scriptures but on the subjects. Second, the year of 1698 was crucial for Henry in that he officially began his publications with revising his sermons and lectures. In that year, Henry visited London for the first time since his settlement at Chester. A friend in London encouraged Henry to publish his sermon: "it is published at

---

work; this body of divinity he had some thoughts of revising and publishing, if God had spared him till he had finished his Exposition on the New Testament, but since that now is become impossible, I think it worth our while to take a view of the general scheme and heads of that great work, which took up so much of his time, for it continued till the year of 1712, and God ordered it so, that this should be the business not only of a considerable part of his life, but of it in which his thoughts must be supposed to be most mature, and he in the best capacity to treat upon a subject of such an excellent nature." Williams, *Memoirs of the Life*, 279; Tong, *Account of the Life and Death of Matthew Henry*, 108.

105. Henry already preached on this subject in the years of 1694 to 1695.

the request of a very worthy friend who heard it preached in London last summer."[106] It can be assumed that Henry had a mind to have an effect on other Christians outside Chester through his published work on the synthesized topics. Third, it is certain that Henry was a very organized minister in terms of his preaching ministry. He did not insert any occasional topics into the subject of the normal Lord's Day worship except for the worship services of the sacraments. Moreover, he was very articulate in pursuing a subject by taking it for several months or even a year or longer.

Main Themes in Henry's Works and Sermons

In order to spell out Henry's thought it is first necessary to analyze the subjects of his sermons. Second, I intend to examine the specific topics and themes in his published works since most of them are his own selections from among his sermons. In his sermons and published works, Henry pursued three important themes in relation to Christian faith: connection between God and humanity, communion with God as a patterned relationship, and the domestic role of religion. The titles in *The Complete Works*, including monographs, present the themes in which Henry was interested. His sermon topics also show that he was concerned with practical aspects for the congregation at Chester.

Relationship between God and Humanity

Henry stressed the connection between God and humanity in his preaching. He clearly indicated the necessity and possibility of the relationship between God and humanity. First, Henry's sermon subjects started from the assumption that there is a distance between God and human beings. The first subject was the "sinful state." This implies that human beings cannot have any appropriate relationship to God since they are in the fallen state that does not allow them to be connected to God. Yet it can be overcome by conversion (the second subject). Humans can recover their relationship with God by conversion. This conversion does not mean a static state; instead, it leads people into a more developed state by requiring of them "a well ordered conversation" (the third subject). This well-ordered conversation does not refer to a manner of speaking. It concerns personal piety

---

106. Henry, *Complete Works*, 1:96.

that has been transformed in the heart by God's grace (the fourth subject). However, Henry did not stop here. Henry developed a patterned relationship: a personal and intimate interaction between humanity and God.

Henry continued to show the way that people can relate to God. "A well ordered conversation" was followed by the subject of the covenant of God's grace, which means God's consolation for the human being.[107] Based on God's consolation, Henry required his congregation to put off the old man and put on the new as a subject of sanctification (his fifth subject).[108] Then Henry suggested a more patterned communal way of relating between the human being and God: worship as a vertical relationship (the sixth subject). He articulated ordinances and opportunities as well as the manner and mediator of worship. At the same time, Henry treated an appropriate patterned relationship among human beings: duty to neighbors as a horizontal relationship (the seventh subject). Last, Henry summarized the subject of relating between the human and God by dealing with "reasonableness of being truly religious" (the eighth subject).

Beginning in 1698 Henry systematized all the subjects of sermons he preached in a new order and structure. He did not change the subjects of preaching, but arranged them in a new way. Based on his eleven years of preaching, he intended a more systematic approach to the close relationship between God and humans. Henry developed his systematic theology based on his preaching ministry. His systematic approach is similar to contemporary approaches to systematic theology. He included God, God's Word and works, man, Jesus Christ and redemption, divine law, faith and repentance, gospel ordinances, church, and last things. These themes resemble contemporary evangelical systematic theology.[109] Systematic doctrines, from Henry's perspective, are not just pedagogical subjects in theological education but real issues for the congregation's patterned relationship to God.

---

107. Williams, *Memoirs of the Life*, 275.

108. Henry selected twenty items that need to be changed: pride: humility; passion: meekness; covetousness: contentment; contention: peaceableness; murmuring: patience; melancholy: cheerfulness; vanity: seriousness; uncleanness: chastity; drunkenness: temperance; deceitfulness: honesty; hatred: love; hypocrisy: sincerity; bad discourse: good discourse; bad company: good company; security: watchfulness; slothfulness: diligence; folly: prudence; fear: hope; a life of sense: a life of faith; self: Jesus Christ. Williams, *Memoirs of the Life*, 276–77.

109. Our contemporary evangelical systematic theology normally includes Prolegomena, Christology, anthropology, ecclesiology, soteriology, and eschatology in theological curriculum, and these topics are similar to the categorized themes of Henry's sermons.

In this way, Henry emphasized the relationship between humanity and God through his preaching. His preaching subjects were deeply related to the *ordo* of human salvation. The human sinful condition needs to be reconciled to God for the appropriate relationship. By grace, humans can connect all of life to God, which promotes a patterned relationship between God and human without ignoring the relationship between humans and each other. He systematically articulated real ways of connecting the person and God.

Communion with God

The patterned relationship that Henry articulated can be summarized and explained as "Communion with God,"[110] the topic articulated by John Owen (1616–1683), a Dissenting Puritan theologian and friend of Philip Henry.[111] Although there is no record that Henry learned from Owen on the theme of communion of God, it may be possible to conclude that he indirectly took the thought of Owen through his home schooling under his father, Philip Henry.[112] Owen wrote *Of the Communion with God the Father, Son, and Holy Spirit, Each Person Distinctly, in Love, Grace, and Consolation* in 1657, and dealt with the communion with God by emphasizing the human's relationship with each person of the Triune God. Henry adopted the same wording of "communion with God." However, his emphasis was much more practical than Owen's. For Henry, communion with God basically meant a pattern of relationship between God and the person: "giving glory to God and receiving grace from God." Henry identified communion with God like this: "I am willing to hope . . . that you are come with a pious design, to give glory to God, and to receive grace from him [God], and in both to keep up your communion with him [God]."[113] Henry's various published works reveal his thought on communion with God.

---

110. William Dyrness articulates a patterned relationship in terms of culture from a Reformed perspective. See Dyrness, *The Earth Is God's*. Also John Owen articulates the concept of communion with the Triune God as a representative thought of Puritan theology.

111. See Henry, *Life of Mr. Philip Henry*, 20.

112. Further work needs to be done in this area. I was not able to discern who Henry read extensively, and this would be an important area of further research.

113. Henry, *Complete Works*, 1:199.

Matthew Henry

First, Henry developed a method for prayer as a practical way of communion with God. Henry defined prayer as a core way of communion with God: "it is a piece of respect and homage so exactly consonant to the natural ideas which all men have of God, that it is certain those that live without prayer, live without God in the world."[114] Prayer, according to Henry, "is the solemn and religious offering up of devout acknowledgments and desires to God, or a sincere representation of holy affections, with a design to give unto God the glory due unto his Name thereby, and to obtain from him promised favors, and both through the Mediator."[115] For Henry, the essence of prayer is not so much a petition or request but humble adoration of and thanksgiving to God.[116] When it comes to communion with God, Henry was convinced that "the scripture describes prayer to be our drawing near to God, lifting up our souls to him, pouring out our hearts before him."[117] Moreover, this prayer as a way of communion with God is at the center of the Christian life:

> A golden thread of heart-prayer must run through the web of the whole Christian life; we must be frequently addressing ourselves to God in short and sudden ejaculations, by which we must keep up our communion with God in providences and common actions, as well as in ordinances and religious services. Thus prayer must be sparsim (a sprinkling of it) in every duty, and our eyes must be ever towards the LORD.[118]

With this conviction, Henry articulated a method of prayer that suggested the sufficiency of the Scriptures in furnishing us for the real practice of prayer. Henry organized his own method of prayer with Scripture expressions in six components: Adoration of God, Confession of Sin, Petition or

---

114. Ibid., 2:1.

115. Ibid.

116. Henry's thought on the essence of prayer was not different from that of Church of England. "The principal kinds of prayer are adoration, praise, and thanksgiving." See "An Outline of the Faith," in *The Book of Common Prayer*, 856: Section of Prayer and Worship. The Puritan came out from the Church of England in order to reform her more strictly according to the Scriptures. So, even though there were struggles between the Puritans and the Church of England in terms of the manner of worship, the Puritan way of prayer was not totally separate from the prayer book of the Church of England (*Book of Common Prayer*). Cf. Rust, *The First of the Puritans and the Book of Common Prayer*.

117. Henry, *Complete Works*, 2:1.

118. Ibid.

Supplication, Thanksgiving for Mercies, Intercession, and Conclusion.[119] At the same time, he included fourteen examples of scriptural prayers for several occasions at the end of *A Method for Prayer*.

Furthermore, Henry articulated a realistic way of communion with God as a practical guideline. He published a book entitled *Daily Communion with God* (1712). The original title of his discourse on daily communion with God was "Directions for Daily Communion with God: Showing How to Begin, How to Spend and How to Close Every Day with God."[120] He attempted to develop a way of experiencing God's presence not only in the acts of ritual but also in common life. His goal was to cultivate godly life in ordinary people: "to the promoting of serious godliness, which is the thing I am at."[121] His approach to the presence of God emphasizes much more time than space. He did not separate holy place from secular place in terms of the presence of God and experience of it. Wherever people stand, according to Henry, they must seek for the presence of God at any time. He clearly categorized every day into three time periods: beginning, spending, and ending. By beginning, spending, and ending every day with God, one can experience communion with God as a patterned relationship. For Henry, the most important thing in human life is to be united with Christ[122] by practicing communion every day: "The most important part of their business lies between God and their own souls, in the frame of their spirits, and the workings of their hearts, in their retirements, which no eye sees but his, that is all eye."[123]

---

119. To put it in more detail, these are the six components of a method for prayer: (1) Of the first part of prayer, which is addressed to God, adoration of him, with suitable acknowledgements, professions, and preparatory requests; (2) Of the second part of prayer, which is confession of sin, complaints of ourselves, and humble professions of repentance; (3) Of the third part of prayer, which is petition and supplication for the good things which we stand in need of; (4) Of the fourth part of prayer, which is thanksgivings for the mercies we have received from God, and the many favors of his we are interested in, and have, and hope for benefit by; (5) Of the fifth part of prayer, which is intercession, or address and supplication to God for others; (6) Of the conclusion of our prayers. *Complete Works*, 2:4–57, 68–70.

120. Ibid., 1:198–247.

121. Ibid., 1:198.

122. "See what need we have of the constant supplies of divine grace, and of a union with Christ, that by faith we may partake of the root and fatness of the good olive continually." Ibid., 1:245.

123. Ibid.

Matthew Henry

Domestic Religion: Raising a Godly Family

Henry heavily emphasized domestic religion in seeking a godly life in daily communion with God as a patterned relationship. Henry defined family as the center of religion: "Look upon houses as temples of God, places for worship, and all your possessions as dedicated things, to be used for God's honor, and not to be alienated or profaned."[124] Moreover, he assumed that "here [family religion] the reformation must begin."[125] Henry published several works on family religion: "A Church in the House: A Sermon Concerning Family Religion, Preached in London, April 16, 1704"; "Christ's Favor to Little Children Displayed, in a Sermon, Preached March 6, 1713"; "A Sermon Concerning the Catechising of Youth, Preached to Mr. Harris's Catechumens, April 7, 1713"; *Treatise on Baptism*. These works stressed the role of family in Christian faith and developed domestic religion.

First, Henry articulated a church in the house. According to Henry, "the families of Christians should be little churches . . . or wherever we have a house, God should have a church in it."[126] Henry saw the nature of church in the family: "Churches are societies, incorporated for the honor and service of God in Christ, devoted to God, and employed for him; so should our families be."[127] The service and honor of God is at the center of a church in the house: "it is a good thing when a man has a house of his own, thus to convert it into a church, by dedicating it to the service and honor of God, that it may be a Bethel, a house of God, and not a Bethaven, a house of vanity and iniquity."[128] Henry furthermore developed three things necessary for a house to be a church: doctrine, worship, and discipline.[129] And, according to Henry, family worship and discipline are based on family doctrine.

---

124. Ibid., 1:250–51.
125. Ibid., 1:248.
126. Ibid., 1:249.
127. Ibid.
128. Ibid., 1:250.
129. Henry applied the necessary conditions of church to family: "where the truths of Christ are professed and taught, the ordinances of Christ administered and observed, and due care taken to put the laws of Christ in execution among all who profess themselves his subjects, and this under the conduct and inspection of a gospel ministry; there is a church. And something answerable to this there must be in our families, to denominate them 'little churches.'" Ibid., 1:251.

Family doctrine is comprised of two parts: reading the Scriptures as a family and catechizing children.[130] Henry emphasized reading the Bible in family worship by requiring "the solemn reading of the Scripture a part of your daily worship in your families."[131] This reading was very important for Henry in that it led to communion with God: "When you speak to God by prayer, be willing to hear him speak to you in his word, that there may be a complete communion with you and God."[132] Moreover, Henry regarded catechism an essential way of raising children. He published his "Sermon on the Catechizing of Youth,"[133] which explains the nature and principle of catechizing. He also organized *A Scripture Catechism*,[134] composed of 107 questions and answers based on the *Westminster Catechism*, and published "A Plain Catechism for Children," composed of five parts, with a short catechism for the Lord's Supper. Henry used the method of catechism as a way for parents to teach their children. Parents need to "oblige them [children] to learn some good catechism by heart, and to keep it in remembrance."[135] This way of catechizing is very important in relation to public teaching at church:

> Public catechizing will turn to little account without family catechizing. The labor of ministers in instructing youth and feeding the lambs of the flock therefore proves to many labor in vain, because masters of families do not their duty in preparing them for public instruction and examining their improvement by it. As mothers are children's best nurses, so parents are, or should be, their best teachers.[136]

In this way, parents have a major minor role in children's spiritual formation. Parents should always consider what their children are capable of and what they are designed for in the world and beyond.[137]

Second, Henry developed the manner of a church in the house. He attempted to apply a method of connecting God and humanity to family.

---

130. For more details on family worship and catechizing children, see the section on family worship in chap. 3.
131. Henry, *Complete Works*, 1:252.
132. Ibid.
133. Ibid., 2:157–73.
134. Ibid., 2:174–265.
135. Ibid., 1:252.
136. Ibid., 1:252–53.
137. See ibid., 1:253.

Matthew Henry

As in the connection between God and humans, Henry emphasized the human heart for the house itself. The most important point connecting God and humanity was the heart. The right method of having a church in the house is this: "first set up Christ upon the throne in your hearts, and then set up a church for Christ in your house."[138] As masters of the family, parents who have Christ at their hearts can keep their authority through family worship. Parents "cannot keep up their authorities better than by keeping up religion in [their] families."[139] For Henry, this family worship was the most important "good work" that needs to be kept up for the family: "you ought to worship God in your families, and that it is a good thing to do so."[140] Henry emphasized the place and importance of family worship in detail:

> Would you have your family relations comfortable, your affairs successful, and give an evidence of your professed subjection to the gospel of Christ? Would you live in God's fear, and die in his favor, and escape that curse which is entailed upon prayerless families? Let religion in the power of it have its due place, that is, the uppermost place in your houses.[141]

For Henry, each godly family needs to begin, revive, and maintain this good work of family worship.

Along with communion with God, Henry also emphasized the communion of people with one other in family religion. First of all, Henry asked people who have a church in their house to "be careful to adorn and beautify it in their conversation."[142] Family worship means not only to pray, read the Scriptures, and sing the psalms, but also to "act under the commanding power and influence of it."[143] Thus, in family worship, real life as a practice of the teaching of worship was very important:

> Let the example you set your families be throughout good, and by it teach them not only to read and pray, for that is but half their work, but by it teach them to be meek and humble, sober and temperate, loving and peaceable, just and honest; so shall you adorn the doctrine of God our Savior, and those who will not be won

---

138. Ibid., 1:262.
139. Ibid., 1:263.
140. Ibid.
141. Ibid.
142. Ibid., 1:265.
143. Ibid.

> by the word, shall be won by your conversation. Your family worship is an honor to you, see to it that neither you nor yours be in anything a disgrace to it.[144]

Then, Henry also developed the communion of families as domestic churches by advocating that "religious families keep up friendship and fellowship with each other, and as they have opportunity, assist one another in doing good."[145] For Henry, upholding one another between religious families is directly related to God's glory:

> Religious families should greet one another, visit one another, love one another, pray for one another, and as becomes households of faith, do all the good they can one to another, forasmuch as they all meet daily at the same throne of grace, and hope to meet shortly at the same throne of glory, to be no more, as they are now divided in Jacob, and scattered in Israel.[146]

In this way, Henry saw domestic religion at the core of the spiritual formation of each family in terms of constant communion with God.

Henry's Theological Method in Developing His Thought

Henry developed his thought on communion with God as a patterned relationship in daily life mainly through articulating domestic religion. With this theme, he treated various issues in relation to cultivating personal piety. He developed this pious thought through sermons and lectures that he delivered primarily at Chester. Henry's published works are based on his sermons and lectures reveal two main characteristics: promoting acquaintance with the Bible and emphasizing the intellectual character of practical applicability.

First, Henry attempted to promote knowledge of the Bible through his sermons and works. During his twenty-five years of ministry, Henry sought a more thorough acquaintance with the Bible. Tong made this point by commenting how Henry "expected both pleasure and advantage in looking into every part of the Bible, and leading his hearers into a more thorough acquaintance with it."[147] Henry was convinced that the history and doctrine

---

144. Ibid., 1:265–66.
145. Ibid., 1:267.
146. Ibid.
147. Williams, *Memoirs of the Life*, 293.

of the Bible contain all the clues for the questions that people have: "for these questions lying everywhere interspersed through the Old and New Testament, and bearing reference to the several cases on which they were proposed, they must need to take in a very considerable part, both of the history and doctrine of the Bible."[148] Through his sermons, Henry organized the themes of the Bible into systematic categories such as God, the human, Christ, the church, and the last things. Thus, familiarity with the Bible is basic to Henry's method for developing his thought.

This method came from his father, Philip Henry. Harman pointed out Philip Henry's influence on Matthew in terms of the familiarity with the Bible:

> Matthew must have been very aware himself of advise his father regularly gave to prospective pastors. Students who had gone through their studies at private academies wanted to spend some time with Philip Henry and his family before they entered into the ministry. When they came to stay, what he did was to impress on them the need above all else to be familiar with the text of the Bible. He reminded them of the maxim, *bonus textarius est bonus theologus*, "the good textual student is a good theologian."[149]

According to this background, as already indicated above, Henry "was able to read a chapter of the Bible very distinctly at about three years old."[150] Moreover, he not only had knowledge of the Bible but also confidence in it—a high sense of the authority of Scripture. According to Old, "the biblical interpretations of Henry are remarkable for their high sense of the authority of Scripture."[151] Old evaluated Henry's method of interpretation of the Bible as "the improving of the biblical imagery":

> A favorite method of interpretation that we find often in Henry's work is what he calls the improving of the biblical imagery. Henry teaches us a great deal about the meaning of Scripture simply by a careful literary analysis of the text and a profound understanding of the literary forms of biblical language. He understood the biblical language because he lived it.[152]

---

148. Ibid.
149. Harman, "Introduction," 24.
150. Tong, *Account of the Life and Death of Matthew Henry*, 2.
151. Old, "Matthew Henry," 523.
152. Ibid.

In this way, Henry regarded knowledge of the Bible as the key method in developing his thought about relating people with God.

Second, Henry stressed the intellectual character for applying the Scriptures to daily life. He did not attempt to simply develop a theoretical doctrine of the Bible. Instead, he strove to apply all the biblical doctrines to real life in a clear and simple way. In order to do so, Henry articulated the way of instructing with questions. Following his father, he used the edifying method of question and answer. For example, Henry continued to develop catechisms that were composed of questions and answers such as his *A Scripture Catechism* and "A Plain Catechism for Children." Moreover, Henry used a systematic and logical approach in developing his sermons and writings. His preaching was composed of two main parts: doctrine and application. In each sermon, Henry first explored the biblical doctrine on a specific topic and then concluded by suggesting very detailed practical applications for that doctrine. Henry expressed the applications in a pungent and emphatic way.

In the funeral sermon for Matthew Henry, Daniel Williams evaluated his manner of expressions: "his words were decent, though familiar, and his proverbial sentences were contrived to affect, and retain in the memory some important truth."[153] Tong also found this quality in Henry: "In his preaching you had a very just and close way of thinking, with the most plain, proper, natural, and easy expression."[154] He furthermore evaluated Henry's preaching by pointing out that "there is generally something pungent and emphatic in what is put by way of question; it is a pointed way of speaking, that strikes the mind more directly; there is in it an immediate application and appeal to one's reason and conscience."[155]

Henry's method of presenting the gospel in a logical way presupposes that "there is an intellectual element in presenting the Gospel."[156] As Harman pointed out, Henry "followed the Puritans in stressing the intellectual character of ministry, both spoken and written."[157] Henry learned this Puritan intellectual style through his tutors, Mr. William Turner and Mr. Thomas Doolittle. Mr. Turner "introduced Mr. Matthew Henry into the

---

153. Williams, *Funeral Sermon*, 33.
154. Tong, *Funeral Sermon*, 31.
155. Williams, *Memoirs of the Life*, 293.
156. Harman, "Introduction," 24.
157. Ibid.

grammar learning";[158] and Henry learned Reformed and Puritan theology through Mr. Doolittle's Academy in Islington.[159] Under their influence, Henry developed his own style. Williams commented on his style:

> It is to the credit of the works under review, that there is in them all an entire absence of garishness and puerility; they never pander to the odious impertinence of vain, and mere curious speculators; neither are there any meretricious ornaments; instruction is never made contemptible by empty declamation.[160]

Clear and simple knowledge with an intellectual character constituted Henry's method of connecting the Bible to real life.

CONCLUSION

Among the numerous resources for interpreting Henry's life and thought, first Tong and Williams contributed to understanding the life and character of Henry by publishing biographies. Following their works, several scholars attempted to interpret Henry's thought and applied his thought for their own people and time. These approaches are only focused on his *Bible Commentary*. While it is certain that Henry's expounding of the Scriptures was a great contribution to evangelical churches, Henry himself published many other works, including sermons and lectures, while he was alive. Contemporary readers have access to almost all of Henry's writings in the *Complete Works*. His unpublished sermons and other writings besides the *Bible Commentary*, might be good resources for understanding Henry's thought, however, few have endeavored to interpret Henry's thought from those materials.

This chapter attempted to briefly introduce the life and thought of Henry by (1) evaluating the works on Henry's life and (2) organizing his thought and theological method in a new way based on his original works. This work made clear that Henry sought communion with God in daily life as a patterned relationship between humanity and God. With that

---

158. Tong, *Account of the Life and Death of Matthew Henry*, 4. In shaping his theological method, Matthew Henry learned from Philip Henry, William Turner, and Thomas Doolittle. As explained above and in chap. 1, Henry was also influenced by Richard Baxter and John Owen. What and how Henry learned about Reformed theology and ministry is another topic worth further research.

159. Williams, *Memoirs of the Life*, 9–16.

160. Ibid., 249.

conviction, Henry endeavored to articulate and develop communion with God in the domestic context. In order to accomplish his vision of human life as communion with God in the ordinary life, Henry developed his own method of connecting the Scriptures to daily life. The patterned relationship between God and humans, for Henry, was more clearly shown and applied in his understanding and practice of worship, the main topic of the next chapter.

3

Matthew Henry on Christian Worship
Communion with God in Liturgical Forms and Patterns

MATTHEW HENRY PRESUPPOSED THAT a gulf existed between God and humanity. His first set of sermons implicated humanity's sinful state, originating from the fall.[1] Keeping this premise in mind, all Henry's ministerial efforts endeavored to help people collapse this distance from God. As discussed in the previous chapter, Henry articulated communion with God in detail as a patterned relationship between people and God. For Henry, communion with God, often visualized by the metaphor of walking with God, was at the core of Christian life.[2] In his last published book, *The Pleasantness of a Religious Life* (1714), Henry stressed that communion with God was not just a duty or obligation but also a goal or pleasure of humanity. He claimed that "the great truth which I desire my heart and yours may be fully convinced of is this: that a holy heavenly life spent in the service of God, and in communion with him, is, without doubt, the most pleasant and comfortable life any man can live in the world."[3] This duty and goal of human life was the foundation of Henry's ministerial thought and practice.

---

1. The first set of sermons at Chester, for three months, 1687, was on the misery of a sinful state. See Tong, *Account of the Life and Death of Matthew Henry*, chap. 4.

2. Henry took communion with God as his main concern and thought from his father, Philip Henry. See Henry, *Life of Mr. Philip Henry*, appendix 12.

3. Henry, *The Pleasantness of a Religious Life*, , 11.

We may also see Henry's understanding and practice of worship as an effort to promote the goal of communing or walking with God. The main purpose of this chapter is to elucidate how Henry understood Christian worship. For Henry, according to the goal of Christian life, worship can be defined as the essential way of drawing people nearer to God's presence by overcoming the deep gulf between God and humanity. Building upon this definition, Henry further developed and articulated his theology of worship and attempted to practice various services of worship as he desired. Henry developed his thought regarding worship in his sermons and expounding notes. He also wrote two main works on the ordinances of worship, especially on the sacraments: *A Treatise on Baptism*[4] and *The Communicant's Companion: Instructions for Receiving the Lord's Supper* (1704).[5] Henry's practice of worship is described in detail by William Tong and John Williams, Henry's two main biographers, so contemporary readers can understand it well.

Understanding Henry's theology of worship, as a case study, will help us clearly see what English Presbyterian worship was like in the late seventeenth and early eighteenth centuries. Furthermore, this research provides insight into what Presbyterian understanding and practice of worship based on the Bible should be like, since Henry developed his theology of worship based on the Scriptures. Following Henry's own thoughts on Christian worship, this chapter will define Henry's understanding of worship with reference to the nature, ordinances, opportunity, manner, and the mediator of worship. While taking into account his understanding of worship, Henry's real practice of worship will be examined with the help of biographers' works as necessary. The conclusion will then analyze some Reformed characteristics in Henry's English Presbyterian theology of worship.

Henry developed his theology of worship mainly through his sermons and expounding notes. After preaching on the subject of sanctification, understood as an individual life being close to God, for about eighteen months (August 1692 to April 1694), Henry treated the subject of divine worship for about twenty months, from May 1694 to December 1695. Thought we do not have access to the manuscripts of his sermons on the subject of worship,[6] through the work of Tong, contemporary readers do have the

---

4. It is not clear when he wrote this treatise.

5. Chapter 4 will explore these two books in detail in order to examine Henry's theology of the sacraments in relation to communion with God.

6. There is no record that the manuscripts of Henry's sermons on worship have

subjects and Scriptures for each sermon on every topic. By examining Henry's expounding notes edited and published in the *Bible Commentary* on several key verses in relation to worship as well as each passage from sermons on the subject of worship, this section will analyze how Henry understood worship. This method implies that Henrys' theology of worship was based on the Bible, not the tradition or ceremony of contemporary worship services. Henry organized his understanding of worship under several categories: ordinances, opportunities or occasions, the manner, and the mediator of worship. Before delving into each category, it is first necessary to consider how Henry defined the nature of worship.

THE MEANING AND NATURE OF WORSHIP

Henry did not define what worship is in one simple sentence. However, he revealed the nature as well as the meaning of worship through his many sermons and writings. In his earlier work "A Scripture Catechism" (1702), Henry taught that the core of religion was a life of communion with God or a walk with God in the whole course of one's thought and behavior.[7] This main thought continued without even minor changes until his death. In his last work, *The Pleasantness of a Religious Life* (1714), he claimed it again: "to be religious is to live a life of communion with God."[8] Communion with God, for Henry, is related to all human life as a primary goal of and process: "we may as truly have communion with God in providences as in ordinances, and in the duties of common conversation, as in religious exercises."[9] In expounding 1 John 1:3, Henry indicated that this communion means fellowship with the Father and the Son Jesus Christ:

> Truly our fellowship [or communion] is with the Father and his Son Jesus Christ. We have communion with the Father, and with the Son of the Father in our happy relation to them, in our receiving heavenly blessings from them, and in our spiritual converse with them.[10]

---

survived.

7. Henry, *A Scripture Catechism*, in *Complete Works*, 2:220.
8. Henry, *Pleasantness of a Religious Life*, in ibid., 1:20.
9. Ibid.
10. Henry, *Bible Commentary* (hereafter abbreviated *BC*), 1 John 1:3.

So, communication between people and God is a crucial part of the communion between them. Henry also summarized the importance of communication in communion with God by mentioning that "herein consists the life of religion, to converse with God, to receive his communications of mercy and grace to us, and to return pious and devout affections to him."[11]

Henry developed his understanding of worship with this concept of communication as a primary function in communion with God. For Henry, communion with God, walking with God, was the core of the life of religion and at the heart of human worship.[12] This thought came from his father, Philip Henry. Henry clearly remembered what his father taught him, and wrote it in the biography of his father:

> To be religious is to know God . . . to know God is to be acquainted with him; to have intimate acquaintance with him, and this includes all religion; it is walking with God. To be religious is also to serve God. . . . This service of God is to wait upon him daily and duly in the duties of his immediate service and worship.[13]

In this way, Henry defined Christian worship as a crucial form of communication between God and humanity. This definition implies two important things regarding the nature of Christian worship: the object of worship and the spiritual aspect of worship.

First of all, Henry clearly presupposed the object of worship as the one with whom we communicate. God as the object of communion should be the only object of worship. Henry's first concern was not the way people worship but the object of worship, since he assumed that the way to worship will flow from the object of worship.[14] In Christian worship, in order to have an appropriate means of communication with God, it is first necessary to know God. For Henry, God cannot be known by human imagination but only by the Scriptures. Henry indicated God, as God is known in the Scriptures, as the object of worship: "[T]hose who by the scriptures have obtained some knowledge of God (a *certain* though not a *perfect* knowledge) may worship him *comfortably* to themselves, and *acceptably* to him, for they *know what they worship*."[15]

---

11. Henry, *Pleasantness of a Religious Life*, in *Complete Works*, 1:20.
12. Henry, *A Scripture Catechism*, 220.
13. Henry, *Life of Mr. Philip Henry*, 362–63.
14. See Henry, *A Scripture Catechism*, 222.
15. BC, John 4:22.

Henry pointed out in his exposition on the same verse that "even Jesus was pleased to reckon himself among the *worshippers* of God: *We worship*."[16] Moreover, in the first subject of his sermons on divine worship based on Matthew 4:10, Henry also emphasized that God is the only object of worship:

> Christ quotes this law concerning religious worship and quotes it with application to himself: First, to shew that in his estate of humiliation, he was himself made under this law; though as God he was worshipped, yet as man he did worship God, both publicly and privately. He obligateth us to no more than what he was first pleased to oblige himself to. Thus it became him to fulfil all righteousness. Secondly, to shew that the law of religious worship is of eternal obligation; and though he abrogated and altered many institutions of worship, yet this fundamental law of nature—that God only is to be worshipped—he came to ratify and confirm, and enforce upon us.[17]

Thus, regarding the nature of Christian worship, Henry stressed that God is the only object of worship. This implies that humans should do as a means of communion with God.

Henry furthermore emphasized the otherness of the object of worship. As a communication between humanity and God, the main focus of worship, for Henry, is not on us but on God. Henry stressed this point when he wrote, "the nature of religious worship is giving to the LORD the glory due to his name."[18] So, "if we would, in hearing and praying, and other acts of devotion, receive grace from God, we must make it our business to give glory to God."[19] In this way, as the sum and substance of the everlasting gospel, worshipping God is crucial in experiencing his otherness.[20]

The other essential element of Christian worship, according to Henry, is its spiritual aspect. Humans can communicate with God, but God as a spiritual being cannot be seen by human eyesight. The invisibleness of God influences worship. In expounding on John 4:24, Henry noted that he regarded worship as a spiritual ordinance, claiming that "Christians shall worship God, not in the ceremonial observances of the Mosaic institution,

---

16. Ibid.
17. *BC*, on Matthew 4:10.
18. *BC*, on Psalm 29:2.
19. Ibid.
20. Ibid.

but in *spiritual* ordinances, consisting less in *bodily exercise,* and animated and invigorated more with divine power and energy."[21] From this perspective, Henry observed that "the way of worship which Christ has instituted is rational and intellectual, and refined from those external rites and ceremonies with which the Old-Testament worship was both clouded and clogged."[22] Henry called this spiritual worship "true worship, in opposition to that which was typical."[23] In this way, "the legal services were figures of the true."[24]

Thus, the most important thing in this spiritual worship is not to follow any particular form but to seek the face of God. For Henry, "the true nature of religious worship is seeking the face of God."[25] This seeking of God's face constituted the core of Christian worship as a way of communion with God:

> This [Seeking the face of God] is in God's precept: "*Seek you my face*"; he [God] would have us seek him for himself, and make his favor our chief good; and this it is in the saint's purpose and desire: "*Thy face, LORD, will I seek,* and nothing less will I take up with." The opening of his hand will satisfy the desire of other living things (Psalm 145:16), but it is only the shining of his face that will satisfy the desire of a living soul.[26]

In this way, seeking God's face, for Henry, had the most important role for communion with God in and through worship. Therefore, "our acquaintance with God is cultivated by religious worship."[27]

Regarding the spiritual aspect of worship, Henry distinguished inward worship from outward worship. According to Henry, inward worship was of "love, desire, joy, hope, and admiration,"[28] and outward worship was of "prayer and praise, and solemn attendance on God's word."[29] Based on this definition, inward worship can be seen as our inward attitude toward God; outward worship can be regarded as our expression in a ritual form. Henry

21. *BC*, on John 4:24.
22. Ibid.
23. Ibid.
24. Ibid.
25. *BC*, Psalm 27:2.
26. Ibid.
27. Henry, "The Sabbath," 284.
28. *BC*, Exodus 20:5–6.
29. Ibid.

emphasized these two kinds of worship as a prior obligation of human beings, saying, "those that truly love God will make it their constant care and endeavor to keep his commandments, particularly those that relate to his worship."[30] Thus, "Gospel worship will have a good influence upon all manner of gospel obedience."[31]

Henry understood Christian worship as a crucial means of communion with God. In emphasizing worship as communication, Henry taught that God not only was the object but also brought about its spiritual aspect. Based on the natures of Christian worship as having only God as its object and therefore as spiritual, Henry continued to develop more specific ways of worship in order to more effectively promote the relationship between God and humanity.

THE ORDINANCES OF WORSHIP

Henry articulated more specific liturgical patterns that comported with communion with God. Since God is the subject in the relationship with humanity, the relationship should follow what God instituted. Therefore we will look at how Henry defined an ordinance and at the different kinds of ordinances in terms of worship.

Ordinances

For Henry, an ordinance was designed for its effectiveness in enabling communion with God. He taught that "those that would have communion with God must not only come to ordinances, but they must abide by them."[32] He also indicated that attending to ordinances is a way of glorifying God: "in all his attendance on God's ordinances he [David] aimed at the glory of God and was much in the thankful praise and adoration of him."[33] Keeping this premise in mind, Henry described an ordinance as it related to the covenant. His sermon on "Ordinances in the Covenant"[34] clarified that "these [instituted means] bear the stamp of a divine appointment, therefore

30. Ibid.
31. Ibid.
32. *BC*, Exodus 24:12–18.
33. *BC*, Psalm 26:8.
34. Henry preached this sermon on April 10, 1692, at Chester. See Henry, *The Covenant of Grace*, 215–30.

we call them ordinances."[35] Henry went on to define the relationship between an ordinance and communion with God: "[I]n them we have more immediately to do with God."[36] After clarifying this, he defined ordinances as "appointed methods of intercourse, channels for the conveyance of covenant comforts and reciprocal returns of covenant duties, acknowledgements, and engagements."[37] Thus, "church members are instructed by ordinances what we must do and how we must do it."[38]

These ordinances belong to the church. To put it in another way, ordinances belong to "all visible church-members, all that profess faith in Christ and obedience to him."[39] In this regard, it can be said that ordinances are ritual forms that embody the confession of church members. However, ordinances "do in a special manner belong to true believers."[40] Church believers do not initiate them; "For their sakes ordinances were instituted."[41] According to Henry, the blessings or advantages of the ordinances are deeply related to communion with God. Among the eight advantages of the ordinances that he described,[42] most of them are directly concerned with communion with God. The seventh advantage is the summary of the deep connection between ordinance and communion:

> They [ordinances] are galleries of communion where the LORD Jesus meets his people, and converse with them, hears from them, speaks to them, shows himself to them, like Mount Horeb where God appointed Moses to meet him (Exod. 34.2) This communion with God in ordinances is a riddle to the carnal foolish world (1 John 1:3). It is the working of the gracious affections in the soul

35. Henry, "Ordinances in the Covenant," 219.
36. Ibid.
37. Ibid.
38. Ibid., 221.
39. Ibid., 219.
40. Ibid., 223.
41. Ibid.
42. (1) They are golden pipes, by which the oil of grace is conveyed from Christ the olive tree to their lamps (Zech 4:12); (2) they are green pastures (Ps 23:2) and they are only the sheep of Christ that find them so—pleasant, refreshing, fattening (Ezek 34:14, 15); (3) they are fountains of salvation (Isa 12:3), wells of living water; (4) they are a feast of fatlings, meat for the soul (Hos 11:4), plenty and variety, as at a feast (Isa 25:6); (5) they are beautiful clothing (Rev 19:8); (6) they are breasts of consolation (Isa 66:11); (7) they are galleries of communion (Cant. 7:5) where the LORD Jesus meets his people, and converseth with them, hears from them, speaks to them, shows himself to them; and (8) they are the gate of heaven (Gen 28:17). See ibid., 225–26.

agreeable to the ordinance we are engaged in, the soul's receivings from God and out-goings towards him.[43]

In this way, Henry attempted to promote communion with God through believers' participation in the ordinances.

Regarding the kinds of ordinances, Henry did not define them in a separate section. He already assumed that church believers had some knowledge of the ordinances. In the preaching on "Ordinances in the Covenant," he addressed the ordinances of church:

> *Baptism*, the door of admission into the visible church—*in the apostles' doctrine*, or under the apostles' teaching—church *fellowship*, the communion of saints in Christian conference and charity, mutual aids—*breaking of bread*, the Lord's Supper; and prayers in public—singing of psalms we have (Col. 3:6), a standing ministry and the Christian Sabbath, or Lord's Day, are gospel ordinances instituted as means, appointed for the due and regular administration of other ordinances.[44]

According to this, several key ordinances provide believers means of God's grace and spiritual privileges: baptism, Word, fellowship, the Lord's Supper, prayer, and singing the Psalms. Among these ordinances, Henry included all except baptism and fellowship in the ordinances of Lord's Day public worship.[45] He subdivided them further into six parts: reading the Word, hearing the Word, prayer, praise, singing the psalms, and the Lord's Supper.[46] Explaining the meaning of each ordinance was very important so that "we may do a reasonable service."[47] Henry stressed that "if either we are ignorant of, or mistaken about, the meaning of holy ordinances, we can neither please God nor profit ourselves."[48]

---

43. Ibid.

44. Ibid., 218–19.

45. It is not clear why Henry excluded these two elements from the ordinance of worship. It seems that people baptized children on weekdays, and that he regarded fellowship not as a separate essential element for public worship, while not ignoring its value for church gathering.

46. This chapter will deal with only five of the six ordinances of public worship; the next chapter will treat baptism and the Lord's Supper as parts of Henry's thought on the sacraments as a liturgical understanding of communion with God in the ordinary life.

47. *BC*, Exodus 12:28.

48. Ibid.

Reading the Scriptures

Henry addressed reading the Scriptures as the first ordinance of worship. In his exposition on 1 Thessalonians 5:27, Henry explained the legitimacy of reading the Scriptures in public worship:

> This is not only an exhortation, but an adjuration by the LORD. And this epistle was to be read to all the holy brethren.... the public reading of the law was one part of the worship of the Sabbath among the Jews in their synagogues, and the Scriptures should be read in the public assemblies of Christians also.[49]

According to Henry, reading the Scriptures in public worship was a way of honoring God as well as edifying people. He clearly indicated the goal and role of reading the Scriptures in worship in his exposition on Nehemiah 8:8: "reading the scriptures in religious assemblies is an ordinance of God, whereby he is honored and his church edified. And, upon special occasions, we must be willing to attend for many hours together on the reading and expounding of the word of God." Moreover, Henry criticized the omission of reading the Scriptures in public worship. In the last preface to the *Bible Commentary*, Henry claimed that "the Lord's day ought to be sanctified by reading books of piety, especially the holy scriptures and to forbid Christians from reading the scriptures is to prohibit the use of the light to the children of light."[50]

While emphasizing the reading of the Scriptures, Henry also noted that reading the Scriptures itself was not enough. Readers need to understand what they read. For this reason Henry stressed expounding as well as reading the Scriptures in public worship: "what they read they expounded, showed the intent and meaning of it, and what use was to be made of it; they gave the sense in other words, that they might cause the people to understand the reading."[51] For Henry, the role of expounding the Scriptures was to connect reading and preaching: "[R]eading is good, and preaching good, but expounding brings the reading and the preaching together, and thus makes the reading the more intelligible and the preaching the more convincing."[52]

---

49. *BC*, 1 Thessalonians 5:27.
50. Henry, preface to vol. 5 of *BC*.
51. *BC*, Nehemiah 8:7–8.
52. Ibid. Henry also explained the attitude of people when the Word was read: (1) with great reverence, (2) with great fixedness and composedness, and (3) with great

Matthew Henry

Hearing the Word

Henry argued that hearing the Word is another important ordinance of worship in relation to the Scriptures.[53] Christian assembly for public worship, for Henry, meant not just gathering together but attending to the ordinance in which people, as worshippers, present themselves unto the LORD.[54] Such attending to this ordinance of hearing the Word is manifested when "[worshippers] are present to hear all things that are commanded by the [preacher] of God, and given [preacher] in charge to be delivered to [them]."[55] Henry also indicated the attitude of hearing the Word:

> How can we hear all? We are desirous to hear all that thou [preacher] are commissioned to preach, though it be ever so displeasing to flesh and blood, and ever so contrary to our former notions, or present secular interests. We are ready to hear all, and therefore let nothing be kept back that is profitable for us.[56]

As with reading the Scripture, hearing the Word itself, for Henry, was not enough. He articulated the need to hear the Word in detail in order to connect the ordinance to everyday life. As Henry pointed out, "it is requisite that those who hear the word should understand it, else it is to them but an empty sound of words."[57] Henry continued to remind his listeners that the Word heard should be kept in the human heart: "[T]hough it is a great privilege to hear the word of God, yet those only are truly blessed, that is, blessed of the LORD, that hear it and keep it, that keep it in memory, and keep to it as their way and rule."[58] Henry even more attempted to connect reading and hearing the Word to way of life by saying that "we read and hear the word acceptably and profitably when we do according to what is written therein."[59] He clearly identified the meaning of hearing the Word:

> It is not enough to be within hearing of it, but we must attend on it, as scholars on the instructions of their teachers; and attend to

---

attention and a close application of mind. See *BC*, Nehemiah 8:3–7.

53. Here Henry followed Calvin in his definition of the church as the place where the Word is (1) preached and (2) heard, i.e., received.

54. Cf. *BC*, Acts 10:33.

55. Ibid.

56. Ibid.

57. *BC*, Nehemiah 8:7–8.

58. *BC*, Luke 11:28.

59. *BC*, on Nehemiah 8:16–17; also see on Colossians 1:6.

it, as servants to the commands of their masters; we must hear and obey it, must abide by the gospel of Christ as the fixed rule of our faith and practice.[60]

In this way, hearing the Word, for Henry, was not limited to that which occurred within the ritual, but what they heard hearers were expected to live out in everyday life.

In order to help people understand and practice what they read and heard in worship service, Henry urged, "it is therefore required of those who are teachers by office that they explain the word and give the sense of it."[61] So, in the ordinance of worship, the Word can be heard through preaching. For Henry, hearing the Word meant "attendance upon the preaching of the Gospel."[62]

Prayer

Henry described prayer as "a principal branch of religious worship."[63] As defined above, religion as communion with God is "so much the business of our lives, and the worship of God so much the business of our religion."[64] Prayer is one of the essential ordinances to promote communion with God through the worship service. Henry articulated the meaning of prayer in detail:

> Prayer is the solemn and religious offering up of devout acknowledgments and desires to God, or a sincere representation of holy affections, with a design to give unto God the glory due unto his name thereby, and to obtain from him promised favors, and both through the Mediator.[65]

By this, Henry understood prayer not only as a petition but also adoration of and thanksgiving to God. Considering the five main parts of prayer (praise, confession, petition, thanksgiving, and intercession), his teaching on prayer in the book *A Method for Prayer* (1710), proved that thanksgiving

60. *BC*, John 5:24.
61. *BC*, Luke 11:28.
62. *BC*, Acts 13:44.
63. Henry, *A Method for Prayer*, 1.
64. Ibid.
65. Ibid.

is a climax in prayer. As Hughes Old pointed out, Henry understood well that "the heart of Christian prayer is Eucharistic."[66]

Furthermore, Henry continued to develop his understanding of prayer from a perspective of communion with God, defining the meaning and function of prayer like this: "it is a piece of respect and homage so exactly consonant to the natural ideas which all men have of God, that it is certain those who live without prayer, live without God in the world."[67] Based on this basic concept, Henry clarified prayer as "conversing with God."[68] This concept is important since it shows that "believers live a life of communion with God."[69] With this understanding of prayer in mind, Henry continued to argue that the Bible indicates that prayer is an essential way of communion with God: "[T]he Scripture describes prayer to be our drawing near to God, lifting up our soul to him, pouring out our hearts before him."[70]

In particular, Henry developed a method of prayer in detail in his book *A Method for Prayer*. It argued that "it is requisite to the decent performance of the duty, that some proper method be observed, not only that what is said be good, but that it be said in its proper place and time."[71] Henry's main concern when developing a method for prayer was also related to understanding, as it was in reading and hearing the Word. Henry stressed that it is good be methodical and sententious in prayer in order to make it understandable:

> As it is good to be methodical in prayer, so it is to be sententious: the Lord's Prayer is remarkably so; and David's Psalms, and many

---

66. Old, "Matthew Henry and Family Prayer," 80.

67. Henry, *A Method for Prayer*, in *Complete Works*, 2:1. Because of this emphasis of communion with God in relation to prayer, for Henry, prayer was not only an ordinance of worship but also an essential part of daily life. He claimed that "a golden thread of heart-prayer must run through the web of the whole Christian life; we must be frequently addressing ourselves to God in short and sudden ejaculations, by which we must keep up our communion with God in providences and common actions, as well as in ordinances and religious services. Thus prayer must be *sparsim*—'a sprinkling of it' in every duty, and our eyes must be over toward the LORD" (ibid.). Henry also defined this in the middle of his book: "it is his will that we should thus acknowledge him in all our ways, and wait upon him for the direction of every step, not prescribing, but subscribing to infinite wisdom, humbly showing him our wants, burdens, and desires, and then referring ourselves to him, to do for us as he thinks fit." Henry, *A Method for Prayer*, in *Complete Works*, 2:57.

68. Henry, *A Method for Prayer*, 1.

69. Ibid.

70. Ibid.

71. Ibid., 2.

of St. Paul's prayers, which we have in his epistles. We must consider, that the greatest part of those who join with us in prayers will be in danger of losing or mistaking the sense, if the period be long, and the parentheses many; and in this, as in other things, they who are strong ought to bear the infirmities of the weak: Jacob must lead as the children and flocks can follow.[72]

In order to promote understanding in prayer, Henry's method for prayer is based on the conviction that "Scripture language will be most intelligible, and the sense of it best apprehended."[73] He illustrated many prayers for providence as well as ordinance in detail.[74]

Prayer, for Henry, was crucial in worship since "the religious meetings of God's people shall be meetings for prayer, in which they shall join together, as a token of their united faith and mutual love."[75] More practically, Henry indicated these two ways of communication in worship: "to hear what he speaks to us out of his word, and to speak to him by prayer."[76] This, for him, was the proper conversation of the Sabbath. Although he was concerned that we should keep up times of prayer, Henry clearly stressed the importance of prayer in the ordinance of worship by claiming that "we must preserve in a particular prayer, not cutting it short, when our hearts are disposed to enlarge, and there is time for it, and our occasions for it."[77] Regarding the manner of prayer, Henry did not develop any written prayers for public worship. Rather, he articulated a comprehensive way of praying in worship by suggesting five main parts (praise, confession, petition, thanksgiving, and intercession) in one prayer. In pubic worship, Henry did not read any written prayers.[78]

---

72. Ibid.

73. Ibid., 3.

74. Henry illustrated various prayers from the Scriptures. These prayers confirm that communion with God was Henry's main concern. See chapter 6 of *A Method for Prayer*, 57–68.

75. *BC*, Isaiah 56:7.

76. Henry, "The Sabbath," 284.

77. *BC*, Ephesians 6:18.

78. Henry was different from Calvin and Baxter in that these two Reformers continued using written prayers in public worship services. It seems that Henry was influenced by the Independent way of prayer since "it was the Independents, led by John Owen, who were most vigorous in their opposition to any kind of prayer formulary." Old, "Matthew Henry and Family Prayer," 90.

Matthew Henry

Praise

Henry also regarded praise as an ordinance of worship, which means "the sacrifices of acknowledgment, not the great sacrifice of atonement."[79] According to this meaning, praise, although it is a sacrifice, is not restricted to the temple; it is "a service of religion as acceptably performed in one place as in another."[80] This is the sacrifice of praise to God, "which we should offer up to God continually."[81] Praise as the sacrifice should include "all adoration and prayer, as well as thanksgiving; this is the fruit of our lips; we must speak forth the praises of God from unfeigned lips."[82] Henry continued to clarify that the only object of praise is God, saying that "this [praise] must be only offered to God, not to angels or saints, or any creature but to the name of God alone."[83] In his commentary on Isaiah's vision of worship, he clarified that when he speaks of God, he intends as the object of praise the Triune God: "it may refer to the three persons in the Godhead, Holy Father, Holy Son, and Holy Spirit."[84]

With this basic understanding, Henry continued to develop the theological implications of praise in worship. Praise was not an expression of feeling or emotion as a result of a religious experience. At the same time, it was not in itself a method of moving people directly toward God in a worship service. Praise could not function in worship without Christ as the mediator. Henry argued that the meaning and function of praise in worship was also totally dependent upon Christ: "it must be by Christ, in a dependence upon his meritorious satisfaction and intercession."[85]

With this theological premise, Henry's comments on the manner and form of praise followed the Reformed tradition.[86] He basically agreed that praise, as all our spiritual sacrifices, "must be free-will-offerings; for God

79. *BC*, Hebrews 13:15.
80. *BC*, Nehemiah 8:6.
81. *BC*, Hebrews 13:15.
82. Ibid.
83. Ibid.
84. *BC*, Isaiah 6.
85. Ibid. Henry understood praises as an offering to God, not as a preliminary part of worship.
86. Among the Reformers, there are different positions on music in worship. Ulrich Zwingli (1484–1531) denied the congregation's singing. However, Calvin (1509–1564), following Luther, recovered but restricted it. See Westermeyer, *Te Deum: The Church and Music*, 141–60.

loves a cheerful giver."[87] Moreover, he confirmed that harmony is the most important way of offering praises: "how this song was sung with zeal and fervency—they cried aloud; and with unanimity—they cried to another, or one with another; they sang alternately, but in concert, and without the least jarring voice to interrupt the harmony."[88] Besides these statements, following Reformed tradition, Henry promoted the active participation of the congregation by letting them sing together in family and public worship.

Singing of Psalms

Singing of psalms was also included among the gospel ordinances. Henry regarded the psalms of David as the most appropriate sources of content for sung music in the worship service. Singing of the psalms was a good answer to the question of how to give praise in worship. However, Henry did not claim that Psalms were the only source of content for praise. In the *Bible Commentary*, expounding on Acts 16:25, Henry says, "they sang praises to [God], in some psalm, or hymn, or spiritual song, either one of David's, or some modern composition, or one of their own, as the Spirit gave them utterance."[89] While considering broad genres of praises, Henry, nevertheless, argued that singing the psalms as an ordinance was the most appropriate among them: "this proves that the singing of psalms ought to be used by all good Christians; and that it is instituted, not only for the expressing of their joys in a day of triumph, but for the balancing and relieving of their sorrows in a day of trouble."[90] This implied that Henry attempted to promote communion with God by choosing David's prayer and confession to God as the main content of singing for worship.

Henry argued that singing the psalms has a significant function as an ordinance of worship. Singing the psalms meant not only praising God but also edifying people. He held that "singing of psalms is a teaching ordinance as well as a praising ordinance; and we are not only to quicken and encourage ourselves, but to teach and admonish one another, mutually excite our affections, and convey instructions."[91] In addition to this, Henry emphasized the pedagogical function of singing the psalms even

87. *BC*, Psalm 54:6.
88. *BC*, Isaiah 6.
89. *BC*, Acts 16:25.
90. Ibid.
91. *BC*, Colossians 3:16.

in family worship, claiming that early Christians "turned their houses into churches—such churches as St Paul speaks of Rom. xvi. 5, Col. iv. 15, and Philem. 2.—by praising God together, and by teaching and admonishing one another in singing of the psalms."[92] In order to promote the function of edification in singing the psalms, Henry stressed not the melody but understanding: "when we sing psalms, we make no melody unless we are suitably affected with what we sing and go along in it with the true devotion and understanding."[93] With this conviction, Henry published *Family Hymns* (1694),[94] mainly composed of David's psalms. Henry himself rendered the psalms in his contemporary English. He regarded *Family Hymns*, with *A Scripture Catechism*, as a main tool for edifying people.

Singing the psalms through *Family Hymns* influenced the manner of worship. Before Henry, one needed to sing praises or psalms in the service of worship one line at a time between the pastor's or leader's reading since congregants did not have their own hymn books. This was "the general practice of the reformed churches abroad."[95] However, in Henry's time each member of the family had their own hymn book so they did not need to follow one leader who read the lyrics for them. Moreover, after memorizing all lyrics at family worship through *Family Hymns*, people gathered at public worship no longer needed to read the lines or lyrics. This change in the way of singing music in public worship did not happen spontaneously. Instead, it was the intention of Henry:

> It is what I chiefly aim at in it—if everyone in the family have a book [of hymns], so that the psalm or hymn—for the distinction is but nominal—may be sung without reading the line betwixt and renders the duty more pleasant and profitable, and takes up less time, and is practicable enough in a family, if not in large congregations.[96]

---

92. Henry, "Family Hymns, Gathered Mostly Out of The Translations of David's Psalms," 413.

93. *BC*, Colossians 3:16.

94. Henry divided this hymn book (with a total of 90 hymns) into seven sections: (1) For Morning Worship, (2) For Evening Worship, (3) For the Lord's Day Morning, (4) For the Lord's Day Noon and Evening, (5) Hymns for Some Particular Occasions, (6) Four Hymns of Instruction, and (7) Hymns of Praise, to be sung to the Tune of the 100th Psalm, and the 148th.

95. Henry, "Family Hymns," 414.

96. Ibid.

It is certain that Henry followed Reformed tradition by promoting singing the psalms in both domestic and public worship. In this way, he applied a part of the Reformed idea of music in worship[97] to the congregation's singing in his own context.

THE OCCASIONS OF WORSHIP

Henry developed several ordinances of worship based on the Scriptures in order to promote human communion with God. These ordinances of worship, for Henry, needed occasions at which they would be enacted. These occasions were essential to glorifying God and reminding people of God's work as one of the goals in communion with God. Henry clarified the necessity and role of the occasion of worship by mentioning that people "must upon all occasions give honor to God";[98] "we should take all occasions to revive the remembrance of the great things God did for our fathers in the days of old."[99] In this regard, occasions of worship, for Henry, were not only a duty but also an opportunity to help them draw near to God.[100] Henry elucidated three opportunities or occasions of worship: "in secret," "in families," and "in public, especially on the Lord's Day." Henry articulated in detail and, even more, practiced these three occasions of worship.

In Secret

Henry developed secret prayer as the first occasion of worship. He asserted that "personal prayer is supposed to be the duty and practice of all Christ's disciples."[101] He was convinced that "if secret devotion be either neglected,

---

97. The Reformed approach to music in worship developed by Calvin can be summarized like this: "Unlike Zwingli, Calvin did not silence music altogether; but unlike Luther, he did not welcome it so eagerly. The strictures he imposed were metrical psalms, a single monophonic line, one note for each syllable of text, without melismas, without polyphony, without instruments, and without choirs except as a group (of children) led the congregation's unison singing." Westermeyer, *Te Deum*, 157. See also Witvliet, "The Spirituality of the Psalter," 280.

98. *BC*, Deuteronomy 6:13.

99. *BC*, Joshua. 4:22.

100. Henry named the occasions of worship "opportunities." See Williams, *Life of the Rev. Matthew Henry*, 277.

101. *BC*, Matthew 6:6.

or negligently performed, the power of godliness will wither and decline."[102] Also, in his book *Communicant's Companion*, Henry indicated that private prayer or devotion was important for communion with God by connecting secret worship to the ordinance of the table thus:

> If indeed thou canst not allow so much time for solemn secret worship in preparation for this ordinance [the Supper], and reflection upon it, as others do, and as thou thyself sometime has done, and wouldst do, yet let not that keep thee from the ordinance; thy heart may be in heaven, when thy hands are about the world; and a serious Christian may, through God's assistance, do a great deal of work in a little time.[103]

According to Henry's basic understanding of worship as communion with God, this private devotion was not optional but a necessary obligation. With this conviction, he went on to explain the necessity of secret prayer:

> Note, Secret prayer is to be performed in retirement, that we may be unobserved, and so may avoid ostentation; undisturbed, and so may avoid distraction; unheard, and so may use greater freedom; yet if the circumstances be such that we cannot possibly avoid being taken notice of, we must not therefore neglect the duty, lest the omission be a greater scandal than the observation of it.[104]

Thus, "it is incumbent on Christians, ordinarily, to set apart that time for prayer by themselves wherein they are most likely to be at liberty from diversions and distractions."[105]

This secret prayer can be regarded as individual worship since there were two main ordinances in this prayer in relation to communication: speaking to God in prayer and hearing God by reading and meditating. It is not clear whether Henry thought that people in their secret prayer should sing praises. However, it is certain that he thought that people in their closet worship should communicate with God by speaking and hearing. He clearly remembered and applied what his father, Philip Henry, advised him on this: "if you do not pray, and read, and hear, you are not God's servant."[106] He also reminded himself of his father's teaching: "Pray alone.

---

102. Williams, *Life of the Rev. Matthew Henry*, 211.
103. Henry, *The Communicant's Companion*, 78.
104. *BC*, Matthew. 6:6.
105. Henry, *Account of the Life and Death of Mr. Philip Henry*, 71.
106. Ibid., 363.

Let prayer be the key of the morning, and the bolt of the night."[107] Based on this conviction, Matthew Henry set time apart for private prayer, and he "shut the door lest the wind of hypocrisy blow in it."[108]

Henry furthermore articulated two benefits of secret prayer. The first benefit was God's acceptance and gracious answer. According to him, "all the prayers that ever should be made in it [closet] according to the will of God, morning, evening, and at noon-day, ordinary or extraordinary, might be accepted of God, and obtain a gracious answer."[109] The second benefit was giving glory to God who is present in all places. Henry exclaimed, "in secret prayer we must have an eye to God, as present in all places; [God] is there in thy closet when no one else is there; there especially nigh to thee in what thou callest upon him for."[110] Moreover, "by secret prayer we give God the glory of his universal presence, and may take to ourselves the comfort of it."[111] Therefore, for Henry, secret prayer was not only a duty but also a privilege through which we can live life in communion with God. In this way, Henry "made conscience of closet-worship, and did abound in it, not making his family-worship to excuse for that."[112]

Besides private prayer, Matthew Henry thought of and practiced two other forms of private devotion: meditation and self-examination. For meditation, he tried to "take a walk every day by faith and meditation to mount Calvary."[113] In this practice, he simply sought to follow his father's teaching: "pray, and hear, and talk, and walk, and live, and all for eternal life."[114] Self-examination, for Matthew Henry, was a private preparation for the Lord's Supper. Matthew Henry "frequently attended to this duty in solitude."[115]

---

107. Ibid., 71.
108. See Williams, *Life of the Rev. Matthew Henry*, 211.
109. Henry, *Account of the Life and Death of Mr. Philip Henry*, 70.
110. BC, Matthew 6:6.
111. Ibid.
112. Henry, *Account of the Life and Death of Mr. Philip Henry*, 69.
113. Ibid., 212.
114. Ibid.
115. Ibid., 213.

In the Family

Henry thought that families "have many errands at the throne of grace, which furnish them with matter and occasion for family prayer every day."[116] Moreover, these errands "cannot be done so well in secret or public, but are fittest to be done by the family in consort, and apart from other families."[117] Keeping this thought in mind, Henry argued that family worship was the second opportunity or occasion for worship. As demonstrated in the previous chapter, Henry understood the family to have a crucial function in shaping Christian faith. For Henry, family worship was a distinctive occasion for each family. This family worship was a "family duty, which must by no means be neglected."[118] On the one hand, Henry held that family worship should not replace secret prayer, exclaiming that "if we perform family-worship, we must not think that this will excuse us from our secret devotions."[119] On the other hand, he also distinguished family worship from public worship: "ministers must not think that their public performances will excuse them from their family-worship."[120] Thus, Henry strongly held that every family should "keep up family worship still, which public worship must not supersede."[121]

Although family worship was distinctively developed in the time of the Reformation and strongly articulated in the time of the Puritans,[122] Henry especially developed domestic worship based on the Scriptures.[123] According to him, family worship was initiated at the time of Abraham. Henry illustrated Abraham as the biblical model of family worship:[124]

---

116. Henry, "A Church in the House," 254.
117. Ibid.
118. *BC*, Psalm 87:2.
119. *BC*, Numbers 29:1–11.
120. *BC*, 2 Samuel 6:20.
121. *BC*, 1 Chronicles 16:37–43.

122. "The Reformation's emphasis on the family began to take on new dimensions with the development of family worship in the late sixteenth century." Williams, "The Puritan Concept and Practice of Prayer," 389.

123. Hughes Old also pointed out that Henry "considered daily family prayer or worship to be of divine institution; it was both taught in Scripture by specific precept and given example by the people of God." Old, "Matthew Henry and the Puritan Discipline of Family Prayer," 69.

124. Based on this, Puritans argued that the first Christian church was the family of Abraham. See Morgan, *The Puritan Family*, 78. He indicated that "the church thus continued to be, for some time after the fall, a purely domestic institution." That is why

> The way of family worship is a good old way, is no novel invention, but the ancient usage of all the saints. Abram was very rich and had a numerous family, was now unsettled and in the midst of enemies, and yet, wherever he pitched his tent, he built an altar. Wherever we go, let us not fail to take our religion along with us.[125]

Henry further established the antiquity of family religion from his expounding on Exodus 12: "God graciously appointed and accepted the family-sacrifice of a lamb."[126] Moreover, for the developing family worship, Henry continued to argue that the role of the master of the family was crucial in family religion. The master of the family, for Henry, should decide for his house:

> That is, his family, his children and servants, such as were immediately under his eye and care, his inspection and influence. Joshua was a ruler, a judge in Israel, yet he did not make his necessary application to public affairs an excuse for the neglect of family religion. Those that have the charge of many families, as magistrates and ministers, must take special care of their own: I and my house will serve God.[127]

Joshua "made his house a little church."[128] In this way, Henry founded the biblical basis of family worship and attempted to maintain its practice.

When it comes to the form or pattern of family worship, there were three elements: the Word, prayer,[129] and praise. In his expounding on 1 Timothy 4:4–5, Henry addressed two elements of family worship: the Word of God and prayer, "must be brought to our common actions and affairs,

---

"in spite of its congregational form, the Puritan church showed signs of its domestic origin, for it included not only individual believers but the children of believers as well" (ibid., 79).

125. *BC*, Genesis 12:7–8.

126. *BC*, Exodus 12.

127. *BC*, Joshua 24:15.

128. Henry, *Account of the Life and Death of Mr. Philip Henry*, 73.

129. In "A Church in the House," his sermon concerning family religion, Henry suggested six things that parents "should endeavor to bring something of each, more or less, into every prayer with [their] families." See *Complete Works*, 1:254. These six things are first, acknowledge your dependence upon God, and his providence, as you are a family. Second, confess your sins against God; those sins you have contracted the guilt of in your family capacity. Third, offer up family thanksgivings for the blessings which you, with your families, receive from God. Fourth, present your family petitions for the mercy and grace which your families stand in need of. Fifth, make family intercessions for others also. Sixth, sing of psalms in your families, as a part of daily worship (ibid., 254–57).

and then we do all in faith."[130] Besides these two, Henry placed praises as an essential element of family worship by translating and publishing David's psalms into the *Family Hymns*. Moreover, Henry distinguished family worship from public worship by pointing out "training and catechizing children" as the parents' duty:

> Train up children in that age of vanity, to keep them from the sins and snares of it, in that learning age, to prepare them for what they are designed for. Catechize them; initiate them; keep them under discipline. Train them as soldiers, who are taught to handle their arms, keep rank, and observe the word of command. Train them up, not in the way they would go (the bias of their corrupt hearts would draw them aside), but in the way they should go, the way in which, if you love them, you would have them go. Train up a child according as he is capable (as some take it), with a gentle hand, as nurses feed children, little and often.[131]

In this regard, one of the main reasons that he published *A Scripture Catechism* was because "it is especially profitable to acquaint children betimes with their Bible," and for that purpose, it was "to the service of governors of families."[132] Therefore, it is certain that Henry thought that family worship should be composed of the Word of God, prayer, and praise with an emphasis on training children through catechism based on the Scriptures.

A crucial contribution of his thought on family worship is Henry's high regard for the value of every person in the family regardless of their sex and age. Henry thought that "women and children have souls to save, and are therefore concerned to acquaint themselves with the word of God and attend on the means of knowledge and grace."[133] In this way, family worship was a crucial place that showed the value of each member of a family. There was no limitation in the family worship that prohibited any one from experiencing a living communion with God. This implies that worship is an important place in which people can express their value without discrimination, regardless of their social and economic status. Henry even encouraged wives to learn how to pray in family worship as he experienced from his parents. As he indicated, "a wife should be sometimes called upon

---

130. *BC*, 1 Timothy 4:4–5.
131. *BC*, Proverbs 22:6.
132. Henry, *Introduction to a Scripture Catechism*, 174–75.
133. *BC*, Nehemiah 8.

Matthew Henry on Christian Worship

to pray with the husband, that she might learn to perform duty in the family in the husband's absence."[134]

Henry himself practiced family worship in his own home according to these thoughts. Henry's friend William Tong confessed, "I have known those that, upon their first acquaintance there, were surprised to see so much beauty of holiness, and were ready to say, "Surely God is in his place; this is no other than the house of God, and the gate of heaven."[135] According to him, Henry "strictly observed his father's example, both in all the parts and circumstances of it; he was constant in family worship; whatever happened, or whoever was present, this duty was never neglected morning or evening."[136]

With the help of Tong's research,[137] Henry's actual practice of daily family worship can be ordered thus:

1. A short invocation of the name of God (begging assistance and acceptance).
2. Reading a portion of Scripture (the Old Testament in the morning and the New Testament in the evening).
3. Exposition (short but judicious and affectionate exposition).
4. Singing the psalm (using *Family Hymns*).
5. Prayer
6. Blessing children

This order shows that he practiced family worship two times every day. He did not omit family worship even on the Lord's Day. Tong delineated in detail the practice of Henry's family worship on the Lord's Day:

> His public work on Lord's Day, great as it was, did not entrench upon family worship. On that day he rose early; and having been some time alone with God and his own soul, about eight of the clock he called his family together. He omitted not his expositions. He sung an hymn as usual, and then took his family with him to the solemn assembly. When he returned home at noon, and had dined, he sung a psalm, and put up a short prayer with his family, and so retired into his closet, till the time of public worship returned. In the evening he generally repeated in his family both

---

134. Henry, *Account of the Life and Death of Mr. Philip Henry*, 72.
135. Tong, *Account of Life and Death of Matthew Henry*, 19.
136. Ibid.
137. Ibid.

the sermons of the day, when many of his neighbors came in; after repetition, sung and prayed, then sung two verses more of a suitable hymn, and so pronounced the blessing, and catechized the younger children. After that was ended, he sung the 136 psalm, then catechized his elder children and servants, and heard them repeat what they could remember of the sermons of the day and so concluded the day with prayer.[138]

The order of family worship on the Lord's Day did not differ much from that of other days except for the addition of catechism. As seen in his practice of family worship, Henry's practice of worship was congruent with what he thought about it.

In Public

In Henry's thought, the third opportunity or occasion of worship was in public. According to Henry, "it is the will of Christ that his disciples should assemble together."[139] He thought public worship was mandated for all Christians through history. He mentioned that "there were in the apostles' times, and should be in every age, Christian assemblies for the worship of God."[140] In this regard, Christians should diligently and constantly attend public worship.[141] However, while regarding public worship as a mandate, Henry did not ignore the other two occasions of worship: in secret and in the family. He held that "public worship will not excuse us from secret worship."[142] Instead, according to him, "the duties of the closet are designed to prepare us for, not to excuse us from, public ordinances."[143] At the same time, he claimed that we should not think "that being employed so much in public worship will supersede the religious exercises of their closets and families."[144]

Henry articulated the goal of public worship as no different from that of worship in any context. Christians should seek for communion with God

138. Ibid., 20.
139. BC, Hebrews 10:25.
140. Ibid.
141. "The public worship of God shall be diligently and constantly attended upon." See BC, Jeremiah 33:10–11.
142. BC, Psalm 119:62.
143. BC, Psalm 5:7.
144. BC, 2 Chronicles 35:10.

in public worship because "in all acts of religious worship, we come into God's presence."[145] Henry proved this thought based on his commentary on Acts 7:44–50. Here he illustrated this goal by narrating the way that "David had the sweet communion with God in public worship which we read of in his Psalms."[146] In our attendance in public worship, we "may expect to meet with Christ [or God], and improve our acquaintance with Him."[147] According to him, "public worship is what Christ chooses to own and grace with his presence and the manifestations of Himself; there they found Him."[148] Thus, "Christ must be sought, and will be found, in the congregations of His people and in the administration of His ordinances."[149]

Although he emphasized daily worship in the world, Henry specified Lord's Day as an appointed particular time for public worship by stating that "the wisdom of God has instituted and appointed a particular time for the special solemnities of it, which is one day in seven."[150] It was because "if God is to be worshipped by us solemnly and in comfort, there must be some fixed and stated times for the doing of it, the designation of which is necessary both to preserve the thing itself, and to put a solemnity upon it."[151] In this way, for Henry, the Lord's Day was a crucial time appointed "as a means of keeping up communion with God in holy ordinances."[152] This communion is our "fellowship with God, with the Father, and with his Son Jesus Christ, by the Spirit."[153] Thus, "it is the work of the Lord's Day to worship God."[154] In this point, when it comes to the Sabbath, although there are some discontinuities between his time and that of the Old Testament, public worship of God is the requirement regardless of the change of time.

What then should God's people observe on the Lord's Day in the service of and in communion with God? Henry articulated the things to be done in public worship and in the remaining part of the day: prayer,

---

145. *BC*, Psalm 100:4.
146. *BC*, Acts 7:44–50.
147. *BC*, John 5:14.
148. *BC*, John 6:59.
149. Ibid.
150. Henry, "The Sabbath," 260.
151. Ibid., 265.
152. Ibid.
153. Ibid., 283.
154. Ibid. In fact, it is the work of Lord's Day to worship "not only in public assemblies but also in secret and in our families, morning, evening, and at noon." See ibid., 260–61.

reading and meditating the Scriptures, and other religious exercises such as praising by means of hymns.[155] In public worship on the Lord's Day, for Henry, communication or conversation with God was the most important thing. In this communication, hearing and speaking are two essential elements. Henry said, "this is a day in which we are with all humility to make visits to God to hear what he speaks to us out of his word, and to speak to him by prayer."[156] For him, public worship, comprised of hearing the Word and praying to God, was essential in cultivating our communion or relationship with God.

Henry attempted to flesh out in practice his theoretical understanding of public worship of the Lord's Day. According to Tong,[157] Henry practiced this order of Lord's Day worship:[158]

1. Singing the 100th Psalm
2. Short prayer
3. Reading some parts of the Old Testament (morning) or the New Testament (afternoon)
4. Exposition
5. Singing another psalm
6. Pastoral prayer[159]
7. Preaching[160]

---

155. See Henry, "The Sabbath," 264. Henry also articulated what needs to be done on the LORDs' Day in order to spend that day appropriately: "reading the Holy Bible and other good books, repetition, catechizing, singing psalms, praying, praising, profitable discourse" (ibid., 285).

156. Ibid., 284.

157. Tong, *Account of Life and Death of Matthew Henry*, 78.

158. For more detailed explanation and analysis on the practice of Henry's public worship, refer to chap. 5.

159. This pastoral prayer looks odd to us since "for at least a generation we have experienced a sort of atrophy in public prayer. It has just dried up." (Old, *Leading in Prayer*, 361).

160. Henry's thought and practice of preaching should be a subject to be taken in another work. However, briefly, As Tong commented, "how great a talent in preaching, the world is not ignorant, so many of his sermons being published, and spread far and wide. He was very happy in the choice of his subjects, there could no occasion happen, either public or private, but as he was ever ready to preach upon it, so he had always an apposite text to preach upon, being a scribe well instructed in the kingdom of God; he had a treasure out of which he could easily bring things new and old" (Tong, *Account of Life and Death of Matthew Henry*, 161).

8. Prayer

9. Singing the 117th Psalm (usually), 134th Psalm, or 136th Psalm (afternoon)

10. Blessing

When he ministered in his own Presbyterian congregations at Chester, Henry followed this order.

The thought and practice of Henry's Lord's Day worship reveal three characteristics. First, as seen in this order, Henry made use of David's psalms in singing. As Tong pointed out, Henry "prefer'd Scripture, Psalms, and Hymns far before those that are wholly of humane Composure, which are generally liable to this Exception, that the Fancy is too high, and the Matter too low, and sometimes such as a wife and good Man may not be able with entire satisfaction to offer up as a Sacrifice to God."[161] Second, Henry offered prayer twice. Of these two prayers, the second is very impressive because he spent about half an hour in that prayer. Tong also commented on that prayer: "In prayer his [Henry's] gifts and graces eminently appeared; he had a wonderful faculty of engaging the attention, and raising the affections of his assembly."[162] The third characteristic is his exposition. He expounded on his reading of the Scriptures, which was different from preaching.[163] As Tong commented, "his father's example led him to take delight in this part of his work";[164] Henry did not ignore or omit this part

---

161. Ibid., 158.

162. Tong continued to highly regard Henry's pastoral prayer: "He was always copious, though never tedious; he was very full in Confession of sin, and very tender and humble, aggravating the evil and guilt of it in a very clear and convincing manner; his prayer was always suited to the state of the congregation, to the season, to the state of the nation, and of the Church of God; in supplication for mercy he was very earnest and particular, pleading the name, and sufferings, and mediation of the LORD Jesus Christ for pardon and peace; he was large and full in praying for grace and used to mention the particular graces of the Holy Spirit, as faith, love, hope, patience, zeal, delight in God, earnestly begging that these graces might be truly wrought in all, and might be preserved, exercised, increased and evidenced to the glory of the God of all grace. . .In supplications for the afflicted he was very particular, seldom forgetting any case that was either known to himself, or put up in writing; his requests were very pertinent to the case, and the sympathy of his heart with the afflicted was very apparent, by the tender and affectionate very apparent, by the tender and affectionate manner in which he used to plead with God for them" (ibid., 158–59).

163. Henry's preaching was not expository. Reading and expounding specific verses of Scripture were separate from preaching.

164. Tong, *Account of Life and Death of Matthew Henry*, 160.

in public worship, even on the Lord's Day.[165] While at Chester, Henry "went through the whole Bible more than once, and by this means his People have been observed to excel in their acquaintance with the Holy Scriptures."[166]

The most impressive lesson from Henry's thought and practice on public worship is that he sought for a clear understanding in communication between humanity and God through the ordinances. He did not seek some typical rubric or form that people should follow in their practice of worship. Instead, Henry preferred to articulate a clear principle of worship, which we see in his claim that "public worship should be performed so as to be understood."[167] In the interactive actions in communion with God through worship, humans cannot have fellowship with God without understanding what they do in that relationship. Thus, public worship should be an ordinance such that people "can hear [God's Word] with understanding."[168] Public worship, according to Henry, could be a great opportunity that helps the attendants to clearly understand their relation with God. Thus, Henry concluded regarding communion with God: "it is to admit into our *minds* the discoveries God has been pleased to make of himself, and of his will and grace, and to dwell upon them in our *thoughts*."[169]

THE MANNER OF WORSHIP

Consideration of the role of ordinances and the various occasions of worship led Henry to a further question: How should people worship God, or what is an appropriate attitude with which to worship God?" This question implies that Henry was much concerned about how we worship, and that there may be better or worse ways of worship: "it is possible that we may be better than our neighbors, and yet not so good as we should be."[170] Henry acknowledged: "it concerns us to be right, not only in the *object* of our worship, but in the *manner* of it."[171]

Before delving into the manner of worship articulated by Henry, it is helpful to understand why he was concerned about it. Henry defined the

165. Ibid.
166. Ibid., 161.
167. BC, 1 Corinthians 14:15.
168. BC, Luke 2:41–43.
169. Tong, *Account of Life and Death of Matthew Henry*, 285.
170. BC, John 4:24.
171. Ibid.

goal of worship like this: "If we would, in hearing and praying, and other acts of devotion, receive grace from God, we must make it our business to give glory to God."[172] In this way, according to him, "when [people] have said and done ou[r] best for the honor of God's name, still [they] come infinitely short of the merit of the subject."[173] Due to the limited ability of humanity to give all glory to God, it is necessary for us to develop the manner of worship. In this way, Henry thought that "when we answer that revelation which [God] has made of himself, with suitable affections and adorations, then we give [God] some of that glory which is due to his name."[174]

Keeping this necessity of suitable affections and adorations in mind, Henry developed the manner of worship by drawing out the connections between worship, beauty, and holiness. Henry presupposed that beauty went together with holiness in worship. "[T]here is a beauty in holiness"; "the glorious majesty of God is called the beauty of holiness."[175] In worship of God, according to Henry, "we must have an eye to the beauty of [God's] holiness";[176] people should seek for the glorious majesty of God in worship. Thus, "it is that [holiness] which puts an acceptable beauty upon all the acts of worship."[177] For "solemn assemblies of Christians (which purity is the beauty of) are the places where God is to be worshipped."[178] In this regard, the place of worship was the center for the beauty of holiness.[179] Based on this concern, Henry articulated the manner of worship in detail.

The inwardness of humanity has the most bearing on the manner of worship. Henry's main interest in relation to the attitude of worship was not so much that of physical participation as of inward engagement. Henry thought that "the heart is the main thing required in all acts of devotion; nothing is done to purpose, in religion, further than it is done with the heart."[180] So when it comes to the manner of worship, "the heart must be

---

172. *BC*, Psalm 29:2.

173. Ibid.

174. Ibid.

175. Ibid.

176. Ibid. It seems that Henry regarded beauty in worship as an entirely spiritual notion because he did not articulate any aesthetic aspects of worship space or decoration besides the beauty of holiness.

177. Ibid.

178. Ibid.

179. Cf. *BC*, Psalm 48:1, 2, and Jeremiah 17:12.

180. *BC*, Psalm 57:7.

fixed, fixed for the duty, fitted and put in frame for it, fixed in the duty by a close application, attending on the LORD without distraction.[181] In this way, he was deeply concerned with the inward part of divine worship. The place where we worship did not matter to Henry. His stress "was laid upon the state of mind in which we worship God."[182] To Henry, developing inwardness in worship was crucial because "the worshippers were generally carnal, and strangers to the inward part of divine worship."[183] However, his intention was not to ignore physical or outward aspects of worship. He was most passionate that worshippers not disregard God as the proper object of worship. God is a spiritual being, so worshippers should not ignore this spiritual nature of God in their manner of worship.

In order to observe this inwardness in worship, Henry first held that the intellectual aspect of worship was crucial in participating in the divine ordinance:

> Christians shall worship God, not in the ceremonial observances of the Mosaic institution, but in spiritual ordinances, consisting less in bodily exercise, and animated and invigorated more with divine power and energy. The way of worship which Christ has instituted is rational and intellectual, and refined from those external rites and ceremonies with which the Old-Testament worship was both clouded and clogged.[184]

Second, he articulated a practical way, suited to the nature of God by drawing upon Jesus' words in John 4, exclaiming that "it is required of all that worship God that they worship him in spirit and in truth."[185] Henry clearly explained the meaning of "in spirit and truth":

> In spirit, we must depend upon God's Spirit for strength and assistance, laying our souls under his influences and operations; we must devote our own spirits to, and employ them in, the service of God, must worship him with fixedness of thought and a flame of affection, with all that is within us. Spirit is sometimes put for the new nature, in opposition to the flesh, which is the corrupt nature; and so to worship God with our spirits is to worship him with our graces. In truth, that is, in sincerity. God requires not only the

181. Ibid.
182. Ibid.
183. Ibid.
184. Ibid.
185. Ibid.

inward part in our worship, but truth in the inward part. We must mind the power more than the form, must aim at God's glory, and not to be seen of men; draw near with a true heart.[186]

For Henry, worship in spirit and truth meant that in worship, people are totally dependent upon God, expecting the work of the Spirit and the Truth. Overall, Henry stressed that "if we do not worship God, who is a spirit, in the spirit, we neither give [God] the glory due to the name, and so do not perform the act of worship, nor can we hope to obtain his favor and acceptance, and so we miss of the end of worship."[187]

Third, Henry articulated other specific ways of cultivating an inward attitude of worship. Most of all, "we cannot worship God acceptably, unless we worship with godly reverence and fear."[188] Moreover, this godly fear did not lead people to worship with obligation; instead, it gave them the opportunity to experience joy in worship. In the time of Old Testament, "the people were not permitted to enter into the holy place; there the priests only went in to minister."[189] But, Henry commented, "let the people be thankful for their place in the courts of God's house, to which they were admitted and where they gave their attendance." In this way, worship "should be special occasion for joy; and it prescribes this as a rule of worship."[190] Thus, "we ought to serve him with holy joy. Gospel-worshippers should be joyful worshippers; if we serve God in uprightness, let us serve him with gladness."[191]

To Henry, the most important function of worship was related not to the eye or ear but to the heart. In medieval worship, people's main role was *seeing*; in Reformed worship, people's main function was *listening*.[192] In both services, people were inactive, not truly participating in the worship. Yet Henry's emphasis on the inwardness of worship did not ignore the participatory nature of worship. Outward activities cannot fully reveal the meaning and function of worship because worship is not just outward activity but also inward participation in the work of God. Comparing these

186. Ibid.
187. Ibid.
188. *BC*, Hebrews 12:28.
189. *BC*, Psalm 100:2.
190. Ibid.
191. Ibid.
192. Refer to Muir, *Rituals in Early Modern Europe*. He explored how early modern Europeans worshipped God distinguishing their use of "upper body" and "lower body."

two aspects of worship, Henry was more concerned with the inwardness of worship. Even more, he hoped to have harmony and cooperation among various congregations, though they were different from each other in the service of worship. As seen in chapter 1, Henry did not intend to recover Baxter's Reformed Liturgy when liturgical liberty came. Instead, he expected a more fundamental principle of unity in worship by seeking out a manner of worship that focused on God, not on the form itself. However, Henry did not criticize any outward forms of worship if the worshippers sought for God as their primary concern. That was why Henry thought that "the most effectual way to take up differences in the minor matters of religion is to be more zealous in the greater."[193]

THE MEDIATOR OF WORSHIP

In the last section of his series of sermons on worship, Henry treated the mediator of worship. Christian worship as communion with God is distinct from a simple performance, which can be done without any divine intervention. Also, worship cannot be regarded as merely the self expression of human beings, since its ordinances, occasions, and even manner are ruled by God, the object of worship. Although he did not address the Trinity in a separate section, Henry clearly assumed the Trinitarian aspect of Christian worship, taking God as the only object of worship and addressing the crucial role of the Holy Spirit in the manner of worship, as seen in the previous sections. God the Father is the object of worship; the Spirit is crucial in leading people into the presence of God in worship; and Christ is the mediator of worship. Henry articulated the nature and necessity of the mediation of Christ in worship, then suggested practical ways to participate in the meditation of Christ.

First, Henry defined the necessity of Christ's mediation. Henry presupposed the Fall of human beings. Because of the resulting depravity, no one now can come into the presence of God without the meditation of Christ. Given this human condition, "fallen man must come to God as a Judge, but cannot come to him as a Father, otherwise than by Christ as Mediator."[194] Worship as a way of coming to God cannot be performed without the help of God. Here, although emphasizing the place and role of Christ as mediator, Henry clearly defined worship from his Trinitarian understanding:

193. *BC*, Psalm 100:2.
194. *BC*, John 14:6.

> We cannot perform the duty of coming to "*God [the Father]*," by repentance and the acts of worship, without "*the Spirit*" and grace of "*Christ*," nor obtain the happiness of coming to God as our Father without His merit and righteousness; He is the high priest of our profession, our advocate.[195]

Worship as meeting with God, by necessity and by its very nature, can be done only with the help of God. Human beings participate in it by coming to God with the help of the mediation of Christ and his Spirit.

Second, Henry defined the nature of the mediation of Christ: "in Him [Christ] God and man meet, and are brought together."[196] People cannot get to the presence of God in the way of innocence. Henry explained the mediation of Christ in relation to worship as follows:

> By Christ, as the way an intercourse is settled and kept up between heaven and earth; the angels of God ascend and descend; our prayers go to God, and his blessings come to us by Him; this is *the way that leads to rest, the good old way.* The disciples followed him, and Christ tells them that they followed the road, and, while they continued following Him, they would never be out of their way.[197]

For Henry, this mediation of Christ works not only at the beginning of worship; Christ "is the beginning, the middle, and the end"[198] in the mediation of *life* as well as worship. "In Him, we must set out, go on, and finish,"[199] both in life and in worship as communion with God. Thus, through all ordinances of worship, Christ is the only mediator who relates people to God.

Third, Henry articulated the difference it makes for our worship to know Christ as mediator, and some specific and practical ways of participating in worship with his help. Getting help from Christ the mediator does not mean taking him as a magic power to lead one into the presence of God. Rather, people have a duty to turn to Christ as the mediator, a duty that is not so much technical as personal. People need to live their lives in communion with Christ. People should know, love, honor, trust in, walk in, and

---

195. Ibid., italics added. Although he did not take up the work of the Spirit in worship in a separate section, Henry did not ignore the work of the Sprit, claiming that "we must worship God in the strength and grace of the Divine Spirit, which is so peculiar to the gospel state, which is the ministration of the Spirit." See *BC*, 2 Corinthians 3:8.

196. *BC*, John 14:6.

197. Ibid.

198. Ibid.

199. Ibid.

rejoice in Christ as the mediator.[200] A main principle permeating these six verbs is that of developing pathways of deep fellowship with Christ. When people walk with Christ and commune with him in daily life, they can more deeply experience communion with God in worship in and through their communion with Christ the mediator.

CONCLUSION: REFORMED PRESBYTERIAN CHARACTERISTICS IN HENRY'S THOUGHT AND PRACTICE OF WORSHIP

Some classic Reformed themes characterize Henry's English Presbyterian theology of worship. First and foremost, Henry attempted to develop a biblical theology of worship. As a Presbyterian minister, Henry articulated and practiced his understanding of Christian worship based on his reading and interpreting the Bible. He organized the form and content of Christian worship, such as ordinances and occasions, in detail based solely on the Scriptures. He sought the most solid foundation for worship, not through traditions, but the Bible. Henry continued to develop the Reformed tradition by constructing a biblical theology of worship without any liturgical manual or book. Unlike other Reformed theologians such as John Calvin[201] and John Knox,[202] Henry did not create or revise any liturgical book as a formulary of worship. In this way, Henry affirmed "the Word of God as the supreme liturgical criterion."[203]

Henry not only kept reading the Bible for public worship but also emphasized the significance of expounding, which was different from expository preaching. Henry fixed exposition as an order of worship. Also, all praises in worship were entirely based on Scripture. Following Calvin, Henry allowed only the psalms and scriptural verses as singing in worship. In addition, Henry attempted to include the Scriptures even in the content of prayer by articulating a method of prayer. Through his biblical theology

---

200. Henry preached on people's duty to Christ the Mediator under these six categories for consecutive weeks.

201. "Forms of Prayer For the Church (1542)."

202. *Forme of Prayer* (1556).

203. This is the title of Horton Davies' book, *The Worship of the English Puritans*. See chap. 5. Davies assumed that English Puritans were followers of John Calvin in theology and ecclesiastical ministry, including worship.

of worship, Henry clearly exemplifies the crucial role of the Scriptures in shaping the form and content of worship in Reformed tradition.

Second, there are Reformed aspects of Henry's theology of worship. A characteristic of Reformed theology of worship articulated by Calvin is a Trinitarian approach to worship.[204] Henry articulated Christian worship from a Trinitarian perspective: God the Father as the object of worship to be glorified, Jesus the Son as the mediator of worship, and the Spirit as the helper to draw us to the ordinances. Moreover, Henry did not ignore human depravity, which influences the condition of worship. One of the main reasons that Henry stressed the necessary work of Christ the mediator in worship was because, as Calvin declared, "the human could not worship God aright however he might wish to."[205] It was important for Henry as a Presbyterian minister to consider the fallen state of humanity in worship practice as well as ordinary life in communion with God. Thus, Henry thought that without the mediating help of Jesus and the Spirit, humans cannot appropriately worship God.

Third, Henry did not separate ordinary life from the act of worship. Henry attempted to integrate worship with ordinary life by seriously considering human life within the liturgical form of worship. Henry first emphasized the ethical aspect of worship. Through reading and hearing the Word, he tried to edify people in a clear and understandable way by expounding and preaching. In Henry's worship ministry, there was no preaching that did not include a practical application of doctrine, which can also be understood as a special characteristic of Reformed Presbyterian preaching.

Moreover, family worship was a crucial devotion that effectively helped people to integrate worship with life. Through keeping up family

---

204. In *The Form of Church Prayers* (1542, Geneva), his Trinitarian approach to Christian worship is clear in the first section on "confession": "Deign, then, O most gracious and *most merciful God and Father*, to bestow thy mercy upon us in the name of *Jesus Christ thy Son our LORD*. Effacing our faults, and washing away all our pollutions, daily increase to us the gifts of *thy Holy Spirit*" (Calvin, "Forms of Prayer for the Church [1542]," 2:100; italics added). Philip Butin nicely summarizes Calvin's Trinitarian structure of Christian worship: "True worship is directed only towards God the Father, as God gives the divine nature to be known and worshipped; true worship is patterned only after God's word, expressed in the incarnation of Jesus Christ, God's living image; true worship is motivated only by the Holy Spirit, who alone can focus human activity and the resources of the created order toward the glory of God's true nature" (Butin, "Constructive Iconoclasm," 135–39).

205. Calvin, *Institutes*, 1.4.4.

worship, Henry intended that religion not be associated only with rituals in the church building. Furthermore, he gave significance not only to individual persons but to the family in relation to religion. For Henry, individual devotion, although necessary for everyone, did not guarantee for the success of public worship. Through family devotion, Henry attempted to promote the communal aspect of life and worship.[206]

Lastly, Henry's pastoral prayer also clearly shows how much he regarded everyday life as an important aspect of worship. Henry did not follow any written or prescribed prayer in worship, as was the case for the Church of England. However, he did not omit the time of prayer in worship. Instead, he added a long spontaneous pastoral prayer that included the life issues of his congregations. This pastoral prayer meant that Henry sought the relevance to the exact condition of worshippers in the service of worship. In this way, ordinary life was a crucial concern of Henry in his developing theology and practice of worship.

As demonstrated in this chapter, Henry articulated his understanding of worship with emphasis on the Scriptures, Reformed theology, and ordinary life in Christian worship. This means that Henry developed worship as a patterned form of human communion with God based on the Scriptures and following the Reformed tradition, as a form related to ordinary life but also rooted in ritual. This chapter attempted to prove that Henry developed and articulated English Presbyterian worship as a liturgical form of communion with God. However, communion with God as a patterned relationship of humanity with God does not simply take liturgical form but also has application in ordinary life. According to Henry, all Christian life should be a walking with God or fellowship with God. Keeping that conviction in mind, Henry also developed ideas about how to walk with God in ordinary life from this liturgical perspective, based on his understanding and practice the sacraments. This is the subject of the next chapter.

---

206. Following Henry's emphasis, J. Ligon Duncan III and Terry Johnson argue that family worship has been a crucial Reformed Presbyterian spiritual legacy and still needs to be recovered for our contemporary Protestantism. According to them, Reformed churches ought to strive (1) for every family unit to become a discipleship group; (2) for every husband and father to become an active, self-denying, spiritual leader in his home; (3) for our congregations to have as many families functioning as "family-based growth groups" as there are families; and (4) for family religion to be the fountain of healthy, robust, corporate worship, as well as worship in all of life. See Duncan and Johnson, "A Call to Family Worship," 317–38.

4

Matthew Henry's Theology of the Sacraments

English Presbyterian Piety of Baptism and the Lord's Supper

AS A PRIMARY FIGURE of the Reformed tradition, Calvin declared that all human self understanding, including the behaviors that shape human life, are totally dependent on God.¹ Regarding this relationship between humanity and God, Henry articulated communion with God as a pattern for this relationship between them. Communion with God was at the core of Henry's thought and ministry, as argued in chapter 2. According to him, "by keeping up daily communion with God, [people] grow more and more meet to partake of that inheritance, and have their conversation in heaven."² He furthermore regarded Christian worship as a liturgical pattern

---

1. The Reformed understanding of human life has been always defined by humanity's relationship with God. The structure of the relationship between humans and God was the basis of John Calvin's understanding of humanity. As originator of the Reformed tradition, Calvin long before tried to connect God with human life as well as human salvation. In his *Institutes of Christian Religion*, Calvin presumes that without knowledge of God there is no knowledge of the human being, titling chapter 1 of book I "The Knowledge of God and That of Ourselves are Connected." See Calvin, *Institutes of the Christian Religion*, 1.1.1–2. According to William Dyrness, this relationship is already set up by God and tied up with God: "[Human] relationships are already embraced by the set of relationships that God sustains with the world" (Dyrness, *The Earth Is God's*, 68).

2. Henry, "Daily Communion with God," 247.

of communion with God. All ordinances of worship including sacraments were to promote human communion with God. For Henry, the Christian life as well as the ordinances of worship[3] should facilitate a deep fellowship or walking with God. On the premise that all areas of human life should be related with God, Henry developed his thought regarding communion with God in ordinary life. His *Directions for Daily Communion with God: How to Begin, How to Spend, and How to Close Every Day with God* (1712)[4] is an example of his thoughts about fellowship with God on a daily basis.

Besides this, Henry developed his thoughts on daily communion with God based on the sacraments. He wrote two works on the sacraments: *A Treatise on Baptism* and *The Communicant's Companion: Instructions for the Right Receiving of the Lord's Supper*. He also published two other baptismal works based on revisions of his sermons, "Christ's Favor to Little Children" (1713)[5] and "The Catechising of Youth" (1713).[6] In these works, Henry explicated the nature, meaning, efficacy, and related purpose of the sacraments. This chapter builds on the conclusion that Henry developed his understanding of the sacraments within the framework of communion with God. The purpose of this chapter is to explore Henry's thought regarding the sacraments as liturgical practices that facilitate communion with God in daily life. By investigating his works on the sacraments, including sermons and the *Bible Commentary*, this chapter will explore Henry's English Presbyterian understanding and piety of the sacraments, and then will evaluate the extent to which he adhered to the Reformed tradition in relation to the sacraments.

HENRY ON THE SACRAMENTS

The Meaning, Nature, and Kind of the Sacraments[7]

The sacraments, for Henry, were crucial to communion with God, which presupposes the capacity for communication between humanity and God.

---

3. Henry regarded reading the Scriptures, hearing the Word, prayer, praise, singing of the psalms and the Lord's Supper as ordinances of worship. See chap. 2 and Williams, *Memoirs of the Life*, 277.

4. In *Complete Works*, 1:198–247.

5. This baptismal sermon based on Mark 10:16 was delivered March 6, 1713. See Henry, *Complete Works*, 2:264–80.

6. Henry, "A Sermon Concerning the Catechising of Youth (April 7, 1713)," 157–73.

7. Sacraments are instituted as signs and seals; ordinances are not necessarily signs

Matthew Henry's Theology of the Sacraments

In this communication, a sacrament is one of the outward means, which can be called the means of grace, "whereby Christ communicates to us the benefits of redemption."[8]

Keeping this in mind, Henry developed his understanding of the sacraments based on the Scriptures. In *A Scripture Catechism*, he defined the Word, the sacraments, and prayer as "the great gospel ordinances"[9] and "public ordinances."[10] He even called them the "principal ordinances" instituted by Jesus Christ.[11] Henry explained how Christians in the early church experienced the sacraments in relation to other ordinances: "Then they that gladly received [Christ's] Word were baptized, and they continued steadfastly in the apostles' doctrine and fellowship, and in breaking bread, and in prayers."[12] In this way, the sacraments, for Henry, were the ordinances of the gospel.[13]

Based on this understanding, Henry gives this definition: "a sacrament is a holy ordinance instituted by Christ, wherein, by sensible signs, Christ, and the benefits of the new covenant, are represented, sealed, and applied to believers."[14] According to this definition, a sacrament is a holy ordinance only instituted by Christ, not by people, and they are instituted to be signs and seals.[15] He defined signs and seals in detail:

> Signs. Not natural signs, as smoke is a sign of fire, but voluntary and instituted. Not purely intellectual signs, as the sign of the prophet Jonas, but sensible and visible. Not signs barely for memorials, as the heap of stones in Jordan, but signs that exhibit, and, as instruments, convey. So that the essence, or formal nature, of a

---

and seals. For Henry, following the Protestants, there are only two sacraments: Baptism and the Lord's Supper. However, there are several ordinances of worship or the Gospel, as explained in chap. 3.

8. Henry, *A Scripture Catechism*, 244.

9. Ibid.

10. Henry, "Ordinances in the Covenant," 221.

11. *BC*, John 20:19.

12. Based on Acts 2:41, 42. See Henry, *A Scripture Catechism*, 244.

13. Henry clearly stated that "the word, and prayer, and the Lord's Supper, and church fellowship, are the ordinances which those who are baptized may (as they become capable) lay claim to" (Henry, *Treatise on Baptism*, 146).

14. Henry, *A Scripture Catechism*, 246.

15. This is Calvin's terminology and the Reformed understanding of the sacraments. So for Henry a sacrament is a special kind of ordinance.

> sacrament, consists in a relative union between the sign and the thing signified.
>
> Seals. Not bare signs, as the map of a Lordship represents that Lordship to everyone who looks upon it: but such signs as deeds, or charters of feoffment, sealed and delivered, which convey the Lordship to the feoffee, upon such conditions; and give him a right and title to the premises, to all intents and purposes, upon the performance of those conditions. Thus the rainbow, Gideon's fleece, the coal from the altar that touched Isaiah's lips, and many others, were not only signs signifying, but signs confirming, the promises to which they were annexed.[16]

When observing the sacraments, mere use of the sign itself, for Henry, did not guarantee its efficacy.[17]

Moreover, Henry understood that intrinsic to the nature of the sacraments was that they functioned as signs and seals of the covenant promises.

> They [sacraments] are signs and seals—signs to represent and instruct, seals to ratify and confirm. They are signs of absolute grace and favor; they are seals of the conditional promises; nay, they are mutual seals: God does in the sacraments seal to us to be to us a God, and we do therein seal to him to be to him a people.[18]

In this way, Henry understood that sacraments were not just signs but also seals of the things signified. He furthermore identified that the sacraments were not magical power but means of grace by which human communion with God as covenantal relationship could be fostered.

Henry also defined the kinds of sacraments based on the Scriptures. He thought that there were different kinds of sacraments in different periods of biblical history. Although there have been different kinds of sacraments in different times, each sacrament presupposes a pattern of relationship between God and people called a covenant. A covenant, for Henry, was a promise for more effective communion with God. Thus, the sacraments are the means of grace by which people sustain their relationship with God, which is conditioned and revealed in a pattern of covenant. Based on this conviction, Henry understood the tree of the knowledge of good and evil

---

16. Henry, *Treatise on Baptism*, in *Family Religion*, 132.

17. For more detailed explanation of the sign and seal, see Q.92 "What is a sacrament?" in Henry, *A Scripture Catechism*, 246–47.

18. *BC*, Romans 4:11.

Matthew Henry's Theology of the Sacraments

(Gen 2:9) and circumcision (Rom 4:11) as sacraments.[19] The tree of life was a sacrament symbolic of innocence;[20] circumcision was an initiating sacrament under the law in the Old Testament.[21] According to him, "the sacraments of the New Testament are baptism and the Lord's Supper."[22] Thus, the sacraments of the gospel for today are only two: baptism and the Lord's Supper.

A Protestant Reformed Position Regarding the Sacraments

As a Presbyterian minister, Henry developed his own understanding of the sacraments from a Protestant perspective over against the Roman Catholic. Henry argued against the Roman Catholic position on the sacraments' validity and virtue. He clarified that sacraments are not dependent on the minister for their validity:

> [Catholics] make the validity and virtue of the sacraments, to depend upon the intention of the priest or minister. So the council of Trent has decreed; and hence it will follow, that if the priest either be carelessly thinking of something else, or willfully and wickedly design something else, when he baptizes, or consecrates the bread and wine, it is no sacrament at all, nor has any virtue in it to the receiver; the person so baptized is no member of the church; the host so consecrated is not the body of Christ, and therefore it is idolatry to worship it.[23]

In contrast, Henry emphasized the working of God in the sacraments. The sacraments become effectual means of grace only by the work of God: "The sacraments become effectual means of salvation, not from any virtue in them, or in him who administers them, but only by the blessing of Christ, and the working of the Spirit in them who by faith receive them."[24] This implied that Henry followed Calvin's tradition, emphasizing the role of the Holy Spirit in the working of the sacrament.[25] A sacrament can be interpreted as an "instrument" by which God's grace is distributed

---

19. Henry, *A Scripture Catechism*, 247.
20. *BC*, Genesis 2:8–15.
21. *BC*, Romans 4:11.
22. Henry, *A Scripture Catechism*, 247.
23. Henry, "Popery, A Spiritual Tyranny," 344.
24. Henry, *A Scripture Catechism*, 246.
25. Calvin, "Short Treatise on the Lord's Supper (1541)," 171–73; *Institutes*, 4.17.38.

to people. When it came to the efficacy of the sacraments, Henry clearly followed Calvin's position by emphasizing that the presence of Christ is a presence in the Holy Spirit. Reformed tradition did not take the Holy Spirit for granted. "There must be prayer for the Holy Spirit."[26] Since Calvin, prayer for the condescension of the Holy Spirit in the sacraments has been a particular emphasis in the Reformed tradition. While following Calvin's emphasis, Henry attempted to connect the Reformed tradition to his own developing context in a complex historical setting.[27] English Presbyterians needed to develop their own manner of observing the sacraments after the Act of Toleration, while Calvin in his time attempted to recover the simple way of primitive churches.

Lastly, Henry also indicated the importance of an intellectual aspect in observing the sacraments. This does not mean that he followed Zwingli's memorialist position on the meaning of the sacraments. Rather, Henry emphasized the necessity of the people's understanding in order to apply the sacraments to their life. As he always conceived of the worship service, he stated, "God's service is reasonable, and it is then acceptable when we perform it intelligently, knowing what we do and why we do it."[28] The sacraments are no exception. Henry promoted greater understanding on the part of those observing the sacraments. Sacraments as signs and seals "have not their meaning so plain and obvious as other ordinances have; therefore we are concerned to search, that we may not offer *the blind for sacrifice*, but may do a reasonable service."[29] According to him, "it is the will of Christ that the sacramental signs should be explained, and that people should be acquainted with the meaning of them."[30] In this way, Henry promoted intellectual understanding in the observance of sacraments so as to help people participate in the ordinance more actively. For this reason, Henry emphasized parent participation and accountability in teaching and raising their children after infant baptism to help their children understand and live out the meaning of the sacraments.

---

26. Bromiley, *Sacramental Teaching*, 30–31.

27. For the development of the history and theology of sacraments in England and Scotland as a legacy of Henry's, see Spinks, *Sacraments, Ceremonies and the Stuart Divines*.

28. *BC*, Exodus 13:14–16.

29. *BC*, Exodus 12:26.

30. *BC*, John 13:12.

Human Life Conforming to the Sacraments

While not ignoring the mode and practice of ritual, Henry was much more concerned that all aspects of human life conform to the sacraments. He attempted to develop his understanding of sacraments as efficacious means of God's action in human life by promoting communion with God in everyday life as expressing the meaning and teaching of the sacraments. For Henry, lessons for the living of ordinary life came from teaching on the sacraments. Sacraments worked not only in the service of ritual, but also permeated every facet of everyday life; the presence of God in the sacraments could be extended into God's action in every area of human life.[31]

Although he treated the mode of the sacraments in his *Treatise on Baptism* and *The Communicant's Companion*, Henry dealt much more with the meaning, practical improvement, and purpose of the sacraments. For example, Henry distinctly connected ordinary human life to the sacraments, especially to baptism: "would you have all our Christian duty in one word, it is, to behave in every respect as those who are baptized; that is, to have our conversation as becomes the gospel of Jesus Christ."[32] Similarly, while Henry did not write any prescribed liturgy for the Lord's Supper,[33] he instead wrote instruction of the right receiving of the Lord's Supper. Among the sixteen chapters of this book, Henry had little to say about the proper mode of celebrating the sacrament; instead, he dealt with practical ways of improving one's Christian life based on the Lord's Supper. In this regard, Henry's main concern in relation to the Lord's Supper was not only where Christ was present but also how to respond to the presence of Christ.

With confidence that the sacraments should be applied to daily life, Henry emphasized this again in his sermon, "Ordinances in the Covenant" (April 10, 1692), where he exhorted his audience: "Understand not only how to improve an ordinance just while you have it, but how to improve it long after it."[34] Henry went on to clarify that "the efficacy is not tied to the administration; they do not work as charms, or by physical agency, but as

---

31. Henry thought that change of life was at the core of applying the sacraments. Contemporary theologians such as Miroslav Volf have also attempted to apply the sacraments to human life. See Volf, *After Our Likeness* and *Exclusion and Embrace*.

32. Henry, *Treatise on Baptism*, 222.

33. For more detailed information on the administration of the sacraments, refer to chap. 5 on the practice of Henry's public worship. In brief, Henry followed the guidance of *The Westminster Directory* for the sacraments.

34. Henry, "Ordinances in the Covenant," 228.

moral instruments."[35] Considering Henry's own intention in his treatment on the sacraments, it is necessary to examine how he articulated his sacramental teaching in relation to daily life in order to promote communion with God.

THE SACRAMENT OF BAPTISM: HENRY'S ENGLISH PRESBYTERIAN BAPTISMAL PIETY

As with the Lord's Day worship services, Henry did not write or revise any prescribed liturgy for baptismal rites. It is not certain whether or not he wanted to follow any particular type of baptismal rite. However, considering his treatises and sermons on baptism, there is no doubt that he regarded baptism as a crucial ordinance in the Christian life and integral to ecclesiastical ministry. The main concern of this section is to explore how Henry articulated his understanding of baptism based on the Scriptures as it relates to the Christian life, as well as ecclesiastical ministry. Henry constructed an English Presbyterian baptismal piety by connecting the sacrament of baptism to ordinary Christian life.

The Meaning and Administration of Baptism

For Henry, the meaning of baptism was more fundamental than its administration, though its meaning for the Christian life has to do with its ritual practice. However, in his *Treatise on Baptism*, Henry first dealt with the meaning of baptism and then treated its administration. He did not interpret the meaning and theological implications on the basis of the contemporary practice of the rite of baptism. Instead, Henry defined the meaning of baptism and then argued for the manner of its practice based on that understanding.

The Institution of Baptism

Since the meaning of baptism comes from its institution, it is first necessary to examine how Henry thought of the institution of baptism. Henry considered that "baptism is a sacrament, wherein the washing with water, in the name of the Father, of the Son, and of the Holy Spirit, does signify

35. Ibid.

and seal our engrafting into Christ, and partaking of the benefits of the covenant of grace, and our engagement to be the Lord's."[36] This definition implies that baptism as an initiating rite grants a new identity to the person baptized, and initiates him or her into a new pattern and meaning of relationship not only with church members but also with God.

Henry clearly defined the institution from his understanding of the Scriptures. He explicated the Scriptures to show that baptism was instituted by Jesus Christ. Nevertheless, he also believed that "washing with water was used long before Lord's time, not only as a common action, but as a religious rite."[37] and so baptism or washing with water was not a new thing to Jesus. According to Henry, Jesus chose water baptism as one of his institutions.[38] Moreover, Jesus "bequeathed this institution to his church at his departure, as a sacred deposit, to be preserved pure and entire, without further alteration, till his second coming."[39] With this basic understanding, Henry based the baptismal rite on Matthew 28:19–20; based on this passage, "we have not only a warrant to make baptismal lawful, but an order to make it a duty."[40]

Among the many meanings and implications of this passage, Henry made a crucial point in relation to baptism. He pointed out that "the word which we translate 'teach' [in v. 19] is, I think, not well translated." He suggested a better English translation, arguing that "it is a different word which is used in v. 20, 'teaching them to observe'; 'Go, disciple all nations,' I think it should be rendered."[41] *Disciple*, for Henry, meant "make them [Jesus'] disciples, that is, admit them [His] scholars or admit them into the school of Christ." In here, "discipling was not of persons already taught, but to the end that they might be taught."[42] And, "in their schools, a person was made disciple, when he [or she] gave himself [or herself] up to be trained up by such a master."[43] Based on this meaning, Henry expressed his position that people should be trained as disciples through life after baptism, and it was mistake to delay baptism until they are thoroughly taught:

36. Henry, *A Scripture Catechism*, 247.
37. Henry, *Treatise on Baptism*, 129.
38. Ibid., 130.
39. Ibid.
40. Ibid., 140.
41. Ibid., 143.
42. Ibid.
43. Ibid.

> I insist so much upon the right sense of the word to vindicate the text from the mistake of those who will have none baptized (of whomsoever born) till they are thoroughly taught, grounding it on the words of the institution, which, if rightly Englished would intimate no such thing; for though infants are not capable of being taught, they are capable of being disciplined.[44]

In this regard, for Henry, Christian life as a disciple was related to the sacrament of baptism in that baptism was followed by catechesis or training as disciple.

The Meaning of Baptism

The meaning of baptism, for Henry, had to do with its institution. Basically, Henry promoted a more developed relationship between God and people. Based on the nature of institution as that which makes people disciples, Henry explained the meaning of baptism as "a solemn admission into the visible church of Christ" and "a seal of the covenant of grace."[45] Following his understanding of the sacrament, Henry defined baptism as the sign of admission into the visible church and the seal of God's covenantal grace.

ADMISSION INTO THE VISIBLE CHURCH

Henry succinctly defined baptism as "an ordinance of Christ, whereby the person baptized is solemnly admitted as a member of the visible church."[46] The church admits all children whose parents are willing by baptizing them. This definition implies three things. First, Henry distinguished the visible church from the invisible church. He clarified baptism as an ordinance of the visible church by saying that "baptism is an ordinance of the visible church members; appointed for the admission of the visible members; admission, not into the internal communion, but only into that which is visible and external, in the profession of faith, and participation of sacraments."[47] The visible church, for Henry, meant the universal (catholic) church. So, he thought that "baptism is not to be looked upon as the door

---

44. Ibid.
45. Cf. Ibid.
46. Ibid., 144.
47. Ibid.

Matthew Henry's Theology of the Sacraments

of admission into any particular church."[48] By defining the visible church as the catholic universal church, Henry defended the authenticity of the Dissenting churches against the Church of England: "hence appears the mistake of those who maintain, that because they were baptized into the Church of England, they are therefore bound never to leave it, nor attempt any alterations in it."[49] In this way, baptism was an ordinance of the visible yet universal church.

Second, Henry thought that baptism was not a completion of catechism but, as the admission into the visible church, the beginning of training to be a disciple. This understanding differed from some believers during the time of the early churches. Henry criticized people who professed faith in Christ but were not yet baptized by pointing out the error of the early churches:

> He who seriously professes faith in Christ, and obedience to him, but is not yet baptized, hath a sort of church-membership, but remote, imperfect, and irregular. Many in the primitive times, upon a mistaken apprehension of the unpardonableness of sin committed after baptism, deferred it long (some even till the dying moment) who yet are not to be looked upon as outcasts. Many of the martyrs died in the state of catechumens.[50]

However, Henry did not ignore the role of catechumen. Instead, he articulated his own way of training baptized people by emphasizing catechism in a new way—with the structure of the family.

Third, Henry connected the meaning of baptism with the core of his thought, communion with God. Henry thought that their admission by baptism entitled people to the privileges of the church, which were related to communion with God. He defined church privileges: "such as are peculiar to true believers, even union and communion with Christ in grace and glory, and fellowship with the Father, and with his Son, by the Holy Ghost." As Henry pointed out, "though baptism does not give a title to these, it seals and ratifies that title to true believers."[51] Baptism entitles us to and invests in us with these privileges. Besides this, Henry addressed other privileges of visible church membership: honor, safety, communion, and opportunity.[52]

48. Ibid.
49. Ibid.
50. Ibid.
51. Ibid.
52. For more detailed explanation, see ibid., 145–46.

Baptism, according to Henry, "gives a title to the ordinances,"[53] such as the word, prayer, and the Lord's Supper, and church fellowship.

A Seal of the Covenant of Grace

The second meaning of baptism that Henry articulated was the way it functioned as a seal of the covenant of grace. Henry drew this meaning from "those words of the institution, baptizing them 'in (or into) the name of the Father, and of the Son, and of the Holy Ghost.'"[54] First and foremost, Henry presupposed that baptism was crucial in that it drew people into the relationship with the Triune God. This pattern of human relationship with God can be called a covenant. According to Henry, "the sum and substance of this covenant is that God will be to us a God, and we shall be to him a people."[55] And this can be called the covenant of grace because it "is founded on free grace, and purchased by the blood of Christ."[56] This covenant of grace, according to Henry, not only has privileges but also duties: "all the privileges of the covenant are summed up in this one, 'that God will be to us a God'; and all the duties of the covenant are summoned up in this, 'that we must be to him a people.'"[57] This pattern of relationship based on the covenant of grace is at the core of human life in communion with God since "it is all our salvation, and should be all our desire."[58]

Henry further articulated how baptism seals the covenant between God and man: sealing the covenant meant "giving the validity to the covenant, and mutual assurance of the sincerity of the covenanters."[59] Baptism as a seal of the covenant of grace implies mutual acts in the relationship between God and human. These mutual acts are to promote a more patterned relationship between God and people. According to Henry, in and by baptism, God first "assures us that he is willing 'to be to us a God' and engages us to be to him a people, according to the tenor of the covenant."[60] At the same time, by baptism, people begin to live in the Triune God by de-

53. Ibid., 146.
54. Henry, *Treatise on Baptism*, 147.
55. Ibid., 149.
56. Ibid., 148.
57. Ibid., 149.
58. Ibid.
59. Ibid.
60. Ibid., 150.

Matthew Henry's Theology of the Sacraments

voting and dedicating themselves to the name. The Triune God in the New Testament, according to Henry, is "not only made known (doctrine) but tendered and offered to us (covenant)."[61] By baptism, people "are brought into that covenant." Henry further articulated how to enter into the covenant with the Triune God through baptism: (1) by renouncing all that is contrary to God and (2) by resigning ourselves to the LORD. These two acts of people, which are symbolized by baptism, presuppose that life is a journey with ongoing rules for making the covenant effective. In this way, baptism meant a seal of the ongoing relationship, "which we find engrossed in the Scriptures, between God and man."[62]

Henry articulated another aspect of this covenant relationship between people and God with a doctrine of the Trinity in the form of baptism. By entering into the name of the Triune God, baptism allows people to have a relationship with the Father, the Son, and the Holy Spirit. By being baptized in the name of the Father, people "give up themselves to God their Creator."[63] In baptism, people confess that God is the Creator as the absolute owner and LORD, supreme governor, chief good, and highest and ultimate end.[64] This acknowledgement of creation in baptism reminds people of the direction of life: "we are not our own, and therefore may not live as we please: we are God's, and therefore must glorify him." In addition to this, by being baptized in the name of the Son, people not only assent to the truth concerning Jesus Christ but also submit to him in his three offices: Prophet, Priest, and King. Lastly, by being baptized into the name of the Holy Spirit, people pledge to submit themselves to "stand in a covenant relation to the Holy Ghost as sanctifier, teacher, guide, and comforter."[65] Henry stressed the place of the Holy Spirit, using the language of the Spirit being "in our heart" or "within us."[66] Although he did not ignore the work of the Spirit in creation,[67] Henry emphasized the Spirit's work in the human heart and life in terms of baptism. In this way, a new relationship resulted from baptism that led people into a more intimate fellowship with the Triune God.

61. Ibid., 152.
62. Ibid., 151.
63. Ibid., 156.
64. Cf. Ibid., 156–58.
65. Ibid., 164–65.
66. Ibid., 165.
67. For example, Henry delineated the work of creation and providence of God as the Spirit; see *BC*, Genesis 1:1.

Matthew Henry

Administration of Baptism

After presenting this understanding of the institution and meaning of baptism, Henry then treated its administration. In the chapter entitled "The circumstances of the administration of baptism" in *A Treatise on Baptism*, Henry dealt with its proper mode, time, place, and manner in detail.

First, when it comes to mode, Henry preferred sprinkling or pouring to immersion while not ignoring the strength of the latter. According to Henry, "in sacraments, it is the truth, and not the quantity, of the outward element, that is to be insisted upon; so in the ordinance of baptism, the application of a little water, provided there be water, and a washing with that water, is sufficient to signify spiritual washing."[68] He thought that the mode of sacrament as a sign should follow a way that was "very much in use in those times and places"; the sign should be "taken from a common action."[69] Based on this thought, Henry held that "in baptism, not dipping, which was then an ordinary way of washing, but sprinkling or pouring water, which is now the usual way of our daily washing, is most proper."[70] Moreover, for Henry, "there is no such convincing evidence from Scripture, that Christ and others were baptized by dipping, as may justly be required to prove it essential to the ordinance."[71] In contrast, he said, "the thing signified by baptism is frequently, in Scripture, set forth by sprinkling or pouring water."[72]

Second, Henry considered the time when baptism should be administered. There are two cases to be considered in relation to time. One is in the case of an adult. Henry clearly held his position that adults should be baptized upon their personal profession of faith without delay, based on the Scriptures: Acts 2:41; 8:38; 9:18; 16:33.[73] As he did when discussing the institution of baptism, Henry again criticized deferral of the baptism of an adult, "till they had long been in the state of catechumens."[74] For Henry, deferring baptism "was an excess of strictness, and making the door of

---

68. Henry, *Treatise on Baptism*, 210.

69. Ibid., 207.

70. Ibid.

71. Ibid.

72. Ibid., 210. Henry also provides Scripture verses illustrating the appropriateness of sprinkling: Isa 44:3; 52:15; Ezek 36:25; Tit 3:5–6; Heb 10:22; 12:24, etc. See ibid., 211.

73. Ibid., 211–12.

74. Ibid., 212.

Matthew Henry's Theology of the Sacraments

the church straiter than Christ and the apostles."[75] The other case is that of an infant. Henry held a moderate position between two extremes: "needless delay" and "superstitious hurry." On the one hand, "it should not be causelessly deferred, as if it were a thing indifferent whether it be done or not."[76] On the other hand, "it should not be superstitiously hastened and precipitated,"[77] because Henry considered it a mistake to think that baptism is absolutely necessary to the salvation of the child.

Third, regarding the place of baptism, Henry did not deal with the architecture of the church building for the baptismal rite.[78] His argument concerning place was related to the meaning of baptism: admission into the visible church. Thus, "it is most fitting and convenient that the ordinance of baptism be administered publicly, in the face of the congregation." According to Henry, administering baptism as an initiating ordinance ought to be public so that "the congregation may be witnesses for the church membership of the person baptized."[79] He also gave the reasons for administering baptism publicly: "for it is an act of solemn religious worship, and therefore should be attended with all due circumstances of solemnity; and the more public to the state and grandeur of the ordinance; it should be performed in a 'holy convocation.'"[80]

Fourth, Henry discussed the manner of the administration of baptism. Henry did not require the rites and ceremonies that were practiced in the Church of Rome.[81] According to him, there are three essential elements in the rite of baptism: the baptismal prayer, the parents' profession of faith, and the words of dedication. The baptismal prayer "was not any set prescribed form but according to the minister's ability."[82] Furthermore, the parents' profession of faith in Christ was mandatory: "it is requisite that at least one of the parents so publicly make that profession in the pres-

---

75. Ibid.

76. Ibid., 213.

77. Ibid.

78. Henry just gave a hint that the baptismal font could be added to near the church doors by mentioning that "in process of time, they erected baptisteria (fonts we call them) near the church doors, to signify that baptism is the door of admission into the church" (ibid., 214).

79. Ibid.

80. Ibid.

81. As illustrations of unnecessary rites in relation to baptism, Henry mentions a kind of exorcism and insufflations, an unction, and triple immersion. See ibid., 218–19.

82. Ibid., 216.

ence of the congregation."[83] Lastly, baptism should be done in the words of dedication prescribed by Jesus: "I baptize thee in the name of the Father, and of the Son, and of the Holy Ghost"; "I do admit this child as a visible church member."[84] After administration of this rite, the minister "should be a remembrance to the parents of their duty in bringing up their child as a Christian," and then, "it is fit to conclude with suitable prayers and praises."[85]

Developing Baptismal Piety

Henry was not satisfied with the administration of baptism only as an ecclesiastical rite. He was much more concerned with developing baptismal piety in and through life. According to him, the baptized children as well as their parents and witnesses "need to be directed in and excited to the practical improvement of their own baptism."[86] This section will explore how Henry developed baptismal piety by articulating its meaning in life.

Living as Baptized People

Most of all, Henry articulated baptism as an essential grace for human life. He assumed that baptism as an admission into the visible church meant not a completion of faith or a manifestation of maturity, but a beginning of human life as a Christian. That was why he did not include three years instruction for the catechumens before baptism in his *Treaties on Baptism*,[87] as did Roman Catholics or the Church of England. Instead, Henry intended to apply baptism to all aspects of life as an essential grace by integrating justification and sanctification as all-encompassing processes. Henry assumed that the Christian life could be divided into justification and sanctification.[88] Yet although he distinguished justification from sanctification,[89] Henry did not

83. Ibid.
84. Ibid., 217.
85. Ibid.
86. Ibid.
87. Ibid., 212.
88. Ibid., 136–38.

89. Puritans clearly separated justification from sanctification. Cf. Calvin did not separate them in applying salvation to human. Cf. Witvliet, "Baptism as a Sacrament of Reconciliation in the Thought of John Calvin," 149–62.

separate them from each other in terms of the efficacy of baptism. Baptism signified not only the beginning of the Christian life but also its ongoing journey or process.

Moreover, although he did not ignore the importance of the debate regarding infant baptism,[90] Henry was much more concerned with the practical improvement of baptism. He presupposed that "infant baptism is questioned, because it is not improved; and then it is not improved, because it is questioned."[91] So Henry emphasized the practice of the doctrine, claiming that "if any man set himself seriously to do his will in this matter, by diligent and conscientious improvement of his baptism, he shall know of the doctrine, whether it be of God, or whether we speak of ourselves."[92] With this conviction, Henry attempted "to find, by experience, the moral influence of baptism, both upon comfort and holiness,"[93] and defined the improvement of baptism as "behaving in every respect as those who are baptized."[94] According to him, "it is the great concern of those who are by baptism admitted members of the visible church, practically to improve their baptism, and to live accordingly."[95] This implies that the meaning of baptism cannot be fully accomplished without its real practice in life. So, Henry even held that "baptism not improved, is no baptism, any more than the carcass is the man."[96] To him, "nominal Christianity is but real hypocrisy."[97] Thus, people "must carry it in everything as a baptized people; and [their] whole conversation must be under the influence of [their] baptism."[98]

---

90. For his treatment of debate on infant baptism, see Henry, *Treatise on Baptism*, 167–98.

91. Ibid., 221.

92. Ibid.

93. Ibid.

94. Ibid., 222.

95. Ibid.

96. Ibid., 223.

97. Ibid. According to Henry, "baptism is a trust, to which we must be faithful; baptism is a talent, which must be traded with, and accounted for; baptism is a privilege, which must be improved; baptism is a profession, which must be lived up to; baptism is an obligation, which must be performed; baptism is an oath, which must be made good. So then, if we do not make use of our baptism, we falsify a trust, we bury a talent, we abuse a privilege, we contradict a profession, we break a sacred bond in sunder, despise an oath, and cast away from us the cords of an everlasting covenant" (ibid., 223–24).

98. Ibid., 222.

Matthew Henry

Baptism in Christian Life

With this understanding, Henry developed his own way of improvement of baptism in the Christian life by connecting the sacrament to life. First, according to Henry, baptized people should "recognize that it [baptismal covenant] cannot be annulled."[99] He encouraged people not to forget it by reminding them of God's faithfulness in the baptismal covenant:

> That time does not wear out the strength of it: though it was administered long ago, yet (being a speciality, a bond sealed) it binds us firmly as if we had been baptized but yesterday.... God remembers "the kindness of our youth, and the love of our espousals"; and we must not forget the covenant of our youth, and the vow of our espousals.[100]

Therefore, baptized people should remember God's faithfulness in the covenant of grace all through their life.

Along with such remembering, Henry strongly held that one's baptismal covenant should be renewed. For him, "it is very good, when [people] grow up to years of understanding, solemnly to renew [their] baptismal covenant; and to make that [their] own act and deed, which [their] parents, as the trustees of [their] wills, to act for [their] good then did for [them]."[101] Moreover, Henry thought that this renewing the baptismal covenant would "help to make the engagement more sensible, and consequently give it a greater and stronger influence."[102] By stressing confirmation, Henry did not ignore the importance of renewing the baptismal covenant throughout one's life.

---

99. Ibid., 225.
100. Ibid., 226.
101. Ibid.
102. Ibid. Henry did not include confirmation in the sacraments. However he knew the rite and regarded it as "a transition from the state of infant church membership, to that of adult." On the administration of confirmation, Henry criticized the way that people should be put into the hands of the bishop. Following the practice of the primitive church and of Baxter, Henry encouraged people to recover the practice of imposition of hands in the rite of confirmation. Moreover, he held that the confirmation should be done in the presence of church community, not in front of the bishop: "it is a riddle to me, why the subordinate constitution of confirmation should be so strictly appropriated to bishops. The recognition of the baptismal covenant, and the profession of faith, repentance, and a holy life, are fittest to be made in the presence of those to whom the right hand of fellowship is to be given in settled stated communion, or their representatives" (ibid., 227).

Thus, Henry stressed that baptized people should acquaint themselves with the meaning and nature of baptism throughout their lives. Based on the Scriptures, Henry pressed holiness and sanctification "from the consideration of the design and tendency of baptism."[103] Henry explained the meaning of improvement of baptism based on the Scriptures as a life conforming to Christ: "by our baptism we are obliged to conform to the burial and resurrection of Christ, in our sanctification; dying to sin, and living to righteousness; putting off the old man, and putting on the new man."[104] As the sign of our union with Christ, baptism signifies and seals our fellowship with him, our walking with God in Christ. In this way, Henry held that "what is done once sacramentally, in baptism, should be always done really, in life."[105]

Practical Improvement of Baptism in Christian Life

Based on his general understanding of baptism and life, Henry continued to articulate practical ways for improvement of baptism in life. Regarding the effect of baptism on life, "it, especially infant baptism, is to be improved, as a restraint from all manner of sin"[106] through life.[107] At the same time, by imposing a lively sense of our relation to the LORD Jesus Christ, Henry also declared that "baptism is also to be improved as an incentive to good works."[108]

Another practical improvement of baptism in the individual's life concerns the way it changes human relationships with God and others. First and foremost, Henry declared the role of baptism as supporting our faith by securing the relationship between the person and God. He encouraged people to "consider that by baptism we were admitted into covenant relations; God did then make over himself to us, to be our God; and take us

---

103. Ibid., 228.
104. Ibid., 231.
105. Ibid., 232.
106. Ibid., 235.
107. According to Henry, "baptism commits us to ongoing repentance" (ibid., 242). For Henry, repentance was an application of baptism in and through their life for reconciliation with God. Thus, it is certain that Henry followed Calvin in that he did not require people to do penance as a requirement for reconciling with God.
108. Ibid.

to himself, to be his people."[109] As a seal of baptism, the covenant of grace strongly holds the person to God by guaranteeing its promises. According to Henry, "by baptism, God had hold of us when we depart from him, so by baptism, we have hold of God when he seems to withdraw from us."[110] For Henry, infant baptism increased this encouragement too. Infant baptism, according to him, "in the parents' right, speaks covenant mercy kept for thousands; the word commanded to a thousand generations; which, if seriously considered, has a great deal in it to encourage faith."[111] Moreover, infant baptism assured people that God "who took [them] when [they] were brought, surely will not cast [them] off when [they] come [themselves], though weak, and trembling, and unworthy."[112] In this way, baptism gives great assurance of the relationship between God and the baptized person through life.

Second, by signifying our dependence on God, baptism, for Henry, was crucial in the Christian life by encouraging and emboldening Christians to pray. Henry presupposed that "a due improvement of our baptism would greatly befriend us in this duty."[113] Based on his premise that in baptism people "took God for [their] God" and "put [them] into the relation of a people to God," Henry gave prayer an important place in the relationship of humans with God: "baptism did signify and seal our dependence upon God, and our submission to him; both of which are in effect denied, and contradicted, if we live without prayer; either wholly neglect it, or frequently intermit it."[114] So, for Henry, if we live neglecting prayer, "we refuse to stand to, and so forfeit its [baptism's] privileges."[115] Moreover, Henry explained how baptism emboldens people to pray: "baptism is one special qualification that fits us for a confident approach to God (as circumcision under the law): by that, we were admitted into the relation of children, which should encourage us to improve the relation, by crying 'Abba, Father' (Gal. 4:6)."[116] Henry also pointed out that "in prayer we stand in need of the Father's smiles, the Son's righteousness, and the Spirit's aid; in reference to

109. Ibid., 245.
110. Ibid.
111. Ibid., 246.
112. Ibid., 247.
113. Henry, *Treatise on Baptism*, 247.
114. Ibid., 248.
115. Ibid.
116. Ibid.

each of which, we should consider, that we were baptized into the name of the Father, and of the Son, and of the Holy Ghost."[117] In this way, baptized people can also participate in prayer and even worship with the confidence and boldness that derives from the seal of baptism.

Third, Henry encouraged people to improve baptism as a powerful engagement to brotherly love. Baptism as a uniting ordinance "induces us to love one another with a pure heart, fervently: and would eradicate all love-killing principles and practices; and overcome all our feuds and animosities."[118] This brotherly love has as its foundation the meaning of baptism: "one baptism" and "baptized into one body." Henry regarded baptism as a center of unity for all Christians. Although people may differ from each other in their apprehensions, "they are baptized into the same great names of the Father, the Son, and Holy Ghost."[119] Based on this common faith professed in baptism—one baptism—Henry regarded oneness among the baptized as a authentic expression of it: "all Christians who are duly baptized, however differing in other things, are interested in one and the same covenant, guided by one and the same rule, meet at one and the same throne of grace, are entitled to one and the same inheritance, and all this by one and the same baptism."[120] Baptized people came to have a new relationship between them since "by baptism [people] are all admitted into the family and kingdom of Jesus Christ, and so become related to one another, yea, are adopted to be the children of the same Father."[121] Thus, according to Henry, when people seriously consider the meaning of one baptism into one body, they are empowered to love one another.

Baptismal Piety and the Family

Henry thought that baptismal piety could be taught in the family, claiming that "baptism is particularly an engagement to family worship: by that, we and ours were taken into covenant with God; therefore, 'we and our households should serve the LORD.'"[122] According to Henry, the family was at the center of developing baptismal piety. He presupposed that baptism,

---

117. Ibid., 249.
118. Ibid.
119. Ibid.
120. Ibid., 252.
121. Ibid.
122. Ibid., 248.

especially infant baptism, was not an individual participation in the rite but a communal engagement in the covenant of God, undertaken in order to connect baptism and life through the family. With this conviction, in order to help children live their lives conforming to their baptism, Henry gave directions to parents concerning the baptism of their children.

Henry taught parents how to bring their children to baptism and train them in relation to it at home in detail. First and foremost, parents should do certain things even before their children's baptism: they should understand it, examine themselves, and pray for a blessing upon that ordinance. Following his theological method, Henry first reminded parents of the importance of understanding with respect to baptism.[123] They should know the nature and reasons for participation in the ordinance of baptism since "there [were] many who brought their children to be baptized, only because it [was] the fashion of the country, and they would [have been] strangely looked upon if they do not do it; but they [knew] nothing of the meaning of this service."[124] Moreover, Henry reminded parents of their communion with God by asking them to examine themselves: "therefore examine yourselves, whether you be in the faith; for though your profession of faith be sufficient, so far as the church can decide, to entitle your children to this ordinance, yet God is not to be mocked."[125] In this way, for their child's baptism, parents should diligently examine their own hearts.

---

123. Part of Henry's theological method was his stress on intellectual understanding for the sake of the real practice of the Scriptures in daily life. See chap. 2.

124. Henry, *Treatise on Baptism*, 256. According to Henry, there are two basic meanings of baptism: parents "give up [their] children (which are parts of parents) to God" (ibid., 256); and they "do hereby oblige their children; bind them to the LORD; to his word and to his law" (ibid., 257). Moreover, Henry gave the meaning of baptism to parents based on the Scriptures: (1) You do it in compliance with the tenor of the covenant; which runs, "to us and to our children," that God will be "a God to us and to our seed." (2) You do it, in conformity to the will of God revealed in the Old Testament administration of the covenant; in that which was not ceremonial, viz. the admission of the children of the covenanters into the same covenant with their parents. (3) You do it in obedience to the appointment of Christ; that "little children should be brought unto him" (Mark 10:14). (4) You do it in pursuance of your own covenant with God; wherein you gave up yourselves, and all near and dear to you, unto him; your children therefore especially, who are in a manner parts of yourselves. (5) You do it out of a natural affection to your children; which prompts you to do all you can for their good. Labor thus to understand yourselves, and act with reason in what you do (ibid., 258).

125. Ibid.

In addition, Henry reminded parents of what they should do during the baptism.[126] They should focus their mind on the purpose of the institution, which is to please God. Henry knew that there was a prevalent societal tendency toward pleasing one's neighbors in baptism: "we see too commonly, that inviting and treating the guests is made the main matter at a christening, as they call it. All the case is to please their neighbors, while there is but little thought how to please God in it."[127] However, he did not condemn the inviting of friends on the ordinance of baptism; rather, Henry was convinced that "friends may be witnesses of our covenanting with God for our seed, and may join with us in prayer for a blessing upon the ordinance."[128] Moreover, Henry continued to ask parents to shape their spirits, with an awareness that God looked upon them. In their children's baptism, parents should be sincere, have faith in Christ, be thankful, sorrow over sin, and rejoice in the covenant of grace.[129] As seen here, all that was necessary for parents in their children's baptism was focused on the human heart's relationship with God, given from the covenant of grace.

Lastly, Henry reminded parents of their obligations concerning training their children after baptism. Baptism was not just a rite in the course of life but a seal of the covenant to be articulated in and through life. Henry instructed parents how to improve the baptism of their children in life: "in praying for them; in teaching them; in providing for them; and in parting with them."[130] According to Henry, "Christian families are the church's nurseries, where the young plants are reared; and parents have, in a special manner, the charge of them; and must be called to account concerning that charge."[131] Among the main duties of parents, Christian worship was the most important thing in raising their children. Henry clarified the place of worship in the family in parenting children after baptism:

> Endeavor, by a reverend carriage in your religious exercises and your sober deportment on the Lord's Day, to possess them with an early apprehension that the worship of God is a serious thing. I think it is good to bring children betimes to the solemn assembly,

---

126. In "A Church in the House." Henry also taught parents the duty of raising their children based on the baptism.
127. Henry, *Treatise on Baptism*, 261.
128. Ibid.
129. Ibid., 262–66.
130. Ibid., 267–68.
131. Ibid., 270.

where there is convenience for it; as soon as they are capable of being kept so quiet as not to give disturbance to others, though they are not able to understand what is said and done.[132]

In order to improve the practice of worship at home after infant baptism, Henry developed *A Scripture Catechism* as an essential aid. Henry also stressed the necessity and importance of training children at home after baptism by publishing his "Christ's Favor to Little Children" and "Sermon Concerning the Catechism of Youth" in the same year, 1713. Henry also reminded parents of their duty to teach their children how to live in the world with this metaphor: "the young tree must not grow always in the nursery; but at length be transplanted into its proper place in the orchard."[133] Therefore, parents should remind their children of "their baptismal engagement"[134] when they send them into the world.

ARTICULATING ENGLISH PRESBYTERIAN UNDERSTANDING OF THE LORD'S SUPPER

Henry also treated the sacrament of Lord's Supper. Instead of a book on the administration of the Lord's Supper, Henry wrote a book assisting the people who attended the table: *The Communicant's Companion* (1704).[135] Although he did not ignore a main issue regarding the Lord's Supper, that is, the presence of God, Henry was much more concerned with "contributing something to the faith, holiness, and joy of those who in this ordinance have given up their names to the LORD Jesus."[136] Following the Reformed tradition, Henry's concern on the Lord's Supper was not so much with the

---

132. Ibid., 270–71.

133. Ibid., 275.

134. Regarding baptismal engagement, Henry told parents to "dismiss [children] with a covenant blessing; as Isaac sent away Jacob (Gen. 28:3–5)." He also asked parents to "tell [children] and tell yourself, that 'the LORD watches between you and them, when you are absent the one from the other' (Gen 31:49)" (ibid., 275).

135. It is certain that Henry was influenced by his former teacher Thomas Doolittle on the Lord's Supper since the themes and specific contents of Henry's book are almost same as Doolittle's. The main contents of Doolittle's book, *A Treatise Concerning the Lord's Supper: With Three Dialogues for the More Full Information of the Weak, in the Nature and Use of this Sacrament* are how to prepare for, participate in, and practice the Lord's Supper.

136. Henry, *Communicant's Companion*, 29.

Matthew Henry's Theology of the Sacraments

elements as with the state and life of the people attending the Supper.[137] In this way, Henry attempted to develop a piety of the Lord's Supper in terms of the faith and life of people rather than to articulate a particular way of administering the Lord's Supper. This section will investigate Henry's view of the Lord's Supper in the following order: (1) how Henry understood the meaning, nature, and practice of the Lord's Supper, and (2) how he developed a piety of the Lord's Supper in relation to his understanding of it.

Henry's Understanding of the Lord's Supper

Henry's understanding of the Lord's Supper includes his thought on the meaning, nature, and practice of the sacrament.

The Meaning of the Ordinance of the Lord's Supper

Henry defined the ordinance of the Lord's Supper as "a sacrament, wherein by giving and receiving bread and wine, [Christ's] death is showed forth and the worthy receivers by faith are made partakers of his body and blood, with all his benefits, to their spiritual nourishment, and growth in grace."[138] Henry discussed this ordinance in detail using its names: a sacrament, the Lord's Supper, the communion, the Eucharist, and the feast. First, Henry called this ordinance a sacrament, "by which we are all bound, and are concerned to improve, and live up to."[139] As a sacrament, this ordinance is a sign, "an outward and visible sign of an inward and spiritual grace,"[140] and an oath, "by which we become members of Christ's mystical body."[141]

Second, he called it the Lord's Supper, according to 1 Corinthians 11:20. According to him, the name of the Lord's Supper implies two aspects: Supper for the soul, "which stands in as much need of its daily bread as the body does,"[142] and Christ the Lord's Supper, which means that "the

---

137. Martha Moore-Keish argued that Calvin was a Reformed theologian who attempted to emphasize the people participating in the Lord's Supper. See "Struggling for Balance," in *Do This in Remembrance of Me*, 15–60.
138. Henry, *A Scripture Catechism*, 249.
139. Henry, *Communicant's Companion*, 31.
140. Ibid.
141. Ibid., 33.
142. Ibid., 34.

sanction of this ordinance, is the authority of Christ; the substance of this ordinance, is the grace of Christ."[143]

Third, Henry called it communion. According to Henry, "in this ordinance, we have communion with Christ, our Head: 'truly our fellowship is with Him.'"[144] Supposing union and fellowship, this communion, for Henry, is at the center of human relationship with Christ: "Christ, by his word and spirit, abides in us: we by faith and love abide in him: here, therefore, where Christ seals his word, and offers his Spirit, and where we exercise our faith, and have our love inflamed, there is communion between us and Christ."[145] At the same time, this communion requires us to have communion with the universal church. All Christians, "though they are many, yet they are one; and we express our consent to, and complacency in that union, by partaking of the Lord's Supper."[146]

Fourth, Henry called it the Eucharist, which signifies a thanksgiving. It is called the Eucharist because "Christ in the institution of it gave thanks and we, in the participation of it, must give thanks likewise."[147] So, Henry supposed that thanksgiving should be the business of this ordinance, saying, "let that [ordinance] turn our complaints into praises; for, whatever matter of complaint we find in ourselves, in Christ we find abundant matter for praise, and that is the pleasant subject upon which, in this ordinance, we should dwell."[148]

Fifth, Henry called it the feast, the Christian feast: a royal feast,[149] a marriage-feast,[150] a feast of memorial,[151] a feast of dedication,[152] a feast

143. Ibid., 35.
144. Ibid.
145. Ibid., 37.
146. Ibid.
147. Ibid.
148. Ibid., 38.
149. "A feast like the feast of a king" (ibid., 38).

150. "It is a feast made by a King, at the marriage of his Son: so our Savior represents it, not only to speak exceeding rich and sumptuous, and celebrated with extraordinary expressions of joy and rejoicing, but because the covenant here sealed between Christ and his church is a marriage-covenant, such a covenant as makes two one; a covenant founded in the dearest love, founding the nearest relation, and designed to be perpetual" (ibid., 39).

151. "It is a feast of memorial, like the feast of the Passover, of which it is said, 'this day shall be unto you for a memorial, and you shall keep it a feast to the LORD,—a feast by an ordinance forever'" (ibid., 40).

152. "In the ordinance of the Lord's Supper, we dedicate ourselves to God as living

upon a sacrifice,[153] and a feast upon a covenant.[154] In his time, "it was very common to approach Communion as the Feast."[155] Henry stressed that an important thing in a feast is communion between the LORD and the LORD's people: "a feast is made for free conversation, so is thus for communion between heaven and earth."[156]

These five names of the ordinance specified the various aspects of human communion with God. According to Henry's naming of the ordinance, the sacrament of the Lord's Supper is a religious rite that promotes deep and intimate fellowship of humanity with God by expressing a grateful heart and living in accordance with that ordinance. He did not limit the presence of Christ to the materials of bread and cup; instead, he articulated the active presence of Christ in the human heart and life through taking the elements.

The Nature of the Ordinance of the Lord's Supper

Based on the names of this ordinance, Henry furthermore defined its nature. According to him, the sacrament of Lord's Supper "was appointed to be a commemorating ordinance, and a confessing ordinance, and a communicating ordinance, and a covenanting ordinance."[157] First, the ordinance of the Lord's Supper is a commemorating ordinance. People "do this in remembrance of Christ."[158] Henry articulated the meaning of whom we should remember in this ordinance by explaining the word "me." People should do this "in remembrance of the person of Christ, as an absent friend of ours,"[159] and "in remembrance of the death of Christ."[160] Henry emphasized the importance of the human heart and its fellowship with Christ by

---

temples: temples of the Holy Ghost, separated from everything that is common and profane, and entirely devoted to the service and honor of God in Christ" (ibid., 41).

153. "Jesus Christ is the great and only sacrifice, who by being 'once offered, perfected forever them which are sanctified'; and this offering need never be repeated; that once was sufficient. The Lord's Supper is a feast upon this sacrifice" (ibid.).

154. "In the Lord's Supper we are admitted to feast with God, in token of reconciliation between us and him through Christ" (ibid., 42).

155. Old, "What Is Reformed Spirituality?," 66.

156. Henry, *Communicant's Companion*, 38.

157. Ibid., 43.

158. Cf. BC, Luke 22:19; Henry, *A Scripture Catechism*, 249.

159. Henry, *Communicant's Companion*, 43.

160. Ibid., 45.

indicating that "we endeavor to revive and incite the remembrance of it in our own hearts."[161]

Second, Henry described it as a confessing ordinance.[162] Through this ordinance, people show their faith by professing not only their value and esteem for Christ but also their dependence upon and confidence in Christ.[163] According to Henry, the Lord's Supper "is a solemnity by which we constantly avow the Christian name, and declare ourselves not ashamed of the banner of the cross under which we were enlisted, but resolve to continue as Christ's faithful servants and soldiers to the end of our lives, according to our baptismal vow."[164] In this way, the Lord's Supper as a confessing ordinance influences the way of our life by helping us take the meaning of that ordinance into all areas of life.

Third, the ordinance of the Lord's Supper is a communicating ordinance. People can communicate with God through this ordinance. In it we are "partakers of Christ of 'his merits and righteousness for our justification' and 'his Spirit and grace for our sanctification.'"[165] According to Henry, this communication meant communion between God and people since he defined the cup of blessing as the communion of the blood of Christ and the bread that we break as the communion of the body of Christ.[166] When it comes to communication between the person and God, Henry emphasized human response to and participation in this ordinance: "by the body and blood of Christ, of which this ordinance is the communion, we are to understand all those precious benefits and privileges, which were purchased *for us* by the death of Christ, and are assured *to us* upon gospel terms, in the everlasting covenant."[167] Moreover, Henry attempted to connect the ordinance of communion to the journey of Christian faith by claiming that "our spiritual life is supported and maintained, and the new man enabled for its work and conflicts, by the spiritual benefits of which we here communicate."[168]

---

161. Ibid., 46.
162. *BC*, 1 Corinthians 11:26.
163. Henry, *Communicant's Companion*, 47–49.
164. Ibid., 47.
165. Ibid., 50.
166. Cf. ibid.
167. Ibid., italics added.
168. Ibid., 52.

Fourth, Henry defined this ordinance as a covenanting ordinance. God relates with God's people in the way of the covenant. The cup in this ordinance, according to Henry, is "the New Testament; not only pertaining to the New Testament, but containing it; it has the whole New Testament in it, and has the sum and substance of it."[169] Moreover, Henry understood this ordinance as an external seal of the covenant. This ordinance "was instituted to assure us that God will never forget [the covenant], and to assist us, that we may never forget it."[170] In and by this ordinance as the seal of the new covenant, "God seals to us to be to us a God and we seal to God to be to God a people."[171] In this way, this ordinance "makes our covenanting with God the more solemn, and consequently the more affecting, and the impressions of it the more abiding."[172]

Henry did not treat the issue of the presence of Christ in the ordinance of the Lord's Supper, other than to criticize the doctrine of transubstantiation, "which makes the bread to be changed into the substance of Christ's body, only the accidents of bread remaining; which affronts Christ, destroys the nature of a sacrament, and gives the lie to our senses."[173] Even though he did not ignore the materials in the ordinance of the Lord's Supper, Henry emphasized the relationship between God and the attendants much more than the mode of the presence of Christ in and around the materials. In this way, Henry defined the nature of this ordinance as one that strengthens the relationship between God and God's people. In and by this ordinance, while commemorating Christ, people should profess their faith by showing their communion with God in the covenant of grace.

The Practice of the Lord's Supper

Although he treated the doctrine of the Lord's Supper thoroughly, Henry did not deal with its administration as much. However, his thought on its administration can be inferred from primary and secondary sources. First and foremost, Henry maintained the English Presbyterian frequency of celebrating the Lord's Supper: once a month.[174] In his time, "there [was] a con-

169. Ibid.
170. Ibid., 55.
171. Ibid., 55–56.
172. Ibid., 55.
173. *BC*, Mathew 26:26–30.
174. This was the same frequency as that of Calvin at Geneva, even though Calvin

siderable diversity of modes of celebration of Communion amongst [the Protestants]."[175] Although they agreed that all manners of worship should follow the guidance of the Scriptures, this principle could not be applied to the case of the Lord's Supper. As Horton Davies pointed out, *The Westminster Parliamentary Directory* "laid down no definite rule as to the frequency of celebration."[176] The Presbyterians in Scotland celebrated it quarterly, following *The Book of Discipline*. The Independents "had a weekly celebration of the Lord's Supper generally, but the interval between one Communion and the next was never longer than a month."[177] However, Henry, following the Presbyterian pattern of his father, Philip Henry,[178] "attended to the ordinance of the Lord's Supper with the members of the church on the first Sabbath in every month."[179] According to Williams, Henry "remarked that among the Jews the beginning of the month was esteemed sacred; and, although he did not consider the Jewish law as to the new moons still in force, yet he thought, from general reasoning, the conclusion a safe one, that whatsoever may be our divisions of time, it is always good to begin such divisions with God."[180] In this way, when it comes to the frequency of the administration of the Lord's Supper, Henry differed from the Scottish Presbyterians[181] but followed the practice of Calvin by celebrating it every month.

With regard to the manner of administering the Lord's Supper, Henry treated the administration of the Lord's Supper as he did that of baptism. Although he followed the pattern of *The Westminster Directory*[182] as he

---

wanted to celebrate the Lord's Supper every Lord's Day.

175. Davies, *The Worship of the English Puritans*, 204.

176. Ibid., 213.

177. Ibid.

178. "Usually once a month he administered the ordinance of the Lord's Supper" (Henry, *Life of Mr. Philip Henry*, 134); "The solemn ordinance of the Lord's Supper he constantly celebrated in his congregation once a month" (ibid., 194).

179. Williams, *Memoirs of the Life*, 127.

180. Ibid., 127–28.

181. They followed *The Westminster Directory*; although there was no clear rule of frequency of the Lord's Supper in the *Directory*, "in the debate it was proposed to require at least a quarterly Communion" (Davies, *Worship of the English Puritans*, 213).

182. *The Westminster Directory* contains seven items: (1) an introductory exhortation with a fencing the Table, (2) the reading of the Institution narrative, (3) Eucharistic prayer, (4) Fraction and delivery of the Elements, (5) an Exhortation to a worthy life, (6) A post-communion prayer, and (7) A metrical Psalm of Praise (Westminster Assembly, *A Directory of Public Worship Westminster*, 24–25). Also refer to Davies, *Worship of the*

learned from his father, Philip Henry, Henry did not articulate the manner of administering the ordinance in detail except clarifying that there is no need to kneel down for prayer at the time of administration.[183] Instead, he suggested eight necessary components to be prepared for administrating the Lord's Supper: (1) a house, the gospel church, (2) a table, which is ready spread in the word and ordinances, (3) a laver, which is ready for people to wash in,[184] (4) ministers, whose work is to direct the attendants to the table, (5) company, the communion of saints that invites the attendants into communion with God, (6) a blessing, which is ready to command a blessing upon our spiritual food, (7) the Master, who is ready to bid the attendants welcome, and (8) the provision, which is ready for the attendants' entertainment.[185] As seen in these eight necessary components for administering the Lord's Supper, Henry was much concerned with people's encountering Christ and his blessings in that ordinance. In this way, Henry stressed not so much the manner and meaning of Christ's presence in the materials by their consecration as people's experience of a deep relationship with Christ in the Lord's Supper.

Piety of the Lord's Supper

Henry's main interest was to develop a piety of the Lord's Supper by attempting to relate that ordinance to human life. The Lord's Supper, for Henry, was related to the ongoing experience of the Christian life since "it is the table in Christ's family, at which we are to eat bread continually."[186] Henry developed his own way to improve the Lord's Supper in human life by articulating how people should prepare before, participate in during, and live out their lives after this ordinance. Henry considered the sacrament of the Lord's Supper as a center of human life, and was therefore crucial in shaping our communion with God not only in the ordinance itself but also in ordinary life.

English Puritans, 215.

    183 Cf. Henry, *Life of Mr. Philip Henry*, appendix 18, p. 396.

    184. This is not familiar to contemporary Presbyterian churches, especially Korean Presbyterian churches.

    185. Henry, *Communicant's Companion*, 57–58.

    186. Ibid., 75.

Matthew Henry

Preparing before the Lord's Supper

A piety of the Lord's Supper, for Henry, began with preparation. Before coming to the Table, people should prepare themselves by examining their own hearts and lives, renewing their covenants with God, and practicing a daily exercise of meditation and prayer. All these preparations were to help people live their life in communion with God as well as promote the ordinance of the Lord's Supper.

First, Henry asked people to prepare themselves, claiming that "the duty most expressly required in our preparation for the ordinance of the Lord's Supper, is that of self-examination."[187] He supposed that "it is not enough that we seek God in a due ordinance, but we must seek him in a due order, that is, we must stir up ourselves to take hold on him."[188] He was also convinced that "much of our communion with God is kept up by the renewing of our conversation with him, and the frequent interchanging of solemn assurances."[189] With these thoughts in mind, Henry declared that "to examine ourselves is to discourse with our own hearts."[190] More particularly, it is "to put serious questions to ourselves, and to our own hearts; and to prosecute them till a full and true answer be given to them." Henry gave six questions: (1) What am I? (2) What have I done? (3) What am I doing? (4) What progress do I make? (5) What do I want? 6) What shall I resolve to do?[191] All these questions imply that people should properly identify themselves and that human life is a journey heading in a direction. The answers to these six questions help people identify themselves and lead their life in a specific direction or goal. Henry gave more specific questions for each of the six broad questions.[192] All these questions help people examine themselves and identify whether they belong not to the world but to God and are willing to live a holy life, transforming their heart, thought, conversation, relations, and so forth. So, before the Lord's Supper, in preparation for it, people must examine the state of their relationship with God, other people, and the world.

---

187. Ibid., 81.
188. Ibid.
189. Ibid., 76.
190. Ibid., 82.
191. Ibid., 85.
192. Ibid., 85–104.

Matthew Henry's Theology of the Sacraments

Second, Henry required people to renew their covenant with God. The covenantal relationship of humans with God began with their baptism. However, according to Henry, "we are not owned and accepted as God's people, 'though we come before him as his people come,' and sit before him as his people sit, if we do not in sincerity 'avouch the LORD for our God.'"[193] He also confirmed that the Lord's Supper is the right place for this by saying that "in our baptism this was done for us, in the Lord's Supper we must do it for ourselves, else we do nothing."[194] Henry addressed the method and manner of renewing the covenant in preparation for the Lord's Supper. In order to enter into the covenant with God, people should be transformed in their heart, thought, and life by repenting of sins, renouncing everything that stands in opposition to God, and resigning themselves to God considerately, humbly, cheerfully, and sincerely. Henry asked people to "bewail the inconsistency of their hearts and lives with the terms of the covenant."[195] After repenting from their sins, people should redirect their way of life by renouncing the devil, the world, and the flesh.[196] According to Henry, this process of transforming life cannot be practiced without God's grace and power, which is guaranteed by the covenant. Thus, people should resign and give up themselves to God with their all hearts and minds. For Henry, without human life being transformed, a renewal of the covenant cannot take place in the ordinance of the Lord's Supper. Therefore, in order to renew the covenant with God, people "must consecrate themselves to God's name, as living temples"[197] before coming to the Lord's Supper.

Third, Henry asked people to practice meditation and prayer on a daily basis in order to prepare for the Lord's Supper, mentioning that "meditation and prayer are the daily exercise and delight of a devout and pious soul."[198] Meditation and prayer lie at the core of humanity's relationship with themselves and with God since "in meditation we converse with ourselves; in prayer we converse with God."[199] Henry connected these two daily practices to the ordinance of the Lord's Supper by pointing out that "they who are frequent and serious in these holy duties at other times, will find them

---

193. Ibid., 106.
194. Ibid.
195. Ibid., 107.
196. Ibid., 108–11.
197. Ibid., 114.
198. Ibid., 125.
199. Ibid.

the easier and the sweeter on this occasion."²⁰⁰ Henry described the practice of meditation: "to meditate is not only to think seriously of divine things but to think of them with concern and suitable affection."²⁰¹ In meditation, people should think of their journey of salvation in and through life: from the sinfulness and misery of man's fallen state to the glory of the divine attributes, shining forth in the work of human redemption, with a focus on Christ's life, suffering, and present glory in heaven. So, before taking the bread and cup, people should have already meditated upon the presence and work of Christ in all their journey of life. Moreover, he regarded the practice of prayer as at the center of a human's relationship with God; "communion with God in prayer prepares and disposes the mind for communion with him in other duties."²⁰² "In prayer, the soul ascends to God, and converses with him; and thereby the mind is prepared to receive the visits of his grace, and habituated to holy exercises."²⁰³ In this way, Henry attempted to connect human life to God by emphasizing the role of prayer in preparing for the Lord's Supper.

Participating in the Lord's Supper

In addition to the need to prepare themselves, people need to "come to this ordinance with earnest desires towards God and communion with him."²⁰⁴ Though Henry did not engage the debate on the presence of Christ in the sacrament, he presupposed that Christ is present and even acts in the participants' hearts and thoughts through taking the bread and cup. With that conviction, Henry taught people that they can take an opportunity to be

---

200. Ibid.
201. Ibid., 127.
202. Ibid., 140.
203. Ibid.

204. Ibid., 153. Human participation in the Lord's Supper begins with coming to this ordinance. Henry treated how to come to this ordinance in detail. Briefly, there are nine attitudes to be taken: (1) a fixedness of thought, (2) an evenness and calmness of affection, (3) a holy awe and reverence of the Divine Majesty, (4) holy jealousy over ourselves and an humble sense of our own unworthiness, (5) a gracious confidence, as children to a father, to a father's table, (6) honest desires towards God and communion with him, (7) raised expectations, (8) rejoicing and thanksgiving, which goes together, and (9) charity with all men and with a sincere affection to all good Christians. For more detailed explanation, see ibid., 144–62.

Matthew Henry's Theology of the Sacraments

transformed by the grace of Christ as they participate in seeing, tasting, and digesting the sacrament.

First and foremost, in this ordinance, Henry required people to contemplate that which is represented and set before them: "[B]ehold we are all invited to see [Christ the Lamb] in a sacramental representation."[205] In order to contemplate, people should see Christ as the Lamb "that had been slain, opening the seals."[206] According to Henry, this helps people see "many other things, which they may infer from that general representation of the sufferings of Christ."[207] They need to see six things: the evil of sin, the justice of God, the love of Christ, the conquest of Satan, the worth of souls, and the purchase of the blessings of the new covenant.[208] Here, Henry intended to motivate the transformation of human life by letting participants see the love and power of Christ in not only saving them from their sinful sates but also giving them the foundation of all their joys and hopes. Thus, by seeing these particular six things, people must resolve to live their new lives as lives that have been given to them by the love and grace of Christ.

Second, in the Lord's Supper, according to Henry, people must not only see, but also eat of the sacrifice, since "the bread which came down from heaven was not designed merely for showing bread; but for bread to be fed upon."[209] By eating and tasting the bread and cup, people can develop their relationship with God in of all life. A most clear benefit to be received by eating in this ordinance is the grace of Christ, since the Lord's Supper is "the ordinary vehicle in which grace is conveyed to the souls of believers."[210] Henry indicated that this grace is not only for justification but also for sanctification, saying that "Jesus Christ, in this ordinance, made of God to all believers not only righteousness, but sanctification; so we must receive him; and having received him, so we must walk in him."[211] In particular, Henry reminded people of the necessity of grace given from the Lord's Supper in ordinary life as well as salvation: "We come to this throne of grace, this mercy-seat, this table of our God, that here we may not only obtain mercy to pardon, but may find grace to help in every time of need, grace to ex-

205. Ibid., 163.
206. Ibid.
207. Ibid., 165.
208. Ibid., 165–79.
209. Ibid., 179.
210. Ibid., 191.
211. Ibid., 190.

cite us to, to direct us in, and thoroughly furnish for every good word and work, according as the duty of every day requires."[212] In this way, Henry stressed that eating and tasting in the ordinance were essential for people in receiving the grace for developing their relation with God in salvation and in all of life.

Third, besides seeing and eating, Henry required people to digest the sacrament in their hearts. He attempted to relate the sacrament to human life by pointing out that "if what is here done do not affect us for the present, it will not be likely to influence us afterwards."[213] For Henry, digesting the sacraments meant affecting hearts, which he regarded as a crucial function in participating in the Lord's Supper, a process of changing the heart from being sorrowful for sins to delighting in God by the grace of Christ.[214] According to Henry, this affecting of the human heart also influences the relationship with God by letting people "be filled with serious desires to know and do their duty, in return for that great love."[215] Thus, the affected participants in the sacrament, before leaving the sacrament, must "make solemn vows to God that they will diligently and faithfully serve God."[216] Regarding duty, Henry remarked that we must "cease to do evil, and learn to do well; that we must put off the old man, and put on the new."[217] To put it another way, participants "must, by a solemn vow, bind themselves against all sin."[218] Moreover, they must promise and vow that they "will live a life of communion with God,"[219] by obliging themselves to "those duties of their respective callings and relations."[220]

As demonstrated above, in and through the sacrament, Henry endeavored to develop a piety of the Lord's Supper by helping people see, taste, and digest it toward the end of fostering a deep relationship with God in Christ. Thus, as Henry pointed out, "a believer receives some of the present benefit of it, in and by this ordinance, both in the comfortable experience

212. Ibid., 192–93.
213. Ibid., 201.
214. Ibid., 202–12.
215. Ibid., 215.
216. Ibid., 219.
217. Ibid., 221–22.
218. Ibid., 222; cf. his first series of sermon topic is related to life conforming to the sacraments.
219. Ibid., 228.
220. Ibid., 232.

of communion with God in grace, and the comfortable expectation of the vision and fruition of God in glory."[221]

Practices Following the Lord's Supper

Henry's piety of the Lord's Supper also articulated a right manner of life after partaking the ordinance. Henry indicated the necessity of practicing the Lord's Supper in life, stating that "the Lord's Supper was instituted not only for the solemnizing of the memorial of Christ's death at certain times but for the preserving of the remembrance of it in our minds at all times."[222] In order to develop an appropriate manner of life from the Lord's Supper, Henry kept applying his thought of communion with God: people that had communion with God through Christ at the table should show their fellowship with God in their lives. The communion with God, for Henry, can be exemplified in the course of human conversation: "we may, in the whole course of our conversation, exemplify the blessed fruits and effects of our communion with God in this ordinance."[223]

Henry held that the Lord's Supper gave the basic rule for human conversation:

> [I]n the Lord's Supper we see what Christ had done for us, and we receive what he bestows on us; and, in consideration of both, we must set ourselves, not only to love and praise him, but to walk before him in the land of the living; that though we cannot return him any equivalent for his kindness, yet, by complying with his will, and consulting his honor, we may show that we bear a grateful mind, and would render again according to the benefit done unto us.[224]

In this way, for Henry, the Lord's Supper must have evidences of a holy and sober conversation in participant's care that they "never say or do anything to be reproach of the gospel, and Christ's holy religion, or which may give any occasion to the enemies of the LORD to blaspheme."[225]

Moreover, Henry supposed that human conversations could be a verification of their communion with God: "our conversation must be such that

221. Ibid., 180.
222. Ibid., 259–60.
223. Ibid., 259.
224. Ibid., 263.
225. Ibid., 260.

we may evidence the communion we have had with God in Christ at the Lord's Table."[226] Therefore, Henry exhorted his followers:

> [W]e must therefore show that we have fellowship with Christ, by walking in the light. By keeping up communion with God in providences, having our eyes ever towards him, and acknowledging him in all our ways; receiving all our comforts as the gifts of his bounty, and bearing all our afflictions as his fatherly chastisements, we evidence that we have had communion with him in ordinances.[227]

So, for Henry, "it is not enough to say that we have fellowship with Christ"; "they that have communion with the holy God should make it appear in all holy conversation, not suffering any corrupt communication to proceed out of their mouth, but abounding in that which is good, and to the use of edifying."[228]

By emphasizing that the communion with God in the Lord's Supper should be verified in human conversation, Henry attempted to develop a Christian piety based on the ordinance. He even chose the topic of a well-ordered conversation as his Lord's Day preaching subject for almost two years, beginning in July 1689.[229] In this regard, a changed life, demonstrated by transformed human speech, was crucial to Henry's thought as he constructed a piety of the Lord's Supper.

CONCLUSION: HENRY'S SACRAMENTAL PRINCIPLE AND ITS EVALUATION

Henry developed the Reformed principle of the sacraments by articulating it in great detail for his ministerial context. Most of all, Henry regarded the sacraments as a means of developing human communion with God through life. As signs and seals, the sacraments, for Henry, played a crucial role in human fellowship with God by providing people with practical guides for Christian life. This was a much more articulated teaching of Calvin's understanding of the sacraments. Calvin regarded the sacraments

---

226. Ibid., 266.
227. Ibid.
228. Ibid.
229 Cf. Williams, *Memoirs of the Life*, 274–75.

as "aid to our faith."[230] He also defined the sacraments, stating that "it is an outward sign by which the LORD seals on our consciences the promises of his good will toward us in order to sustain the weakness of our faith."[231] Henry followed Calvin's definition by understanding that the sacraments were the signs and seals of God's covenantal promise, and furthermore, he articulated Calvin's teaching on the sacraments by regarding them as a principle of Christian life as well as an aid to faith.

Second, Henry emphasized another aspect of Calvin's definition of the sacraments: human piety toward Christ. Calvin gave us a definition of sacrament: "one may call it a testimony of divine grace toward us, confirmed by an outward sign, with mutual attestation of our piety toward him."[232] As seen in this definition, the sacraments, on the one hand, mean a divine grace toward people. On the other hand, they require of people piety toward Christ. As Bromiley indicated, in Reformed tradition, "the supreme thing about the sacraments is that they are the means of the grace of God. But the fact that I am the recipient underlines the fact that the grace of God is for me and that I must accept it."[233] Henry emphasized this aspect of human piety in his understanding and practice of the sacraments. It may seem that Henry regarded the sacraments as the work of people or emphasized the principle *ex opere operantis* (from the work of the one working). However, Henry never denied that the sacraments were the means of divine grace toward people. Yet Henry understood the sacraments as the means of grace working not in us but for us. So the piety toward Christ in and through the Christian life based on the sacraments was not human work leading the grace but human response to God by actively participating in the divine grace.

Third, Henry followed Calvin's position by accepting baptism and the Lord's Supper as the only two sacraments to be kept in the church. Although he practiced confirmation and marriage as important parts of ecclesiastical ministry, Henry did not regard them as sacraments to be performed like baptism and the Lord's Supper. The difference between Calvin and Henry was the particular emphasis based on their ministerial contexts. Calvin attempted to define the meaning of baptism and to argue the issue of the presence of Christ in the Lord's Supper. Unlike Calvin, Henry did

---

230. Calvin, *Institutes*, 4.14.1.
231. Ibid.
232. Ibid.
233. Bromiley, *Sacramental Teaching and Practice in the Reformed Churches*, 19.

not spend much time to articulate the meaning of baptism and the Lord's Supper. Rather, he endeavored to develop more practical improvement of baptism and the Lord's Supper by directing people how to prepare before, participate in, and practice following the sacraments. One of reasons that Henry emphasized this practical way of improving the sacraments was because he was responding to legalistic practice and participation. To Henry's eye, both the Roman Catholic and the Church of England required people to legalistically do the practice without teaching them more practical ways of improving them.

Fourth, Henry followed Calvin by emphasizing that the effect of the sacrament was not restricted to a single moment. It "extends to the whole life of the Christian."[234] Calvin emphasized the lifelong effect of the sacraments by understanding that baptism is a token of cleansing for the whole of life,[235] and the Lord's Supper is a spiritual feeding for our eternal life.[236] Henry's main concern was to extend the effect of the sacraments to all through life; they were not just a single or a periodic rite but also a principle guide of ordinary life. Henry emphasized the new life in relation to the sacraments.[237] He regarded the sacraments as pivotal references to the whole life of believers by emphasizing the pattern of putting off the old humanity and putting on the new.[238] Moreover, as indicated above, *A Treatise on Baptism* and *The Communicant's Companion*, the two main works of Henry on the sacraments, attempted to develop not so much the way of administrating the sacraments as their effect by improving ordinary life in conformity to the sacraments.

In sum, by emphasizing the transformation of human life, rooted in the sacraments, Henry articulated how to develop deep communion or fellowship with God and other people. So, contemporary Reformed

---

234. Ibid., 32.

235. Calvin, *Institutes*, 4.15.3.

236. Ibid., 4.17.4–8.

237. Henry even more emphasized the effect of the sacraments on human life by preaching on the sacramental life as the first subject of his series of sermons, from July 1687 to February 1691. Williams also pointed out "that at which Henry so diligently aimed at was the improvement of the means of grace; and the effects were visible in the whole of his demeanor" (Williams, *Memoirs of the Life*, 218).

238. Geoffrey Bromiley, in *Sacramental Teaching and Practice in the Reformation Churches*, points out that sacraments and their connection to human life was a crucial lesson in the Reformed churches. In addition, Davies points out that "the Calvinist insistence upon a holy life as the worship most acceptable to God was underlined" (Davies, *Worship of the English Puritans*, 160).

Presbyterian churches can find in Henry rich resources as they seek to allow the sacraments to permeate more deeply into all areas of human life.

However, in the study of worship, the actual practice of liturgy is crucial since the meaning of the liturgy is deeply related to its practice. Although he developed and articulated a Reformed sacramental principle by emphasizing human communion with God in ordinary life, Henry did not articulate or leave any prescribed rubrics for the administration of the sacraments. Therefore, it can be difficult for contemporary readers to glean insights from Henry on the actual practice of administering the sacraments in public gatherings. This, of course, does not mean that he ignored the significance of ritual or the actual practice of baptism and the Lord's Supper. Rather, from his writings we understand that Henry was more concerned to connect and apply the sacraments to human life.

5

Reformed Tradition in Henry's Presbyterian Public Worship Service

IN THE PREVIOUS TWO chapters, this book has examined how Henry developed a Reformed Presbyterian understanding of worship and the sacraments, mainly through reference to his own works. Keeping in mind his overarching principle idea of human communion with God (chapter 2), Henry articulated not only a liturgical pattern of relationship between humanity and God in worship (chapter 3) but also a godly life conforming to the sacraments in daily basis (chapter 4). He attempted to show that human life should be lived in communion with God by means of the worship service and godliness expressed in everyday life. He based this conviction on his reading and interpretation of the Bible. By emphasizing the Bible and everyday life in shaping Christian piety, Henry revealed Reformed characteristics in his thought, as demonstrated in previous chapters. Henry did not confine his thoughts to the "theology" of worship. Rather, he extended his practical theological understanding to various ministerial duties of worship such as preaching, praying, and the administration of the sacraments. These practices have already been addressed in the previous chapters.

However, there have been few interpretations and evaluations of the practices of Henry's worship ministry as well as his theology of worship, though there have been some attempts to interpret his general thoughts regarding preaching, as shown in chapter 2. In order to find any lessons from Henry in the sphere of Christian worship, it is also necessary for contemporary readers to understand and interpret the actual practices he

Reformed Tradition in Henry's Presbyterian Public Worship Service

advocated, in addition to his thoughts on worship. This chapter will consider in detail Henry's practice of Lord's Day public worship. As shown in chapter 1, Henry practiced his public worship in a time of freedom of worship. He neither articulated any prescribed liturgy nor wrote any manual of worship for the Presbyterian congregation at Chester. Instead, Henry led and practiced a Presbyterian worship service based on his understanding on the Bible and what he had learned from his own experiences under his father, Philip Henry. His practice of public worship can be regarded as an application of Reformed worship for an English Presbyterian congregation in the late seventeenth and early eighteenth centuries. As an example of Reformed Presbyterian worship, Henry's public worship service may provide contemporary Presbyterian churches with some insights on how to worship God in a similar context of freedom by suggesting a Reformed principle of worship, rather than a strict Reformed formula.[1]

Thus, the main goal of this chapter is to argue that Henry followed the Reformed tradition in the practice of worship as well as in its theology. Although Henry had lived under the influence of Puritans, he himself chose to be ordained as Presbyterian divine. We can infer from this choice that Henry wanted to continue the Reformed tradition instead of being regarded as a nonconformist Puritan minister in his ecclesiastical ministry. And considering his intention to be a Presbyterian minister, it can be argued that Henry's ministry was determined not just by his social and political environment as defined in chapter 1 but also by the Reformed theological tradition. At the time of Henry's ministry, Reformed theology had a history of over a century. Among the main influential Reformers were John Calvin, John Knox, Richard Baxter, the Westminster Assembly, and Philip Henry, who contributed to the development of worship in the Reformed tradition.

In order to examine aspects of the Reformed tradition in Henry's public worship service, this chapter will first describe and analyze the practice of Henry's public worship service in detail. Next, by comparing his worship with previous Reformed worship practice, I will argue that Henry developed Reformed worship not by adopting previous worship patterns but by following the principles of Reformed worship with creative accommodation.

---

1. There is no proof that Henry regarded his practice of public worship as a set form for any time and place. According to Hughes Old, that kind of attempt is called "archaeological reconstruction." Reformed tradition does not take that method since "an archaeological reconstruction rarely meets the needs of the time" (Old, *Worship That Is Reformed According to Scripture*, 158).

Matthew Henry

THE PRACTICE OF HENRY'S PUBLIC WORSHIP SERVICE

This section will explore the practice of Henry's Lord's Day public worship. Simply listing the elements of the worship service is not enough to understand its real practice, although it provides a starting point. To understand Henry's public worship service we need to examine the specific content and practice of each element. So, this section will analyze characteristics in Henry's public worship service in as much detail as possible.

The Lord's Day Public Worship Service

The practice of Henry's public worship was briefly addressed in the discussion of occasions or opportunities of worship in chapter 3. Henry practiced two services of public worship on the Lord's Day: in the morning at nine o'clock and in the late afternoon. His congregation attended the public worship services at their meeting house. In their biographies of Henry, Tong and Williams introduced basic information on the practice of Henry's Lord's Day public worship. However, their descriptions did not include specific content beyond basic information on the order of the worship service. With help from related primary and secondary sources, Henry's practice of public worship on the Lord's Day can be delineated as follows:

Singing the 100th Psalm[2]

With one consent let all the earth
To God their cheerful voices raise;
Serve ye the LORD with awful mirth,
And sing before him songs of praise,
The LORD ye know, is God alone.
Who us without our aid did make,
Us for his flock vouchsafes to own,
And for his pasture-sheep to take.
O enter then his temple-gate,
And to his courts devoutly press,
And still your grateful hymns repeat,
And still his name with praises bless.

   2. Henry's *Family Hymns* included this psalm as Hymn 74. See *Family Hymns*, 439. However, there is no record of the tune for this psalm.

For he's the LORD supremely good,
His mercy is forever sure;
His truth, which always firmly stood,
To endless ages shall endure.

Short prayer[3]

Thou, O God, art greatly to be feared in the assembly of the saints, and to be had in reverence of all them that are about thee. O give us grace to worship thee with reverence and godly fear, because thou our God art a consuming fire. . . .

We come together to give glory to the great Jehovah, who in six days made heaven and earth, the sea, and all that in them is, and rested the seventh day, and therefore blessed a Sabbath-day, and hallowed it. . . . O let us be new creatures, thy workmanship, created in Jesus Christ unto good works. . . .

We come together to give glory to the LORD Jesus Christ, and to sanctify this Sabbath to his honor, who was the stone that the builders refused, but is now become the head-stone of the corner. . . . O that we may this day experience the power of Christ's resurrection, and may be planted together in the likeness of it, that as Christ was raised up from the dead by the glory of the Father, so we also may walk in newness of life. . . .

We come together to give glory to the blessed Spirit of grace, and to celebrate the memorial of the giving of that promise of the Father, in whom the apostles received power on the first day of the week, as on that day Christ arose. . . . O that we may this day be filled with the Holy Ghost, and that the fruit of the Spirit in us may be in all goodness, and righteousness, and truth.

We come together to testify our communion with the universal church; that though we are many, yet we are one; that we worship one and the same God, the Father, of whom are all things, and we in him, in the name of one Lord Jesus Christ, by whom are all things, and we by him; under the conduct of the same Spirit, one and the self-same Spirit, who divideth to every man severally as he will.

---

3. One clear thing in Henry's teaching on prayer is that the contents of prayer must be based on Scripture. At the end of his ministry he published *A Method for Prayer* (1710), and it included a lot of sample prayers for various occasions as well as principles of prayer. The prayer quoted was called prayer "at the entrance upon the public worship on the Lord's day, by the masters of the assemblies." He used this prayer and encouraged other pastors to use it as a sample.

Matthew Henry

Reading some parts of the Old Testament (morning) or the New Testament (afternoon)

Henry read and expounded part (usually less than one chapter) of the Bible, proceeding *seriatim* through the Scriptures, beginning with the book of Genesis.[4]

Exposition[5]

Each reading was expounded in a plain and understandable way.

Singing another Psalm[6]

Pastoral Prayer[7]

Half an hour of extemporaneous prayer.

Preaching[8]

A sermon, roughly one hour in length, on a specific aspect of the nature of God and the Christian life.

---

4. Henry followed neither the Church Calendar nor used the Lectionary in reading and expounding the Scriptures.

5. As is well known, all his expositions were published in the form of Bible commentaries.

6. There was no record of what psalm Henry sang for this time of singing. *Family Hymns* included twenty-four hymns under the title "Hymns of Praise, to be sung to the Tune of the 100th Psalm, and the 148th." These twenty-four hymns were sung to the same tune. It can thus be assumed that Henry may have sung these twenty-four hymns in public worship.

7. As Williams described, "about half an hour was devoted to intercession" (Williams, *Memoirs of the Life*, 110). Although this was an extemporaneous prayer, Henry prepared well for it, concerning the congregation, community, and nation.

8. As examined in chap. 2, Henry's preaching followed a series of subjects.

Reformed Tradition in Henry's Presbyterian Public Worship Service

Prayer[9]

[Lord's Supper][10]

Exhortation
Words of Institution
Matthew 26:26 or 1 Corinthian 11:24–25
Prayer (Thanksgiving)
Taking Bread and Cup
    By delivering the materials to the pews
Prayer

Singing the 117th Psalm (usually)[11]

Let all mankind express their mirth
Unto the LORD in joyful songs,
And render him from all the earth
The homage that to him belongs.
For from his plenteous mercies store
He doth continual grace afford,
His truth likewise lasts evermore;
For ever therefore praise the LORD

---

9. This is a short extempore prayer. There is no record of the content of this prayer.

10. On the first Lord's Day of every month.

11. This psalm is Hymn 75 in *Family Hymns*. In the afternoon Henry sang the 134th Psalm or some part of 136th Psalm. The lyrics of the 134th Psalm of Hymn 76 in *Family Hymns* are this:

Behold, ye servants of the LORD,
Which in his house by night do stand,
Bless ye his name, his praise record,
Devoutly lifting up your hand.
I' the sanctuary bless his name,
Praise him, O praise him thankfully:
The LORD that heaven and earth did frame,
From Sion bless us plenteously.

Matthew Henry

Benediction[12]

Characteristics of Henry's Lord's Day Public Worship Service

Henry consistently followed this pattern for the Lord's Day public worship. This service took about two and half hours, with thirty minutes of exposition, thirty minutes of pastoral prayer, an hour-long sermon, and other orders of singing and reading the Bible.[13] He also practiced the Lord's Supper on the first Lord's Day in every month.[14] As one can see, the structure of this public worship service was not complex. Except for the Lord's Table, the elements of this service were composed of praising, praying, and preaching. Besides these three main elements, there was no provision for offering or announcements. Several common characteristics emerge from a closer look at the practice of Henry's Lord's Day public worship.

First, there were three times of praising in public worship: at the beginning, in the middle, and before the end. People sang together in worship; there was no music by a choir or solo, separate from the congregation as a whole. Henry also included only psalms in public worship, although he compiled some other songs from the New Testament, such as Luke and Revelation, and excerpts from the hymns of St. Ambrose, found in his music book, *Family Hymns*. The first and last psalms in worship were sung to the same tune. Besides this, it is not certain what kind of melody was used in singing the psalms. By singing the psalms, all the attendants actively participated in the service. In addition, as explained in chapter 3, most of those present already knew the lyrics, because each family member had a copy of *Family Hymns* for use in family worship, and Henry chose the metrical psalms from there. In praise, Henry normally "preferred *scriptural* psalms and hymns to those which are wholly of human composition."[15] Williams described how Henry delighted in praising:

> In the work of praise he greatly delighted. It is congenial with devout sensibility, and was eminently suited to his lively and thankful temper. Having, when young, heard his excellent father say, "that our praying-days should be praising-days; that whatever the

12. It is not clear which blessing Henry used as benediction.
13. Williams, *Memoirs of the Life*, 110.
14. Ibid., 127.
15. Ibid., 110.

cup is, we should take notice of the mixtures," he never forgot it. And he, sometimes, devoutly observed, that "a life of praise, and a life of usefulness is a true angelical life."[16]

He preferred scriptural songs and emphasized the attendants' active and delightful participation as they sang together.

Second, there were also three times of prayer in the service of public worship, led by the minister. The first prayer was short, and it focused on inviting people to the worship service. This short prayer, however, was not just an invitation. A Trinitarian approach to Christian worship is clearly evident in this prayer. Through this prayer, people confessed that they came to glorify the Trinitarian God (*We come together to give glory to the great Jehovah, the LORD Jesus Christ, and the blessed Spirit of grace*) and testify to their union with the church catholic (*We come together to testify to our communion with the universal church*). By this short prayer, Henry emphasized that Christian worship was at the center of people's encounter with the Trinity and the universal church.

The second prayer was a more extended, intercessory prayer. This pastoral prayer before preaching emphasized the working of the Holy Spirit, calling upon the Spirit for grace,[17] although he did not call it the "Illuminative Prayer" as Calvin did. Henry spent almost thirty minutes on that prayer. Henry by himself indicated the basic foundation of this intercessory prayer, called pastoral prayer, as follows:

> Our LORD Jesus has taught us to pray, not only with, but for, others; and the apostle hath appointed us to make supplication for all saints; and many of his prayers in his epistles are for his friends: and we must not think, that when we are in this part of prayer, we may be less fervent, and be more indifferent, because we ourselves are not immediately concerned in it, but rather, let a holy fire of love, both to God and man, here make our devotions yet more warm and lively.[18]

Williams described the manner and characteristic of Henry's public prayer in detail:

---

16. Ibid., 111.

17. Williams indicated that "Henry was large and full in praying for grace, and used to mention the particular graces of the Holy Spirit" (Henry, *Memoirs of the Life*, 111).

18. Henry, *A Method for Prayer*, in *Complete Works*, 2:48.

> In the exercise of publick and social prayer, Mr. Henry was almost unrivalled. There was no pompous finery; no abstruse and complex elaboration; no disgusting familiarity; no personal reproofs or compliments; no vain repetitions; no preaching. He prayed, and his style was reverent, humble, simple, and devout. By impressive comprehensiveness; by the happiest adaptation of his petitions to circumstances; and, by peculiar fervency of manner, he successfully stimulated his fellow worshippers.[19]

While the minister led prayers, the attendants must have participated in that prayer by following with their heart.

The third prayer was a short prayer of exhortation following the sermon. Except for this, there is no reference to the style and content of that prayer. Overall, Henry developed the role of prayer as a crucial part of public worship. Although he did not reject the use of written prayers in the worship service, Henry preferred a well-prepared comprehensive prayer over a written set of prayers. In this regard, he emphasized the responsibility of the minister in leading public prayer.[20]

Third, the Word was at the center of Henry's public worship service. People needed to read the Scripture and listen to the preacher expounding what they read. It is not clear whether they read the Scripture aloud together, or if a representative of the congregation such as minister or rector read the passage. Regardless of the specific way, the reading of Scripture, along with its exposition, was a crucial part of Henry's public worship service. Reading and expounding the Scriptures, as Rowland Ward pointed out, was "a practice already common among the Independent in England,"[21] even before *The Westminster Directory*. Also, preaching was something separate from reading and expounding the Scriptures.[22] Henry continued

---

19. Williams, *Memoirs of the Life*, 111.

20. Hughes Old pointed out that Henry was a crucial pastor who developed a principle of ministerial prayer in worship; see Old, *Leading in Public Prayer*, 98.

21. Ward, "The Directory for Public Worship," 122. He also commented that "indeed, strange as it may seem, reading the Scripture as a distinct element in worship was widely absent from Scottish services until the nineteenth century, being swallowed up by the expository comments—hence the direction of the Established Church of Scotland Assembly in 1856" (ibid.). Many contemporary Reformed Presbyterian churches also omitted the reading and expounding of the Scriptures as essential elements of public worship.

22. As Ward pointed out based on Hughes Old's book, *Reading and Preaching of the Scriptures*, 5:28–30, "the exposition of Scripture was favored by the early Reformers and a doctrinal discourse on an isolated text was more usual in the pre-Reformation context" (Ward, "Directory for Public Worship," 122).

Reformed Tradition in Henry's Presbyterian Public Worship Service

to expound the Scriptures as an essential part of public worship. The daily prayer that included exposition that was in Calvin's practice of ministry was, for Henry, worked out at home, not in the church gathering, so there was no exposition upon the Scriptures by ministers during the weekday. As Williams pointed out, "the expounding of Holy Scripture, an ancient and invaluable custom, uniformly formed, on the Sabbath, a part of Mr. Henry's publick services in the evening, as well as the morning."[23] While he was ministering for the congregation at Chester, Henry "explained to them, more than once, the whole of the sacred oracles."[24] By this exposition of the Scriptures, Henry articulated an aspect of edification in the service of public worship as a peculiar characteristic of English Presbyterian worship. With the conviction that "it is the duty of all Christians diligently to search the Scriptures, and it is the office of ministers to guide and assist them therein,"[25] Henry continued to read and expound the Scriptures as significant and separate parts of public worship.

Beside this, Henry spent about one hour on preaching, the central part of his public worship service. His preaching was not directly related to the parts or chapters of reading and expounding Scriptures. He preached a series of topics, as examined in chapter 2. An examination of the characteristics of his preaching is beyond the scope of this work, though a few brief comments may be made here. Williams noted that "in the pulpit . . . Mr. Henry's talents shone with their fullest brilliance."[26] Among many remarkable things in his preaching, the variety of sermon topics and his approach to them were very impressive. His sermon topic developed his doctrine of God and human salvation, as examined in chapter 2.

With regard to Henry's Scripture texts for sermons, Williams commented that "he preferred employing different texts for the discussion of even the same general truth; an improvement well adapted to relieve both the preacher and hearers from the wearisome insipidity inseparable from continued iteration."[27] One last thing to be mentioned is the practice of reading the Scriptures in worship. People in Henry's public worship would have read the Scriptures only for the verses of exposition, not those used for preaching. There was no reading of the Scriptures for the sermon as

---

23. Williams, *Memoirs of the Life*, 112.
24. Ibid.
25. *BC*, preface to vol. 1.
26. Williams, *Memoirs of the Life*, 113.
27. Ibid., 111.

a separate element. In reality, Henry chose only one or two verses as the Scriptures for each Lord's Day preaching. His thematic preaching on the Lord's Day worship service did not include reading the Scriptures for the sermon as an essential order. In Henry's ministry, reading the Scriptures in worship was for the exposition. So, contemporary readers must be aware that reading the Scriptures in worship without expounding them as an essential order had a different meaning from that of Henry's ministry. At the same time, contemporary Reformed Presbyterian churches must recover reading and expounding the Scriptures as essential elements of public worship or public gatherings such as various ministerial programs for learning the Bible besides public worship.

Fourth, Henry celebrated the Lord's Supper once a month, which was the same practice as that of Calvin at Geneva. This was different from that of the Scotland Presbyterian churches' quarterly observance. Except for the frequency, there have been few descriptions of the administrative pattern of Henry's Lord's Supper except for the circumstances of the ordinance.[28] However, it is certain that he included the four essential components for the Lord's Supper (exhortation,[29] words of institution, prayer, and partaking of the elements). There was no record that he used any prescribed prayer or included even the Reformed *Sursum corda* (Let us lift up our hearts)[30] in the Lord's Supper. Henry differed from Calvin in his excluding the Reformed *Sursum corda*. Today contemporary Presbyterian churches, including Korean Presbyterian churches, that were influenced by Henry and other Presbyterian churches tend to ignore the Reformed *Sursum corda* in their administration of the Lord's Supper. Regarding "self-examination," the communicants needed to practice this before the administration of the

---

28. Refer to the section on practice of the Lord's Supper in chap. 4, 194–96.

29. Following Calvin's practice of the Lord's Supper, Henry also placed an exhortation at the beginning. However, unlike Calvin, Henry did not sing the Decalogue before the exhortation.

30. Reformed liturgy in the early Reformation time retained the *Sursum corda* even though there were differences in specific forms. Calvin indicated the significance of *Sursum corda* in the Lord's Supper: "For, in order that pious souls may duly apprehend Christ in the Supper, they must be raised up to heaven. . . . It was established of old that before consecration the people should be told in a loud voice to lift up their hearts. Scripture itself also not only carefully recounts to us the ascension of Christ, by which he withdrew the presence of his body from our sight and company, to shake from us all carnal thinking of him, but also, whenever it recalls him, bids our minds be raised up, and seek him in heaven, seated at the right hand of the Father" (Calvin, *Institutes of the Christian Religion*, 4.17.38).

Supper, as indicated in his *Communicant's Companion*.³¹ In the biography of his father, Philip Henry, Matthew Henry did not describe the administration of the Lord's Supper except to point out that "[Philip Henry's] administration of this ordinance was very solemn and affecting."³² Moreover, he did not write a prescribed formulary for the Lord's Supper. Thus, it is difficult for contemporary readers to discern how Henry practiced the ordinance of the Lord's Supper. However, it proves that Henry's primary emphasis in the Lord's Supper was not on the administration of a rite but on the application of its meaning to everyday life, as examined in chapter 4. The simple order of Henry's administration of the Lord's Supper described above was from *The Westminster Directory*. Williams confirms this: "[T]he formulary which he commonly used on the occasions referred to, but without confining himself to it, was that of the Westminster Assembly."³³ So, there seems no doubt that Henry followed this simple pattern in celebrating the ordinance. With regard to more specifics regarding the Lord's Supper, we may also be reasonably certain that Henry followed the order practiced by his father.³⁴ For delivering the bread and cup, Philip Henry "had been wont to go about in the congregation, and to deliver the elements with his own hand; but, in his latter time, he delivered them only to those near him, and so they were handed from one to another, with the assistance of one who supplied the office of a deacon."³⁵ This was clearly different from the pattern of the Catholic Church and the Church of England at that time, in which people received the elements from the hand of the priests. By this practice, Philip Henry showed that the efficacy of the Lord's Supper in English Presbyterian churches was not dependent on the priest, but on the working of the Holy Spirit. When he began his liturgical ministry, Matthew Henry must have followed this pattern since the meeting house was not designed for a separate table for the Lord's Supper at that time. So, the

---

31. Refer to chap. 4: "Helps for Self-Examination Before We Come to This Ordinance," 81–104.

32. Henry, *Life of Philip Henry*, 194.

33. Williams, *Memoirs of the Life*, 130.

34. This does not necessarily mean that Philip Henry practiced following *The Westminster Directory* for the specific ways of administering the Lord's Supper. However, it is very persuasive that Philip Henry (1631–1696) followed the pattern of the *Directory* since he learned and experienced on the way of administering the Sacraments while The Westminster was the official principle for England.

35. Henry, *Life of Mr. Philip Henry*, 195.

communicants did not need to come up around the table in order to take the bread and cup.[36]

Regardless of differences in specific patterns of celebrating the ordinance, Henry was concerned that his congregants take joy from the Lord's Supper. Williams quoted from Henry's original manuscript on this:

> We have now the pleasure of ordinances; drops of joy; but in heaven we shall bathe ourselves in the ocean of delights; the joy will be spiritual, pure, and unmixed. At present joys are fading and transitory, like the crackling of thorns under a pot: but the joys of heaven will be still flourishing. The light of joy is an everlasting light, which is held too high to be blown out by any of the blasts of this lower region.[37]

As this striking reflection indicates, Henry strongly encouraged his congregation to experience the Lord's Supper not as a gloomy sacrifice but as a joyful feast.[38]

As seen above, Henry's public worship service was neither a tightly prescribed liturgy nor a complex form of service. His public worship was a simple practice, though it did extend over two and a half hours. The congregation, in the public worship, confessed the Word by praising God by means of the psalms and the reading of other Scriptures. Their language in public worship came almost entirely from the Bible since singing the psalms and reading the Scriptures were the only official orders of expression in which they spoke. Beyond this movement of their tongues, the movement of their bodies was fairly limited; instead, they spent most time in listening to the minister's pastoral prayer (thirty minutes), exposition (half an hour), and sermon (one hour). The most important activity of the people in Henry's worship service was listening. They needed to follow the minister's praying, expounding, and preaching, exercising minds and hearts through their ears. In this regard, the hearing of the Word was at

---

36. William Maxwell treated in detail the order of receiving in the Reformed tradition. However, he did not deal with the way of communicants' receiving the bread and cup. See Maxwell, *The Liturgical Portions of the Genevan Service Book*, 205–9.

37. Williams, *Memoirs of the Life*, 128. Henry also expressed this thought in *Communicant's Companion*, 144–62.

38. He defined the Lord's Supper as a Christian feast that implies various meanings such as a royal feast, a marriage feast, a feast of memorial, a feast of dedication, a feast upon a sacrifice, and a feast upon a covenant. See Henry, *Communicant's Companion*, 38–42.

the center of Henry's public worship service.[39] By participating in that worship, people were expected to understand and respond to the Word. For the effective work of God through the Word as well as through intercessory supplication, Henry also spent one half-hour for pastoral prayer before the sermon. That pastoral prayer prompted people's hearts to respond to the Word. Henry regarded not the preacher but the Holy Spirit as the crucial figure to lead worshippers to respond to the Word.

However, none of these elements of public worship were original to Henry. Henry articulated and developed this English Presbyterian pattern of public worship from his study of the Bible and Reformed Presbyterian theology, as well as his experience of public worship while he was growing up. He applied Reformed Presbyterian worship to his own context, accommodating to the needs of his own congregation at Chester. So, it is necessary for contemporary readers to trace the origin and historical development of Henry's public worship in order to understand to what extent Henry developed Reformed Presbyterian legacies in his worship ministry.

HENRY'S PUBLIC WORSHIP PRACTICE AND THE REFORMED TRADITION

Henry developed a practice of English Presbyterian public worship in a time of freedom of worship provided by the Act of Toleration in 1687(9). At the beginning of his ministry, Henry would have chosen a pattern for how to worship God in public. As discussed in chapter 1, Henry did not take Baxter's Reformed Liturgy as the formulary of worship, nor did he write a new prescribed liturgy for the English Presbyterian Church. Rather, Henry followed the pattern that his father Philip Henry practiced at home during the time of persecution, only slightly modifying it. Three main components of family worship that he practiced during the persecution were singing the psalms, praying, and reading the Scriptures. As delineated above, these three main parts became the main orders of English Presbyterian public worship even in the time of liberty, after the persecution.

---

39. At the beginning of the Reformation, listening was very odd to the congregations who were accustomed to seeing in worship. Cf. Kingdon, "Worship in Geneva Before and After Reformation," 41–60. In contrast, at the time of the late seventeenth and early eighteenth centuries in England, seeing without listening and understanding in worship was odd to the Presbyterian congregation.

Henry's pattern of public worship was not formulated by accident in his historical context. Rather, Henry specifically chose and continued the practice of public worship as one of Reformed worship. To put it another way, in a time of freedom of worship, Henry intentionally articulated the simple way of worship described above as the practice of English Presbyterian worship at Chester and Hackney, which has implications for Reformed worship services. Henry placed himself in the Reformed tradition and sought to practice his understanding of Reformed theology in ministry, especially in the worship service. Therefore, it is helpful to understand to what extent and how Henry developed Reformed tradition in his worship practice.

This section will examine Reformed aspects in Henry's public worship by comparing it with other, older Reformed worship practices in order to argue that Henry clearly followed Reformed tradition in his ministry of worship. Henry creatively accommodated Reformed worship in his ministerial context by following the Reformed principle of worship, not just following the form of any Reformed worship practice. Matthew Henry's public worship service will be compared with key Reformed public worship patterns indicated in the introduction of this chapter: Calvin's Liturgy (1542), Knox's Genevan Liturgy (1556), *The Westminster Directory*, Baxter's Reformed Liturgy (1661), and the practices of Philip Henry's public worship.[40] By comparing Henry's public worship with previous Reformed worship services since Calvin, this section will show that keeping to the Reformed tradition in worship was not simply a matter of applying any single pattern or style to another context but rather a creative accommodation of Reformed principles (the Word and life) to each different liturgical context.

Reformed Worship Services before Matthew Henry

Matthew Henry developed and practiced a Reformed theology that fit his ministerial context, yet his practice of public worship did not originate with him. He took over a Reformed pattern by appropriately adapting it to

---

40. In the Reformed tradition, Martin Bucer's Strassburg Liturgy (1539) influenced Calvin's liturgy (1542), and the Waldegrave and Middleburg Liturgy (1586) were the liturgies of the early English Puritans that were based on Calvin's Liturgy. These two English Puritans' worship services did not differ from those of Knox and Calvin since those were the English versions of the Genevan liturgy.

Reformed Tradition in Henry's Presbyterian Public Worship Service

his own context.[41] Calvin's worship practice had became a touchstone for the Reformed tradition,[42] developed with some changes in specific forms and contents, but without losing its principle features during the whole of Protestant history in England. Henry endeavored to articulate Reformed worship as it had been developed by Calvin and transferred to England via Reformed theologians such as Knox and the other writers who labored at the Westminster Assembly.

The origins of Henry's worship service can be found in Calvin's liturgy. Knox brought Calvin's liturgy to the Protestants in England; the Westminster Assembly continued Reformed principles in their worship practice, articulated in the *Directory*. Baxter also tried to recover a Reformed liturgy at the Restoration of the monarchy in 1662 even though it was never practiced. Philip Henry, a Presbyterian minister and theologian, endeavored to keep Reformed worship during the persecution of the nonconformists. Under the influence of the legacy of these five key Reformed worship liturgies, Matthew Henry developed Reformed Presbyterian worship in his own liturgical context.[43] Liturgical shifts in Reformed tradition from Calvin to Philip Henry can be compared below:[44]

---

41. For more detailed information on Henry's liturgical context, refer to chap. 1.

42. Calvin's worship was not his own invention: other Reformed ministers such as Johannes Oecolampadius (1482–1531), Ulrich Zwingli (1484–1531), William Farel (1489–1565), and Martin Bucer (1491–1551) influenced the shape of Calvin's public worship. However, considering the influence of all these Reformed theologians, Calvin has been regarded as a representative of Reformed tradition, especially in Korean Reformed Presbyterian Christianity.

43. These five Reformed worship services are directly related to Henry's worship ministry regardless of differences in specific forms and content. Moreover, Reformed worship services have been developed in various countries beyond Geneva, Scotland, and England.

44. This table does not include the Lord's Supper. It only compares the Lord's Day morning public worship. Although Calvin intended to practice the Lord's Supper every Lord's Day, in reality, he administered it once a month following the decision of the Genevan Council.

Matthew Henry

Calvin's Liturgy (1542)[A]	Knox's Genevan Liturgy (1556)[B]	The Westminster Directory (1644)	Baxter's Reformed Liturgy (1661)	Philip Henry (1687)
1. Invocation	(Scripture Sentence and Exhortation)	1. Prayer	1. A Short Prayer	1. Prayer
			2. The Creeds 3. The Ten Commandments 4. Scripture Sentences	
2. Confession of Sin	1. Confession of Sins		5. The Confession of Sin and Prayer for Pardon and Sanctification	
3. Singing Psalm 4. Prayer for Illumination	2. Singing Psalm 3. Prayer for the Holy Spirit	[Singing Psalms][C]	6. Lord's Prayer	2. Singing Psalm 110
5. Reading the Scripture	4. Reading the Scripture	2. Reading the Scripture	7. Scripture (Gospel) 8. Reading Psalm 95 or 100 or 84 10. Reading the Old Testament Singing a Psalm or Te Deum 11. Reading a chapter of the New Testament 12. Prayer for the King and Magistrates 13. Singing or Reading Psalm 67 or 98 or Some Other Psalm or Benedictus or Magnificat	3. Reading the Scripture 4. Exposition[D] 5. Singing Psalm

Reformed Tradition in Henry's Presbyterian Public Worship Service

		3. Prayer before the Sermon	14. Prayer for the State, Necessities of the Church, and the Subject of the Sermon	
6. Sermon	5. Sermon	4. Sermon	15. Sermon upon Some Text of Holy Scripture	6. Sermon [Prayer]
7. Long Prayer	6. General Prayer	5. Prayer	16. Prayer for a Blessing on the Word of Instruction and Exhortation	7. Singing Psalm 117
8. Lord's Prayer	7. Lord's Prayer			
9. The Apostles' Creed	8. The Apostles' Creed			
10. Singing Psalm	9. Singing Psalm			
11. Blessing[E]	10. Blessing		17. Benediction	8. Blessing

A. *The Form of Church Prayers and Hymns with the Manner of Administering the Sacraments and Consecrating Marriage according to the Custom of the Ancient Church (1542).*

B. The original title of Knox's Genevan Liturgy is "The Forme of Prayers and Ministration of the Sacraments, &c. Used in the Englishe Congregation at Geneua: And Approued, by the Famous and Godly Learned Man, Iohn Caluyn." This *Forme of Prayers* is derived directly from Calvin's service book, *La Forme des Prieres*. In 1559, returning to Scotland, Knox brought copies with him. In 1560 the first General Assembly of the Church of Scotland directed that the sacraments were to be administered according to the Genevan rite, and this was confirmed in 1562. In 1564 the Genevan Forme of Prayers was accepted as the standard of worship in the Church of Scotland. After 1564, it gradually became known as the *Book of Common Order* or *Psalm Book*. And it continued in use until *The Westminster Directory* superseded it in 1645.

C. *The Westminster Directory* included Singing of Psalms as a mandatory order of public worship. However, it did not indicate the place of singing the psalms in the service of worship. Cf. *A Directory for the Public Worship of God (1644)*, 40.

D. He read and expounded a chapter in the Old Testament in the morning and a chapter in the New Testament in the afternoon.

E. There were psalm singings at the beginning and before the benediction only after 1562.

As seen in this diagram, Henry's public worship service was related to the Reformed history that had been developing for about one hundred and fifty years before him. In his actual practice, Henry continued the development of the pattern of his father's public worship by adding a pastoral prayer. Henry's public worship was explicitly or implicitly influenced by previous Reformed worship services such as those of *The Westminster Directory* and key Reformed leaders. In brief, Henry's public worship continued to practice three core elements: praying, singing the psalms, and reading/preaching the Scriptures. At the same time, it omitted some liturgical elements: the Confession of Sin, the Lord's Prayer, and the Apostles' Creed. The most familiar pattern of public worship for Henry was *The Westminster Directory*.

This implies that Henry's public worship service could be interpreted as an illustration of the *Directory*. Yet the *Directory* was not the prescribed formulary of his public worship. It was literally a directory of public worship. So, Henry's public worship could be regarded as an example of applying the *Directory* to a specific context.

Henry's Development of the Reformed Worship Service: Traces of the English Presbyterian Public Worship Service

Although in specific forms of worship some differences appear between Henry and his previous Reformed ministers, Henry's public worship practice had a strong connection with other Reformed practices. Comparison with each Reformed worship service and consideration of their relationships to one another will show the extent to which Henry developed upon previous Reformed worship services.

John Calvin's Liturgy as a Touchstone of Reformed Worship

Henry's Reformed Presbyterian practice had its origin in Calvin's liturgy at Geneva in 1542.[45] John Calvin (1519–1564) was the forerunner of the Reformed understanding and practicing of public worship, although there were some other Reformed theologians and ministers at that time, such as Oecolampadius (1482–1531), Ulrich Zwingli (1484–1531), William Farel (1489–1565), and Martin Bucer (1491–1551). So it is no overestimation to call Calvin a touchstone of Reformed worship. Nicholas Wolterstorff indicated that Calvin's worship service can be regarded as the genius of Reformed worship.[46] He attempted to reform public worship according to the Scriptures and based on the pattern of the primitive church.[47] His theology of worship flowed from the solid theological conviction that human sinfulness led people to not worship God aright when they worshiped according

---

45. Calvin's Geneva liturgy in 1542 was slightly modified at Strassburg in 1545 three years later. Most of all, Absolution was added to the Confession of Sins, and Offering for Poor was inserted between the Sermon and the Long Prayer.

46. For more detailed information on the genius of Reformed worship, refer to Nicholas Wolterstorff, "The Reformed Liturgy."

47. His prayer book was articulated based on the early church, as seen in the title: *The Form of Church Prayers and Hymns with the Manner of Administering the Sacraments and Consecrating Marriage according to the Custom of the Ancient Church.*

to their own whims and desires.[48] That was why "Calvin would only accept what the Bible specifically warranted."[49] In his *Form of Administering Baptism* (1542), Calvin explicated the Bible as the absolute authority with two main reasons: "First, whatever is not commanded, we are not free to choose. Secondly, nothing which does not tend to edification ought to be received into the Church."[50] In *the Institutes of Christian Religion*, Calvin also declared this rule again by saying that "God wills to be worshipped as he commands and we are not to mingle inventions of our own."[51] Henry, as a Presbyterian minister, also regarded the Bible as the norm of public worship and built up his understanding of worship based on the Scriptures following the Reformed tradition, as examined in chapter 3.

When it came to a method of prayer, Calvin used set forms of prayer. However, he did not hold fast to the view that only set prayer was appropriate in worship. Prayer for illumination in the worship service, as a peculiar characteristic of Calvin's worship, needed the minister's discretion. He also "approved of Knox's discretionary liturgy, and [contemporary readers] know of his unwillingness to insist on uniformity in such matters."[52] Hughes Old, a Reformed theologian, pointed out what Calvin intended in relation to the way of prayer:

> [H]e knew that prayer was much more than a form of prayer or an ability to extemporize public prayer. Prayer was for him the principal exercise of religion. Learning to pray was a lifelong discipline that went hand in hand with sanctification. . . . For Calvin, there was no liturgical reform without teaching people to pray. The liturgist of today who would listen to Calvin must be prepared to go beyond questions of liturgical rites and forms.[53]

Henry's pastoral prayer was an exact application of Calvin's teaching on prayer in worship. By using his own discretion, Henry developed a pastoral

---

48. For Calvin's theology of worship, see Eire, *War against the Idols: The Reformation of Worship from Erasmus to Calvin*, 247–76; Old, "Calvin's Theology of Worship," 412–35; Old, "John Calvin and the Prophetic Criticism of Worship," 230–46; McKee, "Context, Contours, Contents," 172–201; Moeller, *Calvin's Doxology*.

49. Davies, *Worship of the English Puritans*, 19.

50. Beveridge, *Selected Works of John Calvin* 2, 118.

51. Calvin, *Institutes of Christian Religion*, 4.10.23.

52. Ward, "Directory for Public Worship," 103.

53. Old, "Calvin's Theology of Worship," 435.

prayer in public worship. This was a strong continuation of Calvin's idea of prayer in worship.

Comparing Henry's worship with Calvin's liturgy, we see two more places where Henry continued to develop Calvin's worship practice. First, Henry took over Calvin's practice of singing metrical psalms as a crucial Reformed principle of worship. Moreover, following Calvin's pattern, Henry's worship had the Word as the climax. Both Calvin and Henry emphasized the reading and preaching of the Word as the center of public worship. These two worship services were conducted mainly from the pulpit.

John Knox's Genevan Liturgy as Successor of Calvin's Worship

Between Calvin and Henry there were developments of Reformed worship; Henry did not follow Reformed tradition from Calvin's practice without encountering and considering other Reformed worship services. John Knox (ca. 1514–1572) introduced the Genevan Liturgy to Scottish and English Reformed churches,[54] and this liturgy was practiced in the churches of Scotland and the Puritans, including the Presbyterians in England. Thus, Henry's public worship was influenced by Knox, who played a pivotal role in the history of the Reformed church,[55] although Henry did not use Knox's worship as a pattern of public worship practice. One of Knox's seminal works was the *History of the Reformation of Religion within the Realm of Scotland*. Among several other publications, many revisions of the *Book of Common Order* (1556–1564), the Scottish service book, were largely his work. On February 10, 1556, "the first Reformed rite in English" was printed at Geneva under the title *The Forme of Prayers and Ministration of the Sacraments used in the English Congregation at Geneva*. This *Forme of Prayers* was derived directly from Calvin's service book, *La Forme des Prieres*. In 1564 the Genevan *Forme of Prayers* was accepted as the standard of worship in the Church of Scotland. After 1564, it gradually became known

---

54. As William Maxwell pointed out, Knox's church as a place of Scottish worship, "became the cradle of the Scottish Reformation and English Puritanism; and its Service Book with slight modifications and additions became the Service Book used in Scotland after 1560 and favored by most English Puritans until displaced eighty-five years later by the Westminster Directory" (Maxwell, *The Liturgical Portions of the Genevan Service Book*, iv).

55. In shaping the *Directory*, "the Scottish influence was considerable and contributed to a directory whose structure was very like the Scottish Book of Common Order of 1564" (Ward, "Directory for Public Worship," 90).

Reformed Tradition in Henry's Presbyterian Public Worship Service

as the *Book of Common Order* or *Psalm Book*. And it continued in use until *The Westminster Directory* superseded it in 1645.[56] In this way, the English congregation at Geneva that had produced the new order was the cradle of English Puritanism, and its liturgy was also of paramount importance as an influence on Puritan worship. Knox slightly modified Calvin's Genevan liturgy for his Scottish and English congregations: Calvin began public worship with the solemn declaration of God's glory and human fall: "Our help is in the name of the LORD, who made heaven and earth. Amen."[57] However, Knox's worship began with Confession of Sins without that declaration. Other than this, the form and content of Knox's liturgy did not differ from Calvin's.

In structure and doctrine, Knox's *Form of Prayers* belonged primarily to the liturgical traditions of Strasbourg and Geneva. It was not a fixed rite; it provided a standard of worship, leaving a great deal to the minister's discretion. Henry's worship, like the *Directory*, emphasized the minister's discretion and role. In addition, as Davies pointed out, "there were three Calvinistic characteristics in Knox's service: Biblical, didactic, and congregational."[58] These characteristics also appear in Henry's public worship. Most of all, Henry's worship was not much different from that of Knox's in that the reading and preaching the Scriptures, along with the singing of psalms, figured at the center of it. Henry developed reading, singing, and hearing the Word as the main components of public worship, as did Knox in his own liturgical context. Moreover, Knox and Henry both emphasized the importance of public prayer as a crucial role of the minister in worship. Knox practiced general prayer as an intercessory prayer in public worship. Henry also developed public prayer as a pastoral prayer in

---

56. Baird, *Presbyterian Liturgies: Historical Sketches*, 138–39. "Until supplanted by the Directory of Worship, it remained the chosen and voluntary formulary of the Calvinistic party in England, as well as the prescribed order of the Church of Scotland."

57. Calvin, *The Form of Church Prayers* (1542; 1545).

58. Davies, *Worship of the English Puritans*, 119. He explained in detail: "First, its Biblical basis is seen in the opening Confession of Sins, based largely on the 9th chapter of the Book of Daniel, in the use of metrical psalms, and in the preference for Biblical blessings as compared with the Anglican blessing. Second, it is didactic in that the climax of the service is approached by a prayer for illumination, and reached in the reading and exposition of the Word of God, while the Apostle's Creed immediately precedes the closing acts of worship. Third, its congregational character is shown by the singing of two metrical psalms and by the particular intercessions for the members of the mystical Body of Christ in the Intercessory prayer (Long prayer), as also in the personal and intimate petition with which this prayer opens" (ibid.).

the public gathering for worship. Following the Reformed tradition, Knox and Henry practiced singing the psalms in public worship.[59]

However, although the main components were similar, there were some differences between them. Most of all, Henry did not use any manual or prayer book for public worship. At the time of the Reformation of the sixteenth century, Knox used a liturgical book as a manual for the public worship service. One century later, Henry did not use any prescribed liturgy or manual of public worship. Moreover, Henry omitted liturgical orders such as the confession of sins, the Lord's Prayer, and the Apostles' Creed from the public worship service, while Knox included them as Calvin did. When freedom of worship was given to him, Henry did not recover these liturgical components. Rather, he kept practicing what he learned from his father and *The Westminster Directory* as a Reformed Presbyterian pattern of worship.

Matthew Henry and *The Westminster Directory*

The Westminster Directory was the rule of public worship for the English Presbyterian churches as well as other Protestant churches in England from 1644 to 1662. "The legal status of the directory disappeared in England with the restoration of the monarch and the royal assent to the Act of Uniformity, May 19, 1662."[60] While Henry was growing up, the *Directory* was not allowed for use by English Presbyterians. Later, after the Act of Toleration, "only in 1690s did the directory begin to have a wide use in the nonconformist churches in England."[61] At that time, as Hughes Old has pointed out, *The Westminster Directory* "was regarded as a key to recovering a simple, sincere, and unpretentious form of worship which was faithful

---

59. "In the English Church at Geneva in 1556, Metrical Psalms were regularly used at their services from the beginning" (Maxwell, *John Knox's Genevan Service Book 1556* in *Liturgical Portions of the Genevan Service Book,* 62). Maxwell also pointed out that singing the psalms was a crucial contribution of the Reformed tradition to England by quoting Strype's description: "From Geneva they spread to England, where as early as 1559 Strype tells us the congregational singing of metrical psalms was introduced into the Church of England 'as was used among the Protestants of Geneva, all men, women, and young folks singing together; which custom was about this time brought also into St. Paul's'" (ibid.).

60. Ward, "Directory for Public Worship," 92.

61. Ibid.

to Scripture, and edifying for the congregation."[62] Although its use was discontinued for about twenty-five years, the *Directory* became the guide for the nonconformists as well as the English Presbyterians thereafter.[63] Although there is no record that Henry referred to the *Directory* for the Lord's Day worship, other than for administration of the Lord's Supper, Henry's public worship embodied the intent of *Directory*. As nonconformist English Presbyterians, Henry's congregation practiced their Lord's Day public worship under the influence of *The Westminster Directory*.

Regardless of the debates about it, the *Directory* pursued the Reformed vision of worship: "wherein our care hath been to hold forth such things as are of divine institution in every ordinance; and other things we have endeavored to set forth according to the rules of Christian prudence, agreeable to the general rules of the word of God."[64] Within this Reformed vision, the *Directory* intended that "there may be a consent of all the churches in those things that contain the substance of the service and worship of God."[65] The *Directory* was not a prescribed liturgy dictating the exact pattern of the worship service. Rather, it provided guides for how worship should be conducted. It "offered a middle way between a fixed liturgy and leaving a minister entirely to his own devices."[66] In using the *Directory*, ministers needed to articulate for themselves portions of the public worship service since it did not provide a set of prayers. The *Directory* also required ministers to fulfill their role:

> The ministers may be hereby directed, in their administrations, to keep like soundness in doctrine and prayer, may, if need be, have some help and furniture, and yet so as they become not hereby slothful and negligent in stirring up the gifts of Christ in them; but that each one, by meditation, by taking heed to himself, and the flock of God committed to him, and by wise observing the ways of Divine Providence, may be careful to furnish his heart and tongue

---

62. Old, *The Reading and Preaching of the Scriptures*, vol. 5: *Modernism, Pietism, and Awakening*, 28.

63. The history of *The Westminster Directory* and related issues should be another research topic. For general information on the history of the *Directory*, refer to Leishmann, *The Westminster Directory*. Also, Ward dealt briefly with the history and principle of *The Westminster Directory* in "Directory for Public Worship," 85–109.

64. *The Westminster Directory*, preface.

65. Ibid.

66. Ward, "Directory for Public Worship," 96.

with further or other materials of prayer and exhortation, as shall be needful upon all occasions.[67]

Thus the *Directory*, on the one hand, articulated Reformed principles of public worship by emphasizing the Word as the rule of reforming it. On the other hand, the *Directory* identified the responsibility and role of ministers by not providing all sets of prayer for public worship. Thus, the *Directory* did not set uniformity in worship services as an ideal.

The meaning and function of *The Westminster Directory* is implied in its title: "A Directory for Public Prayer, Reading the Holy Scriptures, Singing of Psalms, Preaching of the Word, Administration of the Sacraments, and Other Parts of the Public Worship of God, Ordinary and Extraordinary." According to this title, prayer, reading/preaching the Scriptures, and singing the psalms were the main parts of public worship besides the sacraments. Henry's worship practice also emphasized these three parts. Following the rule of the *Directory*,[68] Henry placed reading the Scriptures as a crucial part of public worship, and he developed exposition of the Scriptures as a part of worship separate from preaching.[69] Henry's inclusion of public prayer before and after the sermon also follows *Directory* guidance.[70]

---

67. *The Westminster Directory*, preface.

68. "All the canonical books of the Old and New Testament shall be publiquely read in the vulgar tongue, out of the best allowed translation, distinctly, that all may hear and understand" (*The Westminster Directory*, 7).

69. This was a more strict application than that of the *Directory*, though the *Directory* also gave the principle of expounding the Scripture: "When the minister, who readeth, shall judge it necessary to expound any part of what is read. let it not be done until the whole chapter or psalme be ended: and regard is always to be had unto the time, that neither preaching or other ordinance be straitened, or rendered tedious" (ibid.). According to Ward, "This statement was not a direction to add expository comments, but was soon elaborated in Scotland to an extended lecture/commentary distinct from the subsequent sermon, a practice already common among the Independents in England" (Ward, "Directory for Public Worship," 122).

70. For the prayer before the sermon, the *Directory* included several themes: (1) to acknowledge our great sinfulness, (2) to bewail our blindness of mind, hardness of heart, unbelief, impenitency, security, lukewarmness, barrenness, (3) to acknowledge and confess, that, as we are convinced of our guilt, (4) to draw near to the throne of grace, (5) for the Spirit of adoption, the full assurance of our pardon and reconciliation, (6) to pray for the sanctification by the Spirit, (7) to pray for the propagation of the gospel and kingdom of Christ to all nations, (8) to pray for all in authority, especially for the King's Majesty, (9) to have fellowship with God in the reverend and conscionable use of his holy ordinances, (10) for a more full and perfect communion with God, (11) for the minister himself; for wisdom, fidelity, zeal, and utterance so that he may divide the Word of God aright. Refer to *The Westminster Directory*, 8–10. For the prayer after the sermon, the

His prayers were not read from any prescribed form. Rather, he led a comprehensive extempore prayer, as the *Directory* ruled that "every minister is herein to apply himself in his prayer before, or after his sermon to those occasions; but for the manner, he is left to his liberty as God shall direct and enable him, in piety and wisdom to discharge his duty."[71] Henry's preaching was also an application of the *Directory*, organized as it requested.[72] Lastly, Henry's practice of singing the psalms in public worship followed the guidance of the *Directory*[73] as well as his father's worship practice. Like the rule of the *Directory*, Henry emphasized singing with understanding by encouraging them to memorize and practice at home in advance. Overall, Henry's public worship practice could be regarded as a case of applying *The Westminster Directory* for a specific English Presbyterian congregation.

Richard Baxter's Reformed Liturgy as an Unrealized Vision

Baxter influenced the shape of Henry's thought in the direction of Reformed Presbyterian tradition. Henry had already met him and been influenced by his thoughts on the Christian life. Henry included what he and his friends learned from Baxter in a letter to his father:

> [Baxter] gave us some good counsel to prepare for trials, and said the best preparation for them was a life of faith, and a constant

Directory included three main themes: (1) to give thanks for the great love of God and rich blessings, (2) to pray for the continuance of the gospel; to turn the chief and most useful heads of the sermon into some few petitions; and to pray that it may abide in the heart, and bring forth fruit, (3) to pray for preparation for death and judgment, and a watching for the coming of our LORD Jesus Christ. Refer to *The Westminster Directory*, 18–19.

71. *The Westminster Directory*, 18.

72. *The Westminster Directory* roughly guided preaching to use the following order: (1) Introduction, (2) Analyzing and dividing the text, (3) Raising the doctrine, and (4) Exhorting to duties. See *The Westminster Directory*, 13–18.

73. "It is the duty of Christians to praise God publicquely by singing of Psalms together in the congregation, and also privately in the family. In singing of Psalms, the voice is to be tunable and gravely ordered: but the chief care must be, to sing with understanding, and with grace in the heart, making melody unto the LORD. That the whole congregation may joyn herein, every one that can reade is to have a psalm-book, and all others not disabled by age, or otherwise, are to be exhorted to learn to reade. But for the present, where many in the congregation cannot reade, it is convenient that the minister, or some other sit person appointed by him and the other ruling offices, do reade the Psalms, line by line, before the singing thereof" (*The Westminster Directory*, 40). These brief instructions presume the Reformed principle on music in worship.

course of self-denial. He thought it harder constantly to deny temptations to sensual lusts and pleasures, than to resist one single temptation to deny Christ for fear of suffering.[74]

Moreover, Henry was also acquainted with Baxter's works. Williams described Baxter's influence on Henry:

> With the energetic writings of the puritan and nonconformist divines, he cultivated an enlightened and fond acquaintance. The practical works of Mr. Baxter, especially, occupied a very exalted placed in his esteem; they are more frequently cited in his manuscripts than the products of any other author; and he caught, in a happy measure, the holy flame by which they are animated.[75]

Through conversation and his writing, Baxter influenced the shape of Henry's thought regarding the Christian life. When it came to liturgical ministry, Henry also followed Baxter's idea by continuing to sing the psalms and read the Scripture in public worship. Also, both Henry and Baxter included a comprehensive prayer before the sermon, holding this to be crucial.

However, Henry's public worship differed from Baxter's *Reformed Liturgy*. First of all, unlike Baxter, Henry did not include liturgical elements such as the Creed, the Ten Commandments, Confession of Sin, and Lord's Prayer in the service of public worship. Neither has Henry left us any reasons for this choice. Second, Baxter did not require pastors to interpret or expound the portions of Scripture read in the service, except those used for preaching. Third, unlike Baxter's *Reformed Liturgy* as a prescribed formulary of worship, Henry did not use any prescribed liturgy; he preferred composing worship with the simple elements.

Baxter's *Reformed Liturgy* was never used in practice. So it is difficult to argue that Henry did not follow Baxter's idea of the Reformed worship service only because of the differences between them in some elements of worship. Also, although Baxter included certain liturgical elements in his Reformed vision of worship, his primary emphasis was on the Word: singing the Psalms and preaching the Word. Henry attempted to follow the Word-centered worship service that flowed from Baxter's vision of Reformed worship.

---

74. Williams, *Memoirs of the Life*, 22.
75. Ibid., 221.

Reformed Tradition in Henry's Presbyterian Public Worship Service

Matthew Henry and Philip Henry's Public Worship

It is clear that Philip Henry influenced Matthew Henry in the shaping of worship ministry, as examined in chapter 2. As a nonconformist Presbyterian divine, Philip Henry began his public worship ministry in 1687, right after passage of the Act of Toleration. Matthew Henry also began his worship ministry for a Presbyterian congregation in the same year. Matthew Henry clearly understood and knew how his father Philip Henry practiced public worship at Broad Oak, which was his home town as well as his place of ministry. During the persecution of the nonconformists, Philip Henry could not continue his worship ministry except by way of family worship. As discussed in chapter 1, Philip Henry did not go back to Baxter's idea of Reformed worship when freedom of worship came. According to Matthew Henry's observation, Philip Henry did not regret his choice: "it may be of use to give some account how [Philip Henry] managed his ministerial work in the latter part of his time, wherein he had as signal tokens of the presence of God with him as ever; enabling him still to bring forth fruit in old age, and to renew his youth like the eagles."[76]

Matthew Henry's Lord's Day worship service was almost same as his father's. The pattern of Philip Henry's worship service described above did not change during the last eight or nine years of his ministry until his death. As seen above, the main components of his public worship were prayer, singing the Psalms, and reading and expounding as well as preaching the Scripture. To Matthew Henry's eye, his father's worship was peculiar in two points: (1) singing the Psalms and (2) preaching the Scripture. In the section describing Philip Henry's public worship in the context of political freedom, Matthew Henry delineated how his father practiced singing the psalm:

> He commonly choose a psalm suitable to the chapter he had expounded; and would briefly tell his hearers how they might sing that psalm with understanding, and what affections of soul should be working toward God, in the singing of it; his hints of that kind were of great use, and contributed much to the right performance of that service; he often said, the more singing of psalms there is in our families and congregations on Sabbath-days, the more like they are to heaven, and the more there is in them of the everlasting

---

76. Henry, *Life of Mr. Philip Henry*, 189.

> Sabbath. He would say sometimes, he loved to sing whole psalms, rather than pieces.[77]

According to this observation, there is no doubt that Matthew Henry's practice of singing the psalms in public worship was strongly influenced by his father.

Matthew Henry was also impressed by the characteristics and patterns of his father's preaching.

> As to his constant preaching, it was very substantial and elaborate, and greatly to edification. He used to say, he could not starch in his preaching; that is, he would not; as knowing where the language and expression is stiff, and forced, and fine, as they call it, it doth not reach the greatest part of the hearers.... His sermons were not common place, but even when his subjects were the most plain and trite, yet his management of them was usually peculiar, and surprising.... It might be of use, especially to those who had the happiness of sitting under his ministry, to give some account of the method of his Sabbath subjects, during the last eight or nine years of his ministry.[78]

Thus, Matthew Henry encouraged his congregation to sing the psalms by placing it three times in the order of public worship. Moreover, he regarded the Word as the center of public worship, exemplified by its continued reading, expounding, and preaching. Both Philip and Matthew Henry separated the exposition from the preaching in public worship. Expounding took place only as an accompaniment to the portion of Scriptures that was read on a given Sunday. At the same time, neither of them regarded reading the Scripture that accompanied the sermon as an essential order.

However, Matthew Henry was distinct from his father in that he emphasized and practiced half an hour of pastoral prayer before preaching. Matthew Henry's pastoral prayer was an intercessory prayer that emphasized the working of the Holy Spirit in the life of congregation, which was not much emphasized and practiced in the pastoral ministry of Philip Henry. Nevertheless, apart from this pastoral prayer, Matthew Henry's public worship was quite similar to that of his father.

---

77. Ibid., 191.
78. Ibid., 192–93; see also appendix 20 for the subjects and methods of his preaching.

CONCLUSION: REFORMED PRESBYTERIAN ASPECTS IN HENRY'S PUBLIC WORSHIP SERVICE

Henry contributed to the Reformed tradition by developing a Reformed Presbyterian public worship service in a time of freedom of worship. As investigated above, Henry's public worship service at Chester typified Reformed practice of an English Presbyterian congregation in the late seventeenth and early eighteenth centuries. His practice of public worship had a strong connection with other previous Reformed worship services and can be regarded as a case of applying the Reformed principle of worship in a new context.

First of all, Henry's public worship service had a clear connection with previous Reformed worship practices. He neither wrote any liturgical book nor articulated any directory or rubric for Reformed worship, other than composing the metrical psalms for family and public worship into *Family Hymns*. Moreover, his *Treatise on Baptism* and *The Communicant's Companion* were not manuals for administering the sacraments but simply aids for the full, active participation of believers. However, throughout his liturgical and pastoral leadership, Henry proved that his English Presbyterian worship service was a sound application of the Reformed worship initiated by Calvin. Calvin's Reformed liturgy at Geneva was a formulary liturgy that was reformed to correct the Medieval Mass, although it was still a prescribed liturgy. Knox contributed to Scottish and English Presbyterian worship by introducing Calvin's liturgy in the form of an English translation. He did not just bring it to Scotland and England but also continued to practice what he already had with English congregations at Frankfort and Geneva. *The Westminster Directory* attempted to "produce a more uniformed ethos"[79] in public worship by giving the divine sanction for their order of worship and providing not an invariable prayer book but a general directory. So, the *Directory* did not define any prescribed liturgy to be practiced but provided principles and directions, leaving the specific forms and patterns of worship to be decided by local pastors. Henry, in a time of liturgical plurality or liberty, articulated an English Presbyterian public worship service by following and slightly modifying the pattern of his father, which could be regarded an illustration of the use of the *Directory*. History did not allow Baxter's Reformed Liturgy an opportunity to be practiced in reality; Baxter's Presbyterian idea of Reformed Liturgy was a much more

---

79. Ferguson, "Puritans-Ministers of the World," 26.

liturgical and prescribed pattern of worship, though it emphasized the priority and centrality of the Word. Henry did not attempt to practice Baxter's idea of Reformed worship, as examined in chapter 1. He simply intended to develop English Presbyterian worship in his own context according to the Reformed tradition, which was initiated by Calvin, mediated by Knox, summarized by *The Westminster Directory*, and illustrated in his father's worship service.

In addition, Henry's practice of public worship can be regarded as a case of applying the Reformed principle of worship to a new context. Although each development of the Reformed tradition in different places since the sixteenth century agreed with the principle of worship according to the Bible and the primitive church, their practices have differed in each context.[80] Henry's worship service was not a copy of Calvin's Genevan liturgy even though he followed Calvin's Reformed principle of worship: the Word of God. Rather, it could be interpreted as a contextualization of Reformed worship in his English Presbyterian congregation while staying true to the Reformed tradition.

To be more specific, in a context of freedom of worship, Henry continued to practice what he learned and experienced in relation to worship under the persecution, which, as examined above, can be regarded as an application of *The Westminster Directory*. Henry attempted to follow the decisions of the Westminster Assembly: the *Confession*, the *Catechism*, and the *Directory*. He articulated *A Scripture Catechism* based on the *Westminster Confession* and *Catechism*. And he practiced the service of public worship following the guide of *The Westminster Directory*. English Presbyterian churches have held strongly to the *Confession*, the *Catechism*, and the *Directory* of the Westminster Assembly since the seventeenth century. Although they did not deny other Reformed confessions, patterns of church polity, and ministerial practices, English Presbyterians took these three documents as their main source of teaching in relation to the Reformed tradition. As Henry himself pointed out, his Catechism was "to put the [Westminster] Catechism into such a dress, as to make it both easy and copious, so as that it may not be an insuperable task to the learner, and yet may furnish him with plenty of useful knowledge."[81] Moreover, by

---

80. As Nick Needham reminds us, "all Reformed churches have traditionally claimed a particular concern for shaping the church's worship according to the regulative principle of Scripture and in the light of patristic practice" (Needham, "Worship through the Ages," 411).

81. Henry, *A Scripture Catechism*, in *Complete Works*, 2:174.

his own practice, Henry showed that "the Westminster Directory, like the Confession and the Catechism which bear the Westminster name, contains a wealth of insight on topics relevant to the church in any age."[82] In this way, Henry's public worship service as an illustration of *The Westminster Directory* is congruent with his use of the *Confession* and the *Catechism* of the Westminster Assembly. We learn from studying the case of Henry's practice of public worship that any churches that want to follow Reformed tradition in accord with the *Confession* and *Catechism* of the Westminster Assembly should not ignore the value of practice based in the *Directory* of the Westminster Assembly.

In order for contemporary Reformed Presbyterian churches to apply Henry's worship to their own liturgical contexts, they must first take the Reformed emphasis on the Word and life from his understanding and practice of worship. It is not appropriate for contemporary churches to adopt the practice of Henry's worship in their specific contexts without considering the distance between them. Because Henry's worship can be regarded as an application of *The Westminster Directory*, that is what should be interpreted in detail in order to find out the Reformed Presbyterian principle from Henry's public worship. Regardless of the debate on the *Directory*,[83] it is certain that English Presbyterian worship as developed by Henry followed the *Directory* as a crucial transmitter of Reformed Presbyterian legacy in terms of worship practice. In particular, any Reformed Presbyterian traditions that uphold the *Westminster Confession of Faith* and *Catechism* must also reconsider and attempt to apply the guidance in the *Directory*. Reformed Presbyterian churches need to renew study of the *Directory* in order to practice in ecclesiastical ministry what they believe: The *Westminster Confession of Faith* and *Catechism*.

---

82. Dever, "Preaching Like the Puritans," 41.

83. The principle of worship called the Regulative Principle of Worship (RPW), derived from the *Westminster Directory*, is one of the issues of ongoing debate in Reformed circles. John Frame and R. G. Gore Jr. criticize RPW as a limited application of the Bible to worship ministry. See Frame, *Worship in Spirit and Truth*, and "Some Questions about the Regulative Principle," 357–66; Gore Jr., *Covenantal Worship*. In contrast, William Young defended RPW in his article: "The Puritan Principle of Worship," in *Servants of the Word*. D. G. Hart also defends RPW and advocates its benefits as "a guardian of Christian liberty" in "Acceptable Worship," 77–87. For a short history of the debate on PRW, refer to Clark, *Recovering the Reformed Confession*, 227–57.

6

Conclusion
Liturgical Resources for Renewal of Public Worship in Henry's Theology and Practice of Worship

THIS BOOK BEGAN WITH the assumption that Henry was a Presbyterian minister who held a Reformed understanding of worship and practiced it in his ministerial context. The conclusion of this work is this: Henry did not try to simply adopt a single pattern of worship from previous Reformed ministers such as Calvin, Knox, Baxter, or even Philip Henry. Instead, Henry tried to understand and practice worship in his liturgical context by creatively applying biblical principles with his own pastoral and ministerial discretion. Henry developed and articulated the Word and life as a key principle of worship based on his reading and interpreting the Bible. By articulating communion with God as a patterned relationship between humanity and God, Henry developed a biblical worship that placed the Word at the center of that practice and sought a transformation of ordinary life based on liturgical experiences such as private, family, and public worship as well as the sacraments.

As seen in Henry's case, in order for Reformed worship to be a truly living tradition, contemporary Reformed churches first need to preserve Reformed principles of worship and creatively apply them to each ministerial context with pastoral discretion. To put it another way, there is no single pattern for Reformed worship practice that every Reformed church

Conclusion

can adopt. The Word is at the core of Reformed principles in relation to ecclesiastical ministry as well as theology. With this conviction, Henry did not seek to recover so-called Word and the table pattern of worship as Calvin sought at Geneva. Instead, Henry emphasized transforming human life by extending the experience of the table to ordinary life. Henry did not ignore the value of the sacrament; rather he creatively developed the meaning and function of the sacrament without ignoring the real practice of the sacrament in public worship. In this regard, through articulating the theology and practice of English Presbyterian worship, Henry teaches contemporary Reformed churches that taking the Reformed principle of worship and using pastoral discretion for creatively applying it to each different ministerial context are both necessary to practice Reformed worship in our contemporary context.

Henry's contribution to worship is much more than a general principle about applying the tradition of Reformed worship to a contemporary context. His theology and practice of English Presbyterian worship also provide valuable resources for contemporary evangelical churches as well as Reformed churches. This concluding chapter will briefly summarize Henry's understanding and practice of worship and then suggest liturgical resources for renewal of contemporary churches in more detail. This chapter will finish with a brief comment on the limits of Henry's thought and practice for contemporary churches and suggest further studies on Henry.

BRIEF SUMMARY

This book endeavored to find liturgical resources for the renewal of public worship by examining Henry's English Presbyterian worship ministry with special reference to his theology and practice of worship and the sacraments. In a time of freedom of worship, Henry developed the Reformed tradition by emphasizing the Bible and everyday life in the ministry of worship. Although his understanding and practice of ministry could be interpreted as those of a nonconformist Puritan, Henry regarded himself as a Presbyterian minister. He distinguished Presbyterians from other nonconformists Puritans, such as Independents, Baptists, and Quakers, and also distinguished his thought from that of the Church of England. His development of pastoral thought and practice of ecclesiastical ministry included worship according to his reading and interpretation of the Bible under the influence of Presbyterian ministers such as Baxter, Doolittle, Philip Henry, and Calvin. Although he did not accept and follow everything he learned from them, there is no doubt that Henry was influenced by them in shaping and developing his understanding and practice of pastoral ministry.

As examined in chapter 2, Henry articulated communion with God, a pattern of relationship between humanity and God, as the core of his thought based on his reading and interpretation of the Bible. According to Henry, human communion with God could primarily be sustained and developed through Christian worship. Communion with God in worship is at the core of a patterned relationship between humanity and God (chapter 3). Henry thought that the communion of people with God must also be evident in their ordinary lives in the world by embodying that relationship in their everyday life. Henry regarded the sacraments, Baptism and the Lord's Supper, as the main principle and guide for embodying human relationships with God in the world (chapter 4). By integrating worship and life based on his reading and interpretation of the Bible and the Reformed tradition, Henry continued to extend biblical principles of worship to an English Presbyterian church. His practice of public worship also demonstrated that it continued to follow Reformed tradition by placing the Word as the main rule for form and content of public worship, as discussed in chapter 5. By singing the Scriptures (especially the psalms), praying prayers that used and drew inspiration from the Bible, and promoting understanding of the Word through reading (with exposition) and preaching, Henry's public worship put the Word at the center of the encounter between humanity and God; he expected that it would shape Christian piety and would result in transformed lives.

LITURGICAL RESOURCES OF HENRY'S WORSHIP FOR CONTEMPORARY CHURCHES

With regard to renewal of worship, contemporary churches can learn from Henry by reconsidering the values both *of* and *in* his understanding and practice of ministry. First of all, Henry's worship occupies a crucial position in the history of Reformed worship. Reformed Worship has been developing through history in various contexts and regions. Through Henry's English Presbyterian worship contemporary readers can understand how Reformed worship had been extended to England in the late seventeenth and the early eighteenth centuries after its development by Calvin at Geneva in the middle of sixteenth century. Contemporary Reformed worship has been influenced by this varied history of worship in the Reformed tradition. Calvin and Knox have been regarded as two important figures in worship ministry in Reformed circles. They developed Reformed practices of worship according to their interpretation of the Bible and the pattern of the early church by articulating formularies of liturgy. Many Reformed denominations and ministers have been attempting to articulate their worship practices by examining Calvin's and Knox's worship books as foundational to their understanding and practice of Reformed worship. However, Reformed worship has also been developed and articulated through *The Westminster Directory* and even in ways that did not use any liturgical manuals, as in the case of Henry. Through studying Henry, contemporary Reformed churches can learn that following the pattern of a liturgical book is not the exclusive approach to Reformed worship. In this regard, English Presbyterian worship as seen in Henry's case occupies a crucial place in the development of Reformed worship. Thus, in order to renew worship, contemporary Reformed and even evangelical churches in the Free Church tradition must learn from the values of Henry, using his practice as a case of English Presbyterian worship that was engaged with *The Westminster Directory*, together with the values and practices of Calvin and Knox.

Second, there is much common ground between Henry and contemporary evangelical churches as well as Reformed churches in relation to the context of worship. Henry led public worship in the context of liturgical indulgence, a time of freedom of worship. Contemporary evangelical churches also find themselves in a time of freedom in relation to worship ministry. Although they regard themselves as specific denominational bodies in theology and ecclesiology, each church differs from others in its specific form and style of worship. For example, there is no a strict rule or rubric that is the mandatory pattern of public worship in Reformed Presbyterian churches in Korea, although the denominational judicatory governs Reformed doctrine, theology, and church government, following Calvin and Knox. So, it is very difficult to discern its own aspects in the practice of public worship, although each church may easily regard themselves specific denominational bodies in confession and doctrine. In this regard, each church must appropriately and creatively develop its practice as well as theology of worship with pastoral discretion. Different worship practices in each local church do not necessarily imply that contemporary churches should have only one rubric for public worship. Rather, it means that worship leaders of each local church live in the context of freedom of worship and so they need to choose and apply what they have in mind to their specific contexts. For example, just as Henry developed Reformed worship by emphasizing the Bible and life instead of articulating or modifying a liturgical book, Reformed Presbyterian churches of today must discern ways to develop contemporary Reformed worship in order to sustain Reformed tradition in our contemporary context.

Third, Henry contributed to the liturgical spirituality by articulating the integration of the Word and life as foundational to the Reformed principles of worship and the sacraments. According to Reformed tradition, the Word is the authentic foundation and guide of all human life, including the rites of liturgy. Henry argued that human beings in ordinary life as well as in the service of worship should commune with the Triune God according to the teaching of the Bible. Henry developed a pattern of strongly Word-centered worship, composing it centered around and based upon the Word in singing, praying, and reading/preaching. Also, by emphasizing edification in reading and preaching the Word in the worship service, Henry articulated a principle that is characteristic of Reformed thinking: thoughtful participation in worship. At the same time, by emphasizing the need for human life to conform to the sacraments, Henry also articulated another Reformed characteristic: that how one lives one's life displays evidence of one's worship of God. By so doing, Henry continued to follow the teaching of liturgical spirituality, integrating worship and life based on his reading and interpreting the Bible. According to the Bible, human beings must commune with God in both the worship service and ordinary life. This is the basic principle of Christian teaching in terms of worship and life. For example, Calvin integrated the Word and life by saying that the Word of God is essential "to acknowledge God to be, as He is, the only source of all virtue, justice, holiness, wisdom, truth, power, goodness, mercy, life and salvation."[1] This is not only for the Reformed tradition but also for our contemporary churches that faithfully follow biblical teaching as their center of life and worship. So, even though they do not regard themselves as Reformed churches, any contemporary churches following the biblical teaching in doctrine of faith and practice of ministry can adopt the case of Henry as a practical implication of integrating between the Word and life through ministry of liturgy.

Fourth, Henry emphasized and developed the communal aspect of spiritual formation. For Henry, the family was at the core of spiritual

---

1. Calvin, *Institutes*, 2.8.16.

Conclusion

formation. Family worship as a daily routine was a regular practice of English Presbyterians even before the time of Henry's ministry. The persecution under the Act of Uniformity ironically had made domestic practice of worship the most important liturgical pattern for the nonconformist Presbyterians. Their liturgical pattern of singing the psalms, praying, and reading the Scriptures was almost the same as that of public worship in the time of liturgical freedom given by the Act of Toleration. Historically, at the time of Henry's ministry, English Presbyterians did not take the pattern of family worship from their public worship. Rather, they extended the pattern of family worship to the basic form of public worship in the time of freedom of worship. Not ignoring the practice of private devotion such as reading the Bible and godly books and praying, Henry encouraged and even required Presbyterian congregations to practice family worship as a daily duty. By this emphasis on domestic worship, Henry intended to value the communal aspect of spiritual formation. Especially, Henry thought that children needed to be trained in discipleship as members of the visible church. In that training, parents held the most responsibility for shaping their children's spirituality after professing faith on behalf of their children. For Henry, Christians grow not primarily through individual efforts but through communal commitments, even at the beginning stage of life, since infants cannot think and act when their parents make a confession on their behalf in baptism. In this regard, daily practice of worship in the society of family can be a valuable liturgical legacy for contemporary culture, which tends to overemphasize the value of the individual.

Fifth, Henry contributed to the form of the biblical worship service by emphasizing the public reading of Scripture and by delivering a pastoral prayer before the sermon. Although the exposition was a practice initiated by the Independents in England before Henry, Henry took it over and regulated it as a pattern in the late seventeenth and early eighteenth centuries. A Scripture reading that was not connected to the sermon was a clear, biblical worship practice that was distinctly maintained by Henry. Few contemporary worship services now include reading the Scriptures in public worship at the Lord's Day. In addition, exposition in Henry's worship service was a part of reading the Scriptures. By ignoring the place of reading some parts of the Scriptures in public worship services, most contemporary churches naturally do not treat expounding the reading in the public worship service as an essential element. Contemporary churches can modify the reading and expounding of the Scripture as an essential part of ecclesiastical ministries by including it in a separate Bible study, rather than in the worship service.

Henry also articulated his pastoral prayer before the sermon as a distinctive part of public worship. This was a half-hour-long intercessory prayer for the work of the Holy Spirit and the congregation. This was not a fixed form of prayer to be read by the pastor, but a pastoral prayer that Henry led at his discretion. Following the Reformed tradition that promoted extemporaneous prayer in the public worship service, Henry practiced this pastoral prayer without any prescribed written form, and likewise did not use written prayers in private, family, and public worship, as did the Church of England in both private and public worship. If contemporary pastors are to continue to follow the practice of pastoral prayer in Henry's public worship service, they must consider and articulate extemporaneous but careful pastoral prayer in worship as part of a pastor's crucial ministerial duty, although the prayer may be shorter than Henry's pastoral prayer.

Sixth, when it comes to music in worship, Henry kept to the Reformed tradition by publishing *Family Hymns* and promoting the congregation's singing of the Psalms in public worship. Although not many songs were developed from the Psalms, Henry practiced singing the Psalms with his congregation in the Lord's Day worship service. Moreover, Henry did not organize a choir for the public worship service. Instead, following Calvin, Henry continued congregational praise in worship. Contemporary churches should consider the value of singing the psalms in public worship. Many psalms have been used in liturgical settings throughout Christian history, and the Reformed tradition continues to promote the singing the psalms in worship, acknowledging their profound power to shape and articulate spirituality. Moreover, Contemporary churches should recapture the value of congregational praise. Singing songs together in worship should involve people's active participation. However, though Henry included three psalms in public worship, two of these three psalms were repeated each week. Only one psalm was changed every week. Considering our contemporary worship music and liturgical setting, the pattern of Henry's practice cannot be directly applied to the service of worship for today. Yet by regarding psalms as the best choice for public worship, contemporary churches can develop worship music with lyrics based on the Bible and a more highly developed theological understanding of music.[2]

---

2. Theological understanding of music in worship is another research topic that could be examined in detail.

Conclusion

Seventh, Henry's public worship is an illustration of faithful embodiment of the principles of *The Westminster Directory* and thus can provide a good model of congruence between faith and practice in relation to worship. This is a peculiar contribution of Henry to public worship. Calvin intended to administer the Lord's Supper at every Lord's Day public worship service. However, Calvin found that he could not practice the frequency he intended; there was a conflict between what he thought and what he did in his liturgical practice. However, for Henry, there was no conflict between what he thought and what he practiced in the worship service. English Presbyterians, including Henry, took the *Confession* and *Catechism* of the Westminster Assembly as their primary articulation of the Christian faith. The Westminster Assembly also produced the *Directory* for public worship that guided the church in how to worship God. The *Directory* was intended as the particular guide for English Presbyterians who followed the Westminster *Confession* and *Catechism*. By following the guidance of the *Directory* regarding public worship, Henry demonstrated congruence between what English Presbyterians *believed* and what they *practiced* as his congregations gathered for worship. Contemporary Reformed Presbyterian churches that take the *Westminster Confession* and *Catechism* as their basic rule of faith must attempt to follow the guidance in the *Directory* articulated by the Assembly in order to appropriately embody their faith in ecclesiastical ministry. Interestingly, contemporary Reformed Presbyterian churches, although they teach church members the *Westminster Confession* and *Catechism*, seldom consider and attempt to use the *Directory* as a guide for their practice of public worship. In Reformed history, the *Directory* is a liturgical legacy that was developed mainly by Presbyterians and was practiced in the Presbyterian congregations in England, as seen in the case of Henry. So, contemporary Reformed churches might consider the value of the *Directory* for practicing their public worship when they hold the *Confession* and *Catechism* of the Westminster Assembly as their key profession of faith. Following the case of Henry, contemporary churches should attempt to integrate between what they believe and what they practice in terms of worship.

Matthew Henry

THE LIMITS OF HENRY'S THOUGHT AND PRACTICE FOR CONTEMPORARY CHURCHES

However, Henry's theology and practice of Christian worship is not the only model that may be applied to contemporary Reformed churches. His understanding and practice of ecclesiastical ministry was a contextual application for his own congregation in the late seventeenth and early eighteenth centuries. Although the context of Henry's ministry is similar to that of the contemporary era in having freedom of worship, the specific conditions differ. So, adopting Henry's practice in our contemporary churches without considering the differences between them cannot be an appropriate way of applying Henry's practice to our time. Henry developed and articulated his own Reformed understanding and practice of Christian worship in order to maintain the Reformed tradition within the context of surrounding ministerial options, such as the Church of England and other Protestant churches. Although Henry's order of worship could be followed in contemporary liturgical settings, it would not have the same efficacy because of the differences between his and our situations and attendants. Therefore, contemporary churches may learn biblical principles of worship from Henry, but need to be flexible in adjusting his pattern of worship in order to appropriately develop them in our current context.

Contemporary churches have encountered some strong influences on their worship from other traditions. Some Reformed churches tend to hastily adopt certain traditional and liturgical resources to their worship services without evaluating them from within their own theological perspective. We see this today in attempts to blend liturgical resources from the fourth century or earlier with those of contemporary culture in public worship.[3] This may be attractive to some emerging generations and even older generations. It is certain that contemporary churches can learn from earlier churches in terms of worship practice and church ministry. However, the mere blending of various traditional liturgical resources and contemporary cultures in a worship service cannot guarantee people the best way of worshipping God for today. Without ignoring the values present in earlier worship practices or the contextual elements in contemporary culture, all contemporary churches as well as Reformed churches must continue to develop and articulate their own worship for each generation. The task is not

---

3. This was the effort of Robert Webber in promoting blended worship. For example, see Webber, *Ancient-Future Worship; Ancient-Future Time; Ancient-Future Faith.*

about simply creating some new worship practice but about articulating its own denominational worship in our time and context.

Moreover, contemporary culture has had great influence on the practice of worship. Contemporary churches must consider and evaluate the values of the surrounding culture, such as individualism, consumerism, media, and religiosity. Henry gave contemporary churches basic insights for engaging with culture against individualism and consumerism by emphasizing the communal aspect in daily family worship and Lord's Day public worship, and the true pleasure in walking or communing with God through all the journey of life. However, he did not directly deal with other current cultural issues such as the media and religiosity. These were not issues in his time but are emerging and urgent issues for our contemporary era. So, in order to appropriately apply Henry's liturgical resources today, contemporary churches must seriously seek to understand contemporary culture and articulate practical ways of applying Henry's liturgical sources to contemporary congregations.

SUGGESTION FOR FURTHER STUDY

This book mainly dealt with Henry's theology and practice of worship as an example of English Presbyterian liturgy in order to help contemporary churches renew their worship according to biblical principles. This does not imply that Henry's contribution was limited to the area of worship. There are still more areas to be researched and made known to contemporary readers regarding Henry's thought and ministry. A more practical application of Henry's thought of worship needs to be articulated with consideration of different liturgical contexts. To put it another way, what a contemporary worship should be like needs to be articulated in detail, while considering the Reformed emphasis on the Bible and life in relation to worship, as well as contemporary human life and culture as the social context for worship.

Although there have been some attempts to analyze Henry's *Bible Commentary*, there is still more to be discovered in relation to his Bible exposition. How Henry read and interpreted the Bible can be not only an academic research topic but also part of the real practice of applying Henry's work for the twenty-first century. Likewise, Henry's other works besides the *Bible Commentary* and some books on the sacraments can be good sources for contemporary Reformed spirituality. In the course of revising his sermons, Henry published many books on Christian spirituality. By reading and analyzing Henry's others works besides the *Bible Commentary* and liturgical works, contemporary readers can gain understanding of Henry's thought on Christian spirituality.

Last, there is the historical task of examining Henry's influence on Reformed and other denominational traditions in later centuries. For example, Isaac Watts, Charles Wesley, and George Whitefield are representatives of those who were influenced by Henry. However, how they were influenced by him has not yet been considered in detail. Similarly, Henry's worship ministry had a huge influence on Reformed traditions in England, America, and other countries, including Korea. How and to what extent Henry influenced later Reformed and evangelical traditions remains to be examined in order to fully articulate his contribution to Christian worship.

EPITAPH of Matthew Henry[4]

Stay, stay, passenger!
Here lyes precious dust
Consecrated to the Redeemer;
Which was of old predestinated to be framed
Into a vessel of rich grace,
And at last of angelical glory:
To wit, the remains of
The very reverend MATTHEW HENRY,
Who was an ornament truly eminent
To his most excellent parents.
He was a most happy consolation of two wives successively;
Unless that at his death
He became the cause of perpetual mourning
To the last of these.
He was a lasting honour
To his seven surviving children,
As being a most affectionate father to his family.
He was at first minister at Chester,
And thereafter at Hackney, near London.
He was a most celebrated preacher,
Breathing the light of the gospel
And the zeal of seraphims
Almost every day.
He was a living record of the holy scriptures.

---

4. Tong, *Account of the Life and Death of Mr. Matthew Henry* (1717 edition), 60.

Conclusion

His time was continually employed in the exercise of prayer, or singing of psalms, or in catechizing the people of his charge, or in delivering sermons before crouded audiences, or in composing his sermons.

He was a writer entirely devoted to the promoting of religion, and advancing souls towards heaven.

And, finally, his commentaries upon the Old and New Testament, explanatory and practical, fit to improve the English language, will illustriously recommend him to all those who are seriously concerned about matters of religion, even to the latest posterity.

As to the mysteries contained in the apostolical writings, and in the book of Revelation, he went to view them more closely in heaven.

Well done, good and faithful servant!

Bibliography

THE WORKS OF MATTHEW HENRY

An Account of the Life and Death of Mr. Philip Henry, Minister of the Gospel, Near Whitchurch in Shropshire (1712). Edinburgh: Banner of Truth Trust, 1974.
Commentary on the Whole Bible. 6 vols. Peabody, MA: Hendrickson, 2006.
The Communicants' Companion: Instructions for the Right Receiving of the Lord's Supper. Birmingham, AL: Solid Ground Christian Books, 2005.
The Complete Works of Matthew Henry. 2 vols. Grand Rapids: Baker, 1997.
Vol. 1:
1. The Pleasantness of a Religious Life
2. Sober-Mindedness Pressed upon Young People
3. Against Vice and Profaneness
3.1. An Admonition to Drunkards and Tipplers
3.2. Advice to the Wanton and Unclean
3.3. An Address to Those That Profane the Lord's Day
3.4. A Check to an Ungoverned Tongue
4. Self-Consideration and Self-Preservation
4.1. The Folly of Despising Our Own Souls
4.2. The Folly of Despising Our Own Ways
5. Daily Communion With God:
5.1. How to Begin Every Day with God
5.2. How to Spend the Day with God
5.3. How to Close the Day with God
6. A Church in the House: Family Religion
7. The Right Management of Friendly Visits
8. The Communicants' Companion: Instructions for the Right Receiving of the Lord's Supper
9. Family Hymns
10. Great Britain's Present Joys and Hopes
11. England's Hopes
12. The Work and Success of the Ministry
13. Baptism
14. Funeral Sermon for Dr. Samuel Benion
15. The Life of Samuel Benion, M.D.
16. Funeral Sermon for Rev. Francis Tallents
17. The Life of Rev. Francis Tallents

Bibliography

Vol. 2:
18. A Method for Prayer: With Scripture Expressions Proper to be Used under Each Head
19. Meekness and Quietness of Spirit
20. The Catechising of Youth
21. A Scripture Catechism
22. Christ's Favor to Little Children
23. Faith in Christ and Faith in God
24. Hope and Fear Balanced
25. The Forgiveness of Sin as Debt
26. Popery: A Spiritual Tyranny
27. The True Nature of Schism: A Persuasive to Christian Love and Charity
28. Funeral Sermon for Samuel Lawrence, Minister
29. The Life of Mr. Samuel Lawrence
30. Sermon Preached on the Occasion of Rev. Richard Stretton's Death
31. The Life of Rev. Richard Stretton
32. Sermon Preached on the Occasion of Rev. Daniel Burgess's Death
33. The Life of Rev. Daniel Burgess
34. A Memorial of the Fire of the Lord
35. The Christian Religion Is Not a Sect
36. Disputes Reviewed
37. Sermon Preached to the Societies for Reformation of Manners
38. Ordination Sermon for Mr. Atkinson
39. Ordination Exhortation for Samuel Clark
40. Funeral Sermon for Rev. James Owen
41. The Layman's Reasons for Joining a Congregation of Moderated Dissenters
42. The Life of Lieut. Illidge
43. Sermon Preached on the Occasion of Katharine Henry's Death
44. The Life and Death of Philip Henry

The Covenant of Grace. Edited by Allan Harman. Ross-shire, Scotland: Christian Focus, 2002.

Daily Communion with God; Christianity No Sect; The Sabbath; The Promises of God; The Worth of The Soul. London: Thomas Nelson, n.d.

Family Religion: Principles for Raising a Godly Family. Edited by Allan Harman. Ross-shire, Scotland: Christian Focus, 2008.

The Life and Times of Philip Henry (An Account of the Life and Death of Mr. Philip Henry, Minister of the Gospel, Near Whitchurch in Shropshire). London: Thomas Nelson, 1848.

A Method for Prayer: With Scripture Expressions Proper to be Used under Each Head. Greenville, SC: Reformed Academic, 1994.

The Pleasantness of a Religious Life. Ross-shire, Scotland: Christian Focus, 1969.

The Quest for Meekness and Quietness of Spirit. Eugene, OR: Wipf and Stock, 2008.

"The Sabbath." In *Works of the English Puritan Divines: Matthew Henry*, edited by James Hamilton, 4–50. London: Thomas Nelson, n.d.

The Secret of Communion with God: How to Begin the Day, Spend the Day and End the Day with God. Birmingham, AL: Solid Ground Christian Books, 2005.

Sober-Mindedness Pressed upon Young People. Gale Ecco Print Edition, 2010.

The Young Christian. Ross-shire, Scotland: Christian Focus, 1993.

OTHER SOURCES

Allen, Charles. *The Nevius Plan for Mission Work*. Minneapolis: E. C. Heinz, 1937.

Baird, Charles. *Presbyterian Liturgies: Historical Sketches*. Grand Rapids: Baker, 1960.

Baxter, Richard. *Five Disputations of Church Government and Worship*. London: R.W. for Nevil Simmons, 1659.

Beveridge, Henry, ed. *Selected Works of John Calvin*. Grand Rapids: Baker, 1983.

Bradley, James. "The Religious Origins of Radical Politics in England, Scotland, and Ireland, 1662-1800." In *Religion and Politics in Enlightenment Europe*, 187-253. Notre Dame: University of Notre Dame Press, 2001.

Bromiley, Geoffrey. *Sacramental Teaching and Practice in the Reformed Churches*. Eugene, OR: Wipf and Stock, 1998.

Butin, Philip. "Constructive Iconoclasm: Trinitarian Concern in Reformed Worship." *Studia Liturgica* 19:2 (1989) 135-39.

Calvin, John. *The Form of Church Prayers and Hymns With The Manner of Administering the Sacraments and Consecrating Marriage According to the Custom of the Ancient Church (1542)*. n.p.

———. "Forms of Prayer For the Church (1542)." In *Calvin's Tracts*, vol. 2, translated by Henry Beveridge, 95-112. Eugene, OR: Wipf and Stock, 2002.

———. *Institutes of the Christian Religion*. Edited by John McNeill. Translated by Ford Lewis Battles. Philadelphia: Westminster, 1960.

———. "Short Treatise on the Lord's Supper (1541)." In *Theological Treatises*, 140-66. Philadelphia: Westminster, 1954.

Chapman, Charles. *Matthew Henry, His Life and Times: A Memorial and a Tribute*. London: Arthur Hall, Virtue, 1859.

Church of Scotland: Committee on Public Worship and Aids to Devotion. *Prayers for Sunday Services: Companion Volume to the Book of Common Order*. Edinburgh: Saint Andrew, 1980.

Clark, R. Scott. *Recovering the Reformed Confession: Our Theology, Piety, and Practice*. Phillipsburg: P. & R., 2008.

Cragg, Gerald. *Puritanism in His Great Persecution, 1660-1688*. Cambridge: Cambridge University Press, 1957.

Crump, David. "The Preaching of George Whitefield and His Use of Matthew Henry's Commentary." *Crux* 25:3 (September 1989) 19-28.

Davies, Horton. *The English Free Churches*. London: Oxford University Press, 1952.

———. *Worship and Theology in England*. Vol. 1: *From Cranmer to Baxter and Fox, 1534-1690*. Grand Rapids: Eerdmans, 1996.

———. *Worship and Theology in England*. Vol. 2: *From Watts and Wesley to Martineau, 1690-1900*. Grand Rapids: Eerdmans, 1998.

———. *The Worship of the English Puritans*. Morgan, PA: Soli Deo Gloria, 1997.

Dever, Mark. "Preaching Like the Puritans." In *The Westminster Directory of Public Worship*, 39-70. Ross-shire: Christian Heritage, 2008.

Doolittle, Thomas. *A Treatise Concerning the Lord's Supper: With Three Dialogues for the More Full Information of the Weak, in the Nature and Use of this Sacrament*. London: R.W., 1668.

Duncan, Ligon, III. "Editor's Introduction" to *A Method for Prayer*. Greenville, SC: Reformed Academic, 1994.

Bibliography

Duncan, J. Ligon, and Terry Johnson. "A Call to Family Worship." In *Give Praise to God: A Vision for Reformed Worship*, edited by Philip Ryken, Derek Thomas, and J. Ligon Duncan III, 317–78. Phillipsburg: P. & R., 2003.

Dyrness, William. *The Earth Is God's*. Eugene, OR: Wipf and Stock, 1997.

———. *A Primer on Christian Worship*. Grand Rapids: Eerdmans, 2009.

Eire, Carlo. *War against the Idols: The Reformation of Worship from Erasmus to Calvin*. Cambridge: Cambridge University Press, 1986.

Fagerberg, David. *Theologia Prima: What Is Liturgical Theology?* Chicago: Liturgical Training, 2004.

Fawcett, Timothy. *The Liturgy of Comprehension 1689*. Southend-on-Sea, England: The Alcuin Club, 1973.

Ferguson, Sinclair. "Puritans-Ministers of the World." In *The Westminster Directory of Public Worship*, 5–38. Ross-shire, Scotland: Christian Focus, 2008.

Finlayson, Michael. *Historians, Puritanism, and the English Revolution: The Religious Factor in English Politics Before and After the Interregnum*. Toronto: University of Toronto Press, 1983.

Fletcher, W. G. D., and K. D. Reynolds. "William, John Bickerton." In *Oxford Dictionary of National Biography*, vol. 59, edited by H. C. G. Matthew and Brian Harrison, 249–50. New York: Oxford University Press, 2004.

Frame, John. "Some Questions about the Regulative Principle." *Westminster Theological Journal* 54 (1992) 357–66.

———. *Worship in Spirit and Truth*. Phillipsburg: P. & R., 1996.

Gore, Robert J., Jr. *Covenantal Worship: Reconsidering the Puritan Regulative Principle*. Phillipsburg: P. & R., 2002.

Greaves, Richard. *Enemies under His Feet: Radicals and Nonconformists in Britain: 1664–1677*. Stanford: Stanford University Press, 1990.

Grosart, Alexander. "Matthew Henry: Sanctified Common-Sense." In *Representative Nonconformists: With the Message of Their Life-Work for Today*, 263–346. London: Hodder & Stoughton, 1879.

Guilbert, Charles, ed. *The Book of Common Prayer*. Kingsport: Kingsport, 1977.

Gummer, Selwyn. *Bible Themes from Matthew Henry*. London: Marshall, Morgan & Scott, 1953.

Harman, Allan. "Introduction." In *Family Religion: Principles for Raising a Godly Family*, edited by Allan Harman, 13–26. Ross-shire, Scotland: Christian Focus, 2008.

Harris, Tim. "Introduction: Revising the Restoration." In *The Politics of Religion in Restoration England*, edited by Tim Harris, Paul Seaward, and Mark Goldie, 1–28. Malden, MA: Blackwell, 1993.

Harris, Tim, Paul Seaward, and Mark Goldie, eds. *The Politics of Religion in Restoration England*. West Sussex, UK: Blackwell, 1993.

Hart, D. G. "Acceptable Worship." In *With Reverence and Awe: Returning to the Basics of Reformed Worship*, edited by D. G. Hart and John Muether, 75–88. Phillipsburg: P. & R., 2002.

Joo, Seung-Joong, and Kyeong-Jin Kim. "The Reformed Tradition in Korea." In *The Oxford History of Christian Worship*, edited by Geoffrey Wainwright and Karen Tucker, 484–91. New York: Oxford University Press, 2006.

Kapic, Kelly, and Randall Gleason, eds. *The Devoted Life: An Introduction to the Puritan Classic*. Downers Grove, IL: InterVarsity, 2004.

Kavanagh, Aidan. *On Liturgical Theology*. Collegeville, MN: Pueblo, 1992.

Bibliography

Kilmartin, Edward. *Christian Liturgy: Theology and Practice.* Kansas City, MO: Sheed & Ward, 1988.

Kingdon, Robert. "Worship in Geneva Before and After Reformation." In *Worship in Medieval and Early Modern Europe: Change and Continuity in Religious Practice,* edited by Karin Maag and John Witvliet, 41–60. Notre Dame: University of Notre Press Dame, 2004.

Knox, John. "Forme of Prayer (1556)." In *Liturgies of the Western Church,* edited by Bard Thompson, 287–310. Philadelphia: Fortress, 1961.

Lacey, Douglas. *Dissent and Parliamentary Politics in England, 1661–1689: A Study in the Perpetuation and Tempering of Parliamentarianism.* New Brunswick: Rutgers University Press, 1969.

Lee, Francis. "The Covenantal Home Life of Rev. Matthew Henry." *The Presbyterian,* November 2003, 9–13.

Leishmann, Thomas. *The Westminster Directory.* Edinburgh: William Blackwood, 1901.

Leith, John, ed. *Calvin Studies.* Vol. 7. Davidson, NC: Davidson College, 1994.

London, James. "Biographical Sketch of the Rev. Matthew Henry." In Matthew Henry, *Daily Communion With God; Christianity No Sect; The Sabbath; The Promises of God; The Worth of The Soul,* 11–50. London: Thomas Nelson, n.d.

Marshall, John. *John Locke, Toleration and Early Enlightenment Culture.* Cambridge: Cambridge University Press, 2006.

Maxwell, William. *The Liturgical Portions of the Genevan Service Book.* Edinburgh: Oliver and Boyd, 1931.

McClendon, Murial, Joseph Ward, and Michael MacDonald, eds. *Protestant Identities: Religion, Society, and Self-fashioning in Post-Reformation England.* Stanford: Stanford University Press, 1999.

McKee, Elsie. "Context, Contours, Contents: Towards a Description of Calvin's Understanding of Worship." *Princeton Seminary Bulletin* 16:2 (1995) 172–201.

Mead, Frank, and Samuel Hill. *Handbook of Denominations in the United States.* Nashville: Abingdon Press, 2006.

Moeller, Pamela. *Calvin's Doxology: Worship in the 1559 Institutes with a View to Contemporary Worship Renewal.* Allison Park, PA: Pickwick, 1997.

Moore-Keish, Martha. "Struggling for Balance: John Calvin and the Reformed Tradition." In *Do This in Remembrance of Me,* 15–60. Grand Rapids: Eerdmans, 2008.

Morgan, Edmund. *The Puritan Family: Essays on Religion and Domestic Relations in Seventeenth-Century New England.* Boston: The Trustees of the Public Library, 1944.

Muir, Edward. *Rituals in Early Modern Europe.* Cambridge: Cambridge University Press, 2005.

Needham, Nick. "Worship through the Ages." In *Give Praise to God: A Vision for Reformed Worship,* edited by Philip Ryken, Derek Thomas, and J. Ligon Duncan III, 375–411. Phillipsburg: P. & R., 2003.

Nevius, John. *Methods of Mission Work.* New York: Foreign Mission Work, 1895.

"Memoirs of the Rev. Matthew Henry, Author of Commentaries on the Holy Bible." *Methodist Review* 17:1 (January 1835) 5–33.

Old, Hughes. "Calvin's Theology of Worship." In *Give Praise to God: A Vision for Reformed Worship,* edited by Philip Ryken, Derek Thomas, and J. Ligon Duncan III, 412–35. Phillipsburg: P. & R., 2003.

———. "Daily Prayer in the Reformed Church of Strasbourg." *Worship* 52:2 (1978) 121–38.

Bibliography

———. "John Calvin and the Prophetic Criticism of Worship." In *John Calvin and the Church: A Prism of Reform*, edited by Timothy George, 230–46. Louisville: Westminster John Knox, 1990.

———. *Leading in Prayer: A Workbook for Worship*. Grand Rapids: Eerdmans, 1995.

———. "Henry, Matthew" In *Dictionary of Major Biblical Interpreters*, edited by Donald McKim, 521–24. Downers Grove, IL: InterVarsity, 2007.

———. "Matthew Henry and Family Prayer." In *Calvin Studies*, vol. 7, edited by John Leith, 72–89. Davidson, NC: Davidson College, 1994.

———. *The Reading and Preaching of the Scriptures in the Worship of the Christian Church*. Vol. 4, *The Age of the Reformation*, Grand Rapids: Eerdmans, 2004.

———. *The Reading and Preaching of the Scriptures in the Worship of the Christian Church*. Vol. 5: *Modernism, Pietism, and Awakening*. Grand Rapids, Eerdmans, 2006.

———. "What Is Reformed Spirituality?" In *Calvin Studies*, vol. 7, edited by John Leith, 63–71. Davidson, NC: Davidson College, 1994.

———. *Worship That Is Reformed According to Scripture*. Atlanta: John Knox Press, 2002.

Packer, James. "Introduction" to *The Pleasantness of a Religious Life*. Ross-shire, Scotland: Christian Focus, 1998.

Pederson, Randall, ed. *Matthew Henry Daily Reading*. Ross-shire, Scotland: Christian Heritage Imprint, 2009.

Plum, Harry. *Restoration Puritanism: A Study of the Growth of English Liberty*. Port Washington, NY: Kennikat, 1972.

Ramsbottom, John. "Puritan Dissenters and English Churches, 1630–1690." PhD diss., Yale University, 1987.

Reynolds, John. *Sermon Upon the Mournful Occasion of the Funeral of the Reverend and Excellent Mr. Matthew Henry, Minister of the Gospel*. London: John Clark, 1714.

Roberts, H. D. *Matthew Henry and His Chapel, 1662–1900*. Liverpool: The Liverpool Booksellers Company, 1901.

Routley, Erik. "Charles Wesley and Matthew Henry." *Congregational Quarterly* 33 (October 1955) 345–51.

Rust, Paul. *The First of the Puritans and the Book of Common Prayer*. Milwaukee: Bruce, 1949.

Spinks, Bryan. *Liturgy in the Age of Reason*. Burlington: Ashgate, 2008.

———. *Sacraments, Ceremonies and the Stuart Divines*. Burlington: Ashgate, 2002.

Spurr, John. "From Puritanism to Dissent, 1660–1700." In *The Culture of English Puritanism, 1560–1700*, edited by Christopher Durston and Jacqueline Eales, 238–64. New York: St. Martin's, 1996.

———. *The Restoration Church of England, 1646–1689*. New Haven: Yale University Press, 1991.

Stell, Christopher. "Puritan and Nonconformist Meetinghouses in England." In *Seeing Beyond the Word*, edited by Paul Finney, 49–82. Grand Rapids: Eerdmans, 1999.

Theology and Worship Ministry Unit for the Presbyterian Church. *Book of Common Worship*. Philadelphia: Westminster, 1966.

Thompson, Bard. *Liturgies of the Western Church*. Philadelphia: Fortress, 1980.

Tong, William. *An Account of the Life and Death of Mr. Matthew Henry, Minister of the Gospel of Chester, Who Died June 22, 1714*. London: M. Lawrence, 1716.

———. *Funeral Sermon Preached at Hackney on Occasion of the Much Lamented Death of the Reverend Mr. Matthew Henry*. London: J. Lawrence, 1714.

Bibliography

Volf, Miroslav. *After Our Likeness: The Church as the Image of the Trinity.* Grand Rapids: Eerdmans, 1998.

———. *Exclusion and Embrace.* Nashville: Abingdon, 1996.

Wainwright, Geoffrey. *Doxology: The Praise of God in Worship, Doctrine, and Life: A Systematic Theology.* New York: Oxford University Press, 1980.

Wainwright, W. "Henry, Matthew." In *Dictionary of Biblical Interpretation*, 495. Nashville: Abingdon, 1999.

Ward, Rowland. "The Directory for Public Worship." In *Scripture and Worship*, edited by Richard Muller and Rowland Ward, 85–140. Phillipsburg: P. & R., 2007.

Watts, Michael. *The Dissenters.* Oxford: Oxford University Press, 1978.

Webber, Robert. *Ancient-Future Faith.* Grand Rapids: Baker, 1999.

———. *Ancient-Future Time.* Grand Rapids: Baker, 2004.

———. *Ancient-Future Worship.* Grand Rapids: Baker, 2008.

Westermeyer, Paul. *Te Deum: The Church and Music.* Minneapolis: Augsburg Fortress, 1998.

Westminster Assembly. *A Directory for the Publique Worship of God throughout the Three Kingdoms of Scotland, England, and Ireland (1644).* London: printed for Thomas Simmons at the Bull and Mouth neer Aldersgate, 1659.

Whiting, Charles. *Studies in English Puritanism from the Restoration to the Revolution, 1660–1688.* New York: Augstus M. Kelley, 1968.

Williams, Daniel. *Funeral Sermon Upon Occasion of the Death of the Reverend Mr. Matthew Henry.* London: W. Wilkins, 1714.

Williams, John. *Memoirs of the Life, Character, and Writings of the Rev. Matthew Henry (The Life of Matthew Henry).* Carlisle, PA: The Banner of Truth Trust, 1828.

Williams, Roy. "The Puritan Concept and Practice of Prayer: Private, Family, and Public." PhD diss., University of London, 1982.

Witvliet, John. "Baptism as a Sacrament of Reconciliation in the Thought of John Calvin." In *Worship Seeking Understanding*, 149–62. Grand Rapids: Baker, 2003.

———. "The Spirituality of the Psalter: Metrical Psalms in Liturgy and Life in Calvin's Geneva." *Calvin Theological Journal* 32:2 (November 1997) 273–97.

———. "The Transformation of Christian Worship: Recent History of Protestant and Catholic Practices." Seminar, Calvin College, June 26–July 7, 2006.

Wolterstorff, Nicholas. "The Reformed Liturgy." In *Major Themes in the Reformed Tradition,* edited by Donald McKim, 274–304. Grand Rapids: Eerdmans, 1992.

Wykes, David. "Henry, Matthew" In *Oxford Dictionary of National Biography*, edited by H. C. G. Matthew and Brian Harrison, 26:582–84. New York: Oxford University Press, 2004.

Young, William. "The Puritan Principle of Worship." In *Servants of the Word: Puritan Conference Papers 1957,* edited by D. M. Lloyd-Jones, 43–52. London: Banner of Truth Trust, 1957.

Zagorin, Perez. *How the Idea of Religious Toleration Came to the West.* Princeton, NJ: Princeton University Press, 2003.

www.ingramcontent.com/pod-product-compliance
Lightning Source LLC
Chambersburg PA
CBHW051521230426
43668CB00012B/1698